Clear and

Simple as

the Truth

Clear and Simple as the Truth

Writing Classic Prose

Second Edition

Francis-Noël Thomas and Mark Turner

PRINCETON UNIVERSITY PRESS   *Princeton and Oxford*

Published by Princeton University Press, 41 William Street,
Princeton, New Jersey 08540
In the United Kingdom: Princeton University Press, 6 Oxford Street,
Woodstock, Oxfordshire ox20 1tw

press.princeton.edu

Library of Congress Cataloging-in-Publication Data

Thomas, Francis-Noël, 1943–
    Clear and simple as the truth : writing classic prose / Francis-Noël Thomas and
Mark Turner. — 2nd ed.
        p.   cm.
    Includes bibliographical references and index.
    ISBN 978-0-691-14743-7 (pbk. : alk. paper)   1. English language—Rhetoric.
2. English language—Style.   3. Report writing.   I. Turner, Mark, 1954–   II. Title.
    PE1408.T4155 2010
    808ʹ.042—dc22   2010035977

British Library Cataloging-in-Publication Data is available

This book has been composed in Minion Pro
Printed on acid-free paper. ∞
Printed in the United States of America

10 9 8 7 6 5 4 3 2 1

Contents

Acknowledgments

The first edition of this book was planned and shaped at the National Humanities Center, Research Triangle Park, North Carolina.

Mark Turner gratefully acknowledges the subsequent support of the John Simon Guggenheim Memorial Foundation; the University of Maryland; and the Department of Cognitive Science, the Department of Linguistics, and the Center for Research in Language at the University of California, San Diego. Francis-Noël Thomas gratefully acknowledges the assistance of the University of Chicago Computing Organizations. The authors thank Wayne C. Booth, Robert E. Brown, Frederick Crews, Peter Dougherty, Jason Epstein, Jeanne Fahnestock, Beth Gianfagna, Peter Lang, and members of the Board of Princeton University Press for comments. We also thank the students—especially Jennifer Bacon and William FitzGerald—in Prose Style and in Classic Prose Style at the University of Maryland, who used this book in earlier drafts.

We thank Anne Savarese for suggesting that we undertake a second edition and for guiding the Studio to completion. We thank Arthur Evenchik, David Lee Rubin, and Vera Tobin for comments on the Studio.

Clear and
Simple as
the Truth

Clear and Simple as the Truth

J'ai sur-tout à cœur la clarté. . . . Mon style

ne sera point fleuri, mes expressions seront

simples comme la vérité.

—Jean-Baptiste Le Brun

The teaching of writing in America is almost entirely controlled by the view that teaching writing is teaching verbal skills—from the placing of commas to the ordering of paragraphs. This has generated a tremendous industry, but the effect of this teaching is dubious. Why is American prose as bad as it is, even though we have more writing programs than ever?

Our answer is that writing is an intellectual activity, not a bundle of skills. Writing proceeds from thinking. To achieve good prose styles, writers must work through intellectual issues, not merely acquire mechanical techniques. Although it is true that an ordinary intellectual activity like writing must lead to skills, and that skills visibly mark the performance, the activity does not come from the skills, nor does it consist of using them. In this way, writing is like conversation—both are linguistic activities, and so require verbal skills, but neither can be mastered just by learning verbal skills. A bad conversationalist may have a very high level of verbal skills but perform poorly because he does not conceive of conversation as distinct from monologue. No further cultivation of verbal skills will remedy his problem. Conversely, a very good conversationalist may have inferior verbal skills, but a firm grasp on concepts such as reciprocity and turn-taking that lie at the heart of the activity. Neither conversation nor writing can be learned merely by acquiring verbal skills, and any attempt to teach writing by teaching writing skills detached from underlying conceptual issues is doomed.

But it is possible to learn to write by learning a style of writing. We think conceptual stands are the basis of writing since they define styles. To be sure, it is only through the verbal level that the conceptual level can be observed, and verbal artifacts—like plumage—help identify a style. Nevertheless, in general, a style cannot be defined, analyzed, or learned as a matter of verbal choices.

Writing is defined conceptually and leads to skills. This is true of all intellectual activities. There are skills of mathematical discovery, skills of painting, skills of learning a language, and so on. But in no case is the activity constituted by the skills. Great painters are often less skillful than mediocre painters; it is their concept of painting—not their skills—that defines their activity. Similarly, a foreigner may be less skillful than a native speaker at manipulating tenses or using subjunctives, but nonetheless be an incomparably better writer. Intellectual activities generate skills, but skills do not generate intellectual activities.

A style is defined by its conceptual stand on truth, presentation, writer, reader, thought, language, and their relationships. Classic style, for example, adopts a conceptual stand on these elements that can be expressed briefly, as it was by the eighteenth-century picture merchant Jean-Baptiste Le Brun in a book attempting to instruct amateurs in how to judge pictures: "J'ai sur-tout . . . à cœur la clarté. . . . Mon style ne sera point fleuri, mes expressions seront simples comme la vérité." 'Above all, I have clarity at heart. My style will not be at all florid; my expressions will be simple as the truth.' Classic style is in its own view clear and simple as the truth. It adopts the stance that its purpose is presentation; its motive, disinterested truth. Successful presentation consists of aligning language with truth, and the test of this alignment is clarity and simplicity. The idea that presentation is successful when language is aligned with truth implies that truth can be known; truth needs no argument but only accurate presentation; the reader is competent to recognize truth; the symmetry between writer and reader allows the presentation to follow the model of conversation; a natural language is sufficient to express truth; and the writer knows the truth before he puts it into language.

Le Brun's own writing could never be the result of any collection of verbal skills. It derives instead from the classic conception of the activity of writing, in which language can be fitted to truth and writing can be an undistorting window on its subject. Le Brun's concept of writing depends upon his stand on truth: there exist good and bad paintings; their qualities are independent of him or anyone; a lifetime of experience has refined his vision so that he can see the quality of a painting; the order of his presentation follows the order of truth, not of sensation; once he positions his reader to see what he himself has learned to see, the reader will be competent to recognize it. His concept of truth and its corollaries are intellectual stands, not technical skills. They define his performance—and their ability to do so is independent of their validity.

Le Brun's stand—that he knows something true and can position his reader to see it—allows him to claim that his writing is clear and simple as the truth. It also justifies his model scene of conversation in which one person speaks to another, unmotivated by gain or interest. This conceptual stand elevates clarity and simplicity to the position of prime virtues of classic style. It is apparent that a writer who does not adopt the stand that truth can be known or recognized could not claim that his writing is clear and simple as the truth.

It is equally apparent that any writer can simply learn the classic stand and, writing from that stand, achieve its virtues. Le Brun's stylistic stand was, for him, probably a conviction, but it offers access to the same stylistic virtues when taken as an enabling convention. Classic style comes from adopting a particular stand on intellectual issues for the specific purpose of presentation; it is not a creed. Once adopted, the classic stand offers a general style of presentation suitable to any subject whatever. It is obviously not limited to the judgment of paintings. The feature of classic style that makes it a natural model for anyone is its great versatility. The style is defined not by a set of techniques but rather by an attitude toward writing itself. What is most fundamental to that attitude is the stand that the writer knows something before he sets out to write, and that his purpose is to articulate what he knows to a reader. The style does not limit the writer's subject matter or efface his individuality, but the writer's individuality will be expressed principally by his knowledge of his subject.

The first part of our book shows why learning to write cannot be reduced to acquiring writing skills, why learning to write is inevitably learning styles of writing, and how styles derive from conceptual stands. We coach our readers in the conceptual stand that defines classic style, and contrast the classic stand with some others: reflexive, practical, plain, contemplative, romantic, prophetic, oratorical. The second part of the book is a museum of examples with commentary, ranging from Thomas Jefferson to Junichirō Tanizaki, and including Madame de Sévigné, Descartes, Jane Austen, and Mark Twain.

While a particular conceptual stand is the foundation of classic style, acquiring an active mastery of the style requires practice. In the third part—the Studio—the focus changes from observation and analysis, the activities featured in the Museum, to a series of exercises that will lead the reader to an active mastery of the style. Since classic style can be recognized across all boundaries of language and era, the book ends with a list—meant to be suggestive—of writing in classic style from the *Apology* of Socrates to *Lulu in Hollywood*.

ONE

Principles of Classic Style

■ The Concept of Style

"Style" is a word everybody uses, but almost no one can explain what it means. It is often understood as the inessential or even disreputable member of a two-term set: style and substance. This set of terms is elastic but in all its many applications, style is the subordinate term and, in the traditional American idiom, there is a persistent suggestion that we would be better off without it. Style is, at best, a harmless if unnecessary bit of window dressing. At worst, it is a polite name for fraud. There used to be a cigar company whose motto was "All Quality. No Style."

When style is considered the opposite of substance, it seems optional and incidental, even when it is admired. In this way of framing things, substantive thought and meaning can be prior to style and completely separable from it. The identical thought or the identical meaning, it is suggested, can be expressed in many styles—or even in none at all, as when just plain integrity or the unvarnished truth is offered as an alternative to the adornments of style. Style, conceived this way, is something fancy that distracts us from what is essential; it is the varnish that makes the truth at least a little harder to see.

The notion that style is something completely separate from substance, so that substance can be offered "straight," lies behind both the motto of the cigar company and William Butler Yeats's description of Bernard Shaw's writing, but in the second case the poet puts a high value on style and views writing in no style, while possible, to be something monstrously mechanical. Yeats apparently thought of his own characteristic poetic voice as "style." It was a voice so compelling that attempts to imitate it have ruined quite a number of aspiring poets. Shaw's voice was not poetic in Yeats's sense, so Yeats considered Shaw to be a writer "without style." Because he held the view that style is optional, Yeats could simultaneously view Shaw as "the most formidable man in modern letters," able to write "with great effect," and yet view Shaw's writing as "without music, without style, either good or bad." He described Shaw as a nightmare sewing machine that clicked, shone, and smiled, "smiled perpetually."

Whether style is viewed as spiritual, fraudulent, or something in between, any concept of style that treats it as optional is inadequate not only to writing but to any human action. Nothing we do can be done "simply" and in no style, because style is something inherent in action, not something added to it. In this respect, style is like the typeface in which a text is printed. We may overlook it, and frequently do, but it is always there. The styles we acquire unconsciously remain invisible to us as a rule, and routine actions can seem to be done in no style at all, even though their styles are obvious to experienced observers. A printer, a proofreader, or a type designer cannot fail to notice the type in which a text is printed, but for most of us, that typeface will have to be laid down beside a contrasting face before we even notice it exists. We thought we were looking at words pure and simple and did not notice that they are printed in a specific typeface.

When we do something in a default style acquired unconsciously, we do not notice the style of our activity. In such cases, we have an abstract concept of action that leaves style out of account. We can have a concept of lying without being aware—as a good investigative reporter is—that, in practice, we must have a style of lying. We can have a concept of quarreling without being aware— as a good marriage counselor is—that, in practice, we must have a style of quarreling.

Despite a lifetime of speaking, we can remain unaware of having a style of speaking. Yankees in Maine or Good Ol' Boys in Louisiana think that people from Brooklyn talk funny. WASPS in the Chicago suburbs think that Poles or Lithuanians in Chicago speak English with an accent, as if the suburban WASPS, the Yankees, and the Good Ol' Boys speak just plain American English with no accent. Coastal Californians think—just as the ancient Greeks did—that everybody else sounds barbarous. A moment's reflection will convince anyone that it is impossible to speak without an accent. But people who feel they set the local tone do not consider their own accents to be accents. It is hard to think of a child who is just learning to speak wanting to learn a style of speaking. The style is folded into the activity as it is learned: we think that we have learned to speak a language, not that we have learned a regional dialect. Children in Maine do not think they are learning to speak English with a Yankee accent; they think they are learning to speak English.

Although there are certainly a lot of English accents to be heard, even if we restrict the field to America, only a few people consciously choose theirs. Professional broadcasters, of course, do; sometimes people interested in acting careers do. Many politicians with degrees from prestigious universities have learned to speak with one accent in the capitals where they make laws and policy and quite a different one back home where they campaign for office. Senator Fulbright was a Rhodes scholar with an Oxford education. Before he went to the Senate, he had been the dean of a law school and the president of a university. His background was perfectly congruent with what he sounded like in action as chairman of the Senate Foreign Relations Committee conducting hearings on the Vietnam War, but when he campaigned in rural Arkansas, where he got his votes, there was no hint of Oxford, or even Fayetteville. On the stump, he sounded completely down home. After the election, that sound dissipated with every mile he got closer to Washington until he was sworn in for a new term and reassumed both the seat of power and the music of policy.

Senator Fulbright could maintain two dramatically distinct styles of speech in his personal repertory because he was aware of both as styles and consequently did not mistake either of them for just plain English. His awareness of his own styles allowed him to switch back and forth between them and fit them to circumstances. Everyone does this to some extent, but not everyone is aware of doing so. Speakers who are not consciously aware of their styles run into problems when none of their habitual styles fits a particular circumstance very well. We are trapped by our unconscious styles if we cannot recognize them as styles. When all of our styles are effectively default styles, we choose without knowing we are choosing and so cannot recognize the practical possibility of alternative styles.

People who unconsciously have acquired a full complement of routine conversational styles can deliberately and consciously add a new style of conversation to their collection, a style invented for new purposes and situations, once they have an operating concept of style. A novice receptionist at the headquarters of a large corporation consciously acquires the standard impersonal business style of conversation. The receptionist already possesses an underlying competence in conversation; he consciously acquires a new style meant for a special and unusually well-defined purpose.

Because writing is an activity, it too must be done in a style. But the domain of writing, like the domain of conversation, is enormous, not limited by just a handful of occasions or purposes. Consequently, there are many styles of writing. Common wisdom to the contrary, no one can master *writing* because *writing* is too large to be encompassed. It is not one skill; it is not even a small bundle of routine skills. A single style of writing invented for particular purposes, however, can be like a receptionist's conversation, something small enough to be walked around. It is possible to see where it begins and where it ends, what its purposes and occasions are, and how it selects its themes. These styles of writing can be acquired consciously as styles. Classic style is one of them.

Although nearly anybody who can read a newspaper can write, the styles we acquired unconsciously do not always serve our needs. Most of us have no unconscious writing style available to use when, after becoming engaged in a problem, we have thought it through, reached confident conclusions, and want to make our thought accessible to a permanent but unspecified audience. Even the best-educated members of our society commonly lack a routine style for presenting the result of their own engagement with a problem to people outside their own profession. Writers with a need to address such readers invented classic style. It is not a routine style in our culture, and unlike most of the writing styles we acquire, it is unlikely to be picked up without deliberate effort.

Classic style was not invented by one person or even by a small group working together. It was not invented just once, nor is it specific to one culture or one language. It was used with notable skill and effect by some of the outstanding French writers of the seventeenth century, and their achievements have left an echo in French culture that has no direct English or American equivalent. The seventeenth-century French masters of classic style, for one reason or another, conceived of themselves as addressing an intelligent but nonspecialist reader. They were all writers who had no doubt about the general importance of what they had to say. They shared the idea that truth about something is, in some sense, truth about everything, and they adopted the view that it is always possible to present a really significant conclusion to a general audience.

Classic style is focused and assured. Its virtues are clarity and simplicity; in a sense, so are its vices. It declines to acknowledge ambiguities, unessential qualifications, doubts, or other styles. It declines to acknowledge that it is a style. It makes its hard choices silently and out of the reader's sight. Once made, those hard choices are not acknowledged to be choices at all; they are presented as if they were inevitable because classic style is, above all, a style of presentation with claims to transparency.

To write without a chosen and consistent style is to write without a tacit concept of what writing can do, what its limits are, who its audience is, and what the writer's goals are. In the absence of settled decisions about these things, writing can be torture. While there is no single correct view of these matters, every well-defined style must take a stand on them. Classic style is neither shy nor ambiguous about fundamentals. The style rests on the assumptions that it is possible to think disinterestedly, to know the results of disinterested thought, and to present them without fundamental distortion. In this view, thought precedes writing. All of these assumptions may be wrong, but they help to define a style whose usefulness is manifest.

The attitudes that define classic style—the attitudes that define any style—are a set of enabling conventions. Some of the originators of classic style may have believed its enabling conventions— such as that truth can be known—but writing in this style requires no commitment to a set of beliefs, only a willingness to adopt a role for a limited time and a specific purpose.

The role is severely limited because classic prose is pure, fearless, cool, and relentless. It asks no quarter and gives no quarter to anyone, including the writer. While the role can be necessary, true, and useful, as well as wonderfully thrilling, it can hardly be permanent. For better or worse, human beings are not pure, fearless, cool, or relentless, even if we may find it convenient for certain purposes to pretend that we are. The human condition does not, in general, allow the degree of autonomy and certainty that the classic writer pretends to have. It does not sustain the classic writer's claim to disinterested expression of unconditional truth. It does not allow the writer indefinitely to maintain the posture required by classic style. But classic style simply does not acknowledge the human condition. The insouciance required to ignore what everyone knows and to carry the reader along in this style cannot be maintained very long, and the masters of the style always know its limits. The classic distance is a sprint.

■ Recognizing Classic Style

Classic style never became the standard for English prose that it has been at various times for French. The most admired prose writers in English have never been as successful in creating any dominant style as the most admired French prose writers of the seventeenth century were in making classic style a cultural norm. The reasons are many and defy simple summary, but they probably include the existence of an exceptionally influential line of verse writers in English—a line with no French counterpart; the profound influence of the King James translation of the Bible on English prose style; the great diversity of styles among admired English prose writers; and the fact that English prose before the eighteenth century cannot serve as a direct model for later writing. Seventeenth-century English prose seems archaic to later English readers; seventeenth-century French prose is perfectly normal even to a contemporary French reader.

Certain classic French writers—Descartes, Pascal, the duc de La Rochefoucauld, Madame de Lafayette, the Cardinal de Retz, Madame de Sévigné, and La Bruyère—have been taken as models of French prose practically from their day to ours. Indeed, for many, their French *is* French. Those who admire it rarely fail to single out for praise its clarity, suppleness, and elegance.

Propagandists, in the course of promoting the use of French as an international diplomatic language, attributed these marks of style to something inherent in the French language. Antoine Rivarol is the author of the best-known version of this primitive excursion into salesmanship as essentialist linguistics. Language, Professor Rivarol observes, is clear when it follows the order of reason, and unclear when it follows the movements and order of our experience. But, behold, French has a unique privilege among languages: its natural order *is* the order of reason. It is, therefore, necessarily clear where Greek, Latin, Italian, and English are not. In the absence of the uniquely French syntax of reason, writing in other languages is heir to all the fog and filthy air that passion and sensation impart. Rivarol won a prize for a disquisition based on these observations in the eighteenth century; today both his argument and his conclusion sound like a parody of alchemy. In the age of Derrida and Lacan, French prose has triumphantly displayed its capacity to be as incomprehensible, elephantine, and turgid as double-Dutch.

The almost transparent silliness of attributing marks of style to the inherent qualities of particular languages has not discouraged the practice even among accomplished writers who ought to know better. T. S. Eliot, in observing that English writers at no time looked to a common standard, attributes this fact to what he takes to be an inherent characteristic of the language. "The English language," he pronounces, "is one which offers a wide scope for legitimate divergences of style; it seems to be such that no one age, and certainly no one writer, can establish a norm."

It seems superfluous to argue that classic style does not issue from French or from any other language as such. All we have to do is look at its history. French classic style was invented by drawing together and refining attitudes and practices found in antiquity among writers of Greek and Latin, and the invaluable instrument that resulted has long been employed by classic stylists in English, although no English philosopher with the cultural standing of Descartes consistently employs it, nor was there ever such a remarkable group of classic writers in English at any one time as there was in the French *grand siècle*.

Consider, as an example of classic style, the following passage from La Rochefoucauld:

> Madame de Chevreuse had sparkling intelligence, ambition, and beauty in plenty; she was flirtatious, lively, bold, enterprising; she used all her charms to push her projects to success, and she almost always brought disaster to those she encountered on her way.

> Mme de Chevreuse avait beaucoup d'esprit, d'ambition et de beauté; elle était galante, vive, hardie, entreprenante; elle se servait de tous ses charmes pour réussir dans ses desseins, et elle a presque toujours porté malheur aux personnes qu'elle y a engagées.

This passage displays truth according to an order that has nothing to do with the process by which the writer came to know it. The writer takes the pose of full knowledge. This pose implies that the writer has wide and textured experience; otherwise he would not be able to make such an observation. But none of that personal history, personal experience, or personal psychology enters into the expression. Instead the sentence crystallizes the writer's experience into a timeless and absolute sequence, as if it were a geometric proof. The sentence has a clear direction and a goal. It leads us to that goal, which coincides with its final phrase; it is constructed to telegraph its direction. We know that it will bring us to its goal, and stop cleanly when it has done so.

By contrast, consider the opening sentence of Samuel Johnson's "Preface to Shakespeare," which is a master's recital piece, but is not classic:

That praises are without reason lavished on the dead, and that the honours due only to excellence are paid to antiquity, is a complaint likely to be always continued by those, who, being able to add nothing to truth, hope for eminence from the heresies of paradox; or those, who, being forced by disappointment upon consolatory expedients, are willing to hope from posterity what the present age refuses, and flatter themselves that the regard which is yet denied by envy, will be at last bestowed by time.

This sentence does not telegraph its structure from the opening. We must follow it through complex and unexpected paths. In La Rochefoucauld's classic sentence, the last section is the conclusion of all that has gone before it; the beginning of the sentence exists for the end, and the sentence is constructed so that we can anticipate arriving at such a conclusion. In Johnson's sentence, by contrast, the final phrase, "flatter themselves that the regard which is yet denied by envy, will be at last bestowed by time," is not a conclusion upon which the rest of the sentence depends. It might have come in the middle of the sentence. The end of the sentence might have been "be always continued by those, who, being able to add nothing to truth, hope for eminence from the heresies of paradox." This does not make the sentence inadequate in any way, but it is characteristically unclassic. The classic sentence, once written, seems to have been inevitable.

La Rochefoucauld's sentence was of course difficult to write, but it looks easy. The writer hides all the effort. Johnson's sentence was clearly difficult to write, and its writer wants to display it as if it were a trophy won through his personal effort.

La Rochefoucauld's classic sentence pretends that it could be said. It would take a true master of speech to construct such a sentence spontaneously. In fact we sense that the rhythm is too perfect to be spontaneous. Still, it sounds like ideally efficient and precise speech. If angels spoke French, it would sound like this. Johnson's sentence, by contrast, can only be writing that took effort. In its rhythms, we do not hear someone speaking spontaneously. One could memorize it and repeat it in speech, but even then it would sound like memorized writing, not like speech. In the theology behind Johnson's sentence, writing is hard and noble, because truth is the reward of effort and cannot be captured in spontaneous speech. In the theology behind La Rochefoucauld's sentence, writing should look easy even as it looks masterful. Truth is a grace that flees from earnest effort. The language of truth is ideally graceful speech.

La Rochefoucauld's sentence is a prototype of classic style. The conceptual and linguistic environment associated with classic style is extremely rich and complex. No classic text—not even a prototype—incorporates all of it. Any list of criteria would be misconceived: some texts lack central attributes of classic style and yet are obviously classic; other texts are faintly classic throughout; still others have isolated parts that are strongly classic; some texts incorporate only a few elements of classic style; some clearly unclassic texts contain marks of classic style; some texts have the verbal marks of classic style but none of its theology; some texts lie between classic style and another style.

Consider the gradient between plain style and classic style. "The truth is pure and simple" is plain style. "The truth is rarely pure, and never simple" is classic style. The plain version contains many elements of classic style without being classic; the classic version contains all of the plain version without being plain.

The concept of classic style assumes that plain style already exists. The classic version introduces a refinement, a qualification, a meditation on the plain version that makes it classic. Classic style takes the attitude that it is superior to plain style because classic style presents intelligence as it should be presented: as a sparkling display, not weighed down by grinding earnestness. The classic writer wants to be distinguished from others because she assumes that truth, though potentially available to all, is not the common property of common people, and that it is not to be perceived or expressed through common means unrefined. The classic writer sees common sense as only an approximation which, left untested and unrefined, can turn out to be false. The plain writer wants to be common because she assumes that truth is the common property of common people, directly perceived and expressed through common means. For the plain writer, common sense is truth. Unlike plain style, classic style is aristocratic, which is not to say artificially restricted, since anyone can become an aristocrat by learning classic style. Anyone who wants to can attain classic style, but classic style views itself as an intellectual achievement, not a natural endowment.

There are many features of classic style besides a simple and elegant shape and the introduction of some refinement in the thought. Behind these features is a complicated, polished, and fascinating view of truth and language, writers and readers. The rest of this essay is an attempt to lay out the features of classic style and their underlying conceptual stand.

■ **The Elements of Style**

Elementary does not always mean easy. It often means fundamental. Euclid's mathematical classic is called *The Elements of Geometry*. If we ask what Euclid means by "elements," we will discover that they consist of a short list of twenty-three definitions, such as "a line is breadthless length," five postulates, such as "all right angles are equal to one another," and five common notions, such as "if equals be added to equals, the wholes are equal." From these elements, all of Euclid's geometry follows. For a mathematical genius like Sir Isaac Newton, the book is really over once these elements are laid out, since everything else is implicit within them. *The Elements of Geometry*, the most successful textbook in history, establishes a set of expectations for other textbooks that present the structure of a field. So, when we look into a book called *The Elements of Accounting* or *The Elements of Boatbuilding* or the elements of anything—every field has at least half a dozen books with such a title—we expect what we find in Euclid: a small number of starting points at a high level of generality from which all the details of the subject follow.

In the eighteenth century, when chemistry was separated from alchemy, the field came to be structured around the concept of chemical elements, only a handful of which were known. Chemical elements, like Euclid's elements, are the fundamental starting points of their domain; unlike Euclid's elements, they are also elemental in constituting everything more complex. The origin of this concept of chemical elements is often attributed to Antoine Lavoisier (1743–1794), whose presentation in *Traité élémentaire de chemie, presenté dans un ordre nouveau et d'après les découvertes modernes* (1789) was embraced by almost everyone who read it, partly because he wrote in classic style; other books on the subject were written in styles too complicated to be widely understood.

The concept of chemical elements is similar to Euclid's concept of elements, inasmuch as everything in the domain of chemistry can be said to be implicit in them. Even today, when there are 118 elements instead of the handful known to Lavoisier, it is possible to put them all on a chart inside the cover of a chemistry textbook or on the wall of a classroom. The concept that all matter is a combination of elements is fundamental to the science of chemistry; but some of these elements are less central as constituents than others. Oxygen, for example, is central; unnamed elements that are known to exist but have not been isolated experimentally are peripheral. The physical world, unlike geometry, is not invented. There are a multitude of geometries that derive from a multitude of starting points. There is only one physical world, whose starting point is not a human invention. So while the concept "elemental atom" is fundamental and distinct, the actual table of these elements has slightly fuzzy margins. New elements have been added or created within the past fifty years, but they are all exotic and have little to do with our understanding of the fundamental nature of the chemical world.

The periodic table of chemical elements is implicitly modeled on the alphabet. The chemical elements are a kind of alphabet of the physical world. The Roman alphabet, used to write English and most European languages, is itself a set of elements. With just twenty-six letters, we can write every word in these languages, even words that are obsolete, even tomorrow's words that have not yet been coined. When the letters of this alphabet are arranged on a typewriter keyboard, we can see that while they are not all equally important—we would miss the z if it were broken a lot less than the e—they exist like Euclid's axioms on the same level of generality; they are all fundamental: no one of them derives from any other. When the original typewriter keyboard became the more complex computer keyboard, it was expanded. It added exotic function keys, all of which are convenient, none of which is elementary in the sense that the letters of the alphabet are elementary. The computer keyboard, like the table of chemical elements, acknowledges in its spatial layout the marginal nature of the exotic additions.

Elements in all of these cases are definite and few and are the starting points of everything in their domain. We should expect the same limits to apply to the elements of prose style. These elements cannot be an indefinite and miscellaneous list of surface features and mechanical rules. The authors of this book think the elements of style legitimately can be expressed as a short series of questions concerning a set of relationships among truth, presentation, writer, reader, thought, and language. These questions are addressed to fundamental issues that must be answered deliberately or by default before we can write at all. The issues are all on the same fundamental level. None concerns a surface phenomenon—like sentence length—and however closely related they are, none derives from another.

These questions concern a series of relationships: What can be known? What can be put into words? What is the relationship between thought and language? Who is the writer addressing and why? What is the implied relationship between writer and reader? What are the implied conditions of discourse? In any given style, positions will be assigned to truth, language, the writer, and the reader. Classic style is a group of closely related decisions. It defines roles and creates a distinctive network of relationships; it takes a consistent stand on the elements of style. Other stands constitute other styles.

The concept that a style follows from a set of fundamental decisions is commonplace in musicology and art history. For example, when Charles Rosen describes the origins of the classical style in music, he begins by describing what he calls "needs" that the existing high baroque style was incapable of meeting. In Rosen's analysis, high baroque style was invented to present static states: it rendered sentiment or a theatrical moment of crisis. Classical style was invented to present dynamic action. Handel, a master of high baroque style, juxtaposed different emotions. Mozart, a master of classical style, represents a single character passing from one emotion to another in a sequence. In Rosen's formula, "Dramatic sentiment was replaced by dramatic action." Classical style differs from the style of the high baroque because it has made different decisions about the object of presentation. Although it is possible to catalogue surface differences between high baroque style and classical style, the motive and character of the change cannot be understood as a replacement of one set of surface features by another. For Rosen, the first significant examples of the capacity of the classical style to represent dramatic sequence are to be found in the harpsichord sonatas of Domenico Scarlatti. Scarlatti made classical decisions about fundamental questions although he lacked many of the surface features of the style: "the changes of texture in his sonatas are the dramatic events, clearly set off and outlined, that were to become central to the style of the generations that came after him." "Although there is little sign in his works of the classical technique of transition from one kind of rhythm to another, there is already an attempt to make a real dramatic clash in the changes of key. . . ."

In art history as well, there is normally an awareness that style follows from fundamental decisions rather than surface features. Émile Mâle, in his analysis of the iconographic sources of religious art in Western Europe, for example, notes that theologians of the thirteenth, fourteenth, and fifteenth centuries share a conception of the world as a "vast symbol." But while this theological concept of the world as an integrated symbolic form is the source of the stylistic decisions of the thirteenth century, it has no such role in the style of religious art of the fifteenth century. In Mâle's words, "A profound symbolism had governed the arrangement of the sculptured figures on the portals of . . . thirteenth-century churches," so that "the statues of Chartres formed a perfectly coherent system of ideas."

By contrast, the fifteenth-century façade of Saint-Vulfran at Abbéville, which Mâle describes as magnificent and compares for its beauty and the richness of its decoration to the great achievements of the thirteenth century, is stylistically a world away from the thirteenth-century conception of a church as a learned encyclopedia. The style of the sculptural program of Saint-Vulfran is not informed by any such governing plan because, in common with the other great achievements in religious art of its century, it does not derive from a symbolic conception of the universe. The symbolism of the thirteenth century that was the foundation of a style of iconography has yielded to a less learned, less literary style of iconography in the fifteenth. Sentiment and emotion have replaced symbol and encyclopedic organization.

The thesis that a style follows from a set of fundamental decisions and not from a catalogue of surface features is far less common in books about style in writing. Almost every book about writing contains the word "style" in its title or as a significant section heading, and many magazines and journals include a style sheet defining their house style. Let us consider a selection of these: *The Chicago Manual of Style*, the *MLA Style Manual*, the final section ("Style") of *The Harvest Reader*, chapter 6 ("Style") of Kate Turabian's *Manual for Writers of Term Papers, Theses, and Dissertations*, Strunk and White's *The Elements of Style*, and Joseph M. Williams's summary of his collaboration with Gregory Colomb, *Style: Toward Clarity and Grace*.

The word "style" does not mean the same thing to the writers of these guides, textbooks, and manuals. In *The Chicago Manual of Style*, "style" refers to those arbitrary decisions that must be made for consistency's sake in copy text, but have no consequence for intellectual content or conceptual organization. For example, with respect to intellectual content or conceptual organization, it makes no difference how a date is written—"March 24, 1954" or "24 March 1954"—but it is desirable that dates be written in a consistent manner throughout a text, and *The Chicago Manual of Style* gives a standard, arbitrary way to achieve consistency. "Style" here means necessary but arbitrary decisions about surface features of copy text.

Joseph Williams's *Style*, by contrast, views surface features of copy text as peripheral to its project, which is to explain how to revise "pointed" prose so that it can be easily parsed.

Yet all six of our selections, which stand for an indefinite number of others, characterize "style" as something external to the core decisions that define style in the sense that Rosen and Mâle have discussed it.

The *MLA Style Manual* is just a shorter and arbitrarily different version of *The Chicago Manual of Style*. Kate Turabian offers rules—many of them "adapted from *The Chicago Manual of Style*, 13th edition"—suitable for term papers. The final section ("Style") in *The Harvest Reader* implies that style is a decorative element that comes after all the serious work has been completed, like paint on a house.

Even Strunk and White's famous textbook *The Elements of Style*—whose title might lead you to expect a writer's equivalent to Euclid's *Elements of Geometry*—treats style as composed of distinguishing surface marks. If you open Euclid's *Elements* to the first page, you see a few fundamental definitions and axioms. If you open Strunk and White's *Elements* to the first page, you see:

1. Form the possessive singular of nouns by adding 's.
   Follow this rule whatever the final consonant. Thus write,

   > Charles's friend
   > Burns's poems
   > the witch's malice.

   Exceptions are the possessives of ancient proper names in *-es* and *-is*, the possessive *Jesus*', and such forms as *for conscience' sake, for righteousness' sake*.

If you look at chapter 5, "An Approach to Style," where the authors propose to treat "style in its broader meaning," you will find a discussion not of core decisions but rather of "what is distinguished and distinguishing" about the surface of language: "When we speak of Fitzgerald's style, . . . we mean the sound his words make on paper."

In Strunk and White, all style is finally said to be a "high mystery" because it cannot be learned from a catalogue of the only elements of style that they consider, the surface elements. "Who knows why certain notes in music are capable of stirring the listener deeply, though the same notes slightly rearranged are impotent?" Charles Rosen, working from the core decisions that define a musical style, rather than from individual notes, sees an intelligible historical process instead of high mystery.

Joseph Williams's book, *Style*, is completely free of high mystery and intelligently suspicious of rules of usage. Even his final chapter, "Usage," which treats basic rules, regards points of usage as peripheral to writing. *Style* is entirely invulnerable to any accusation that it offers a mechanical approach to *writing* since it is quite explicit that it is not a guide to writing at all but rather a guide to solving a problem in writing: if the writer has finished the intellectual work of writing and has written a draft, but finds that his text frustrates his reader's attempt to understand it, then *Style* will show the writer ways to change the structure of expression so as to accommodate the reader's routines. To this extent, Williams's approach to style is distinguished from that of everyone else on our list. His book is not meant as a guide to arbitrary conventions or matters of taste but rather as a model of how people read what Williams calls "pointed discourse"—which includes arguments, instructions, memos, and so on. Knowing this model allows a writer to shape his discourse to fit the expectations of his readers. Williams's book is effective and helpful as a guide to higher mechanics. But it presents itself as concerned with revision—an activity independent of decisions on the fundamental questions of truth, language, reader, and writer. In this way, Williams inadvertently and inevitably presents himself as describing *style*, rather than *a style*. There is a consistent set of decisions on fundamental matters lying behind the style Williams treats, but he does not acknowledge them or acknowledge that there are alternatives.

For every item on our list that treats prose style, there is an assumption made at the beginning that is linked to a mistake that comes at the end. If you start off with the view of style as a list of surface mechanical elements at any level, then you can end up with the correct list and present it as constituting *style*, rather than *a style*.

In music and in painting, different fundamental decisions define different styles. In geometry or logic, different fundamental axioms define different systems. In writing, different stands on the elements of style define different families of prose styles. A failure to view style as a fundamental stand on central issues entails a failure to see the possibility of other stands that constitute other styles.

The domain of style is what can be chosen. A fundamental stand is a choice open to the writer. By contrast, to know a language is to know a great range of things that are not open to choice: it is not open to every writer, for example, to decide that sentences shall begin with a period and end with a capital letter, that the word "dog" shall refer to cats, that predicates shall not agree in number and person with their subjects, or that six fine brick houses shall be called "brick fine houses six." You can, however, decide whether to call a certain dog a "dog" or a "hound," to say "Sally devoured the roast beef" rather than "The roast beef was devoured by Sally," to write in sentences that are short and clipped rather than baroque and periodic, or to write "24 March 1954" rather than "March 24, 1954," but these are surface features. Books that talk about style in writing treat these moments of choice at the surface level but typically ignore the elements of style, which is to say, the fundamental choices from which surface features derive.

We propose to describe the fundamental questions that are the elements of style in writing, and the answers to these questions that define classic style. The elements come under five topical headings: truth, presentation, scene, cast, thought and language.

■ **The Classic Stand on the Elements of Style**

Truth

René Descartes provides a kind of philosophic patronage for classic style in its seventeenth-century French expression. Because the fundamental problem he addresses and the solution he offers commanded attention throughout Europe, he helped to make the attitudes that define the style, as well as the style itself, widely plausible and attractive. Although classic style does not itself depend upon specifically Cartesian assumptions or conclusions, some of Descartes's characteristic attitudes and emphases are fundamental to the style. Not least among these attitudes is Descartes's conception of his audience's access to truth. In his view, the most important issues in philosophy are of general human concern and can be understood by nonspecialist readers. One expression of this attitude is the very fact that Descartes's most famous book, usually called (misleadingly) in English *Discourse on Method* (1637), is written in French, not in Latin, the conventional language of advanced study and erudition at the time.

A philosophic treatise called *Discourse on Method* might lead its reader to expect an abstract discussion about method in general rather than a book about a particular method for doing one thing. Descartes was not, however, interested in discussing method in general, and his original title, while long, was not misleading: DISCOURSE ON THE METHOD *of rightly directing one's Reason and of seeking Truth in the Sciences.* There is a remarkable and attractive freshness to this book, which in little more than fifty pages of disarming narrative offers a method for separating a few certain truths from the morass of uncertain opinions and simple prejudices that everyone manages unconsciously to acquire. He presents his subject according to the order of reason, represented—not coincidentally, for the supremely rational classic mind—as identical to the order of discovery. Assimilating intellectual experience to the order of reason is a matter of course in classic style.

Descartes's little book is among the most accessible of recognized philosophic classics in the Western tradition. It is not a book by an erudite addressed to other erudites. Descartes explicitly devalues erudition. His thesis is that everybody has what is essential for identifying truth—natural reason—whether or not that person has any special educational formation. Failure to identify truth comes either from directing natural reason to the wrong objects—which can include the recondite lore of erudition—or from uncritically accepting opinion and custom.

Descartes frames his *Discourse* as a personal account of what he himself did and suggests that anyone who wants to do what he did can. At least ostensibly, he is not arguing a case; he is merely trying to place the reader where he himself stood in order to make his subsequent actions intelligible. His method of expression mirrors his contention that once we clear away received opinion, custom, and prejudice, what is certainly true is immediately apparent because of its distinctness and clarity. Everyone who has cleared away the normal mental impediments is equally capable of perceiving what is certainly true and can personally stand behind his perception. What is certainly true can be personally verified by each individual—whether that individual has mastered Latin and the liberal arts or speaks only low Breton and has spent his life farming—and without the need of any outside authority.

From one point of view, classic style can been seen as a version of Descartes's approach to truth in which the domain of truth has been expanded to include, first, conventional information, and then those very opinions and customs that Descartes filtered out. For Descartes, there are very few certain truths, but everybody has a natural endowment that, once purified, gives access to them. Classic style treats all its objects as if they were equally available to every observer and as if every reader has whatever may be necessary to verify what the writer presents. What is a natural endowment in Descartes becomes a kind of cultural competence in classic style. The certain truths Descartes perceived are internal and essentially timeless. To verify them we need to return to a sort of state of nature as it was before we had acquired any local conventions. Classic style treats external objects, contingent facts, and even opinions as if they too are beyond doubt or discussion. To verify them we need to acquire local conventions so widespread within the relevant culture that the style treats them as if they were natural endowments.

To see how this attitude about verification applies in practice, suppose someone wants to know the color of a house two blocks away. The competence needed to check and report back is so widespread that we might think it pedantic to object to the claim that

"anyone" could do it. Let us leave to the fine print all the qualifications: anyone old enough to know his colors, anyone with normal vision, anyone we can trust not to lie, anyone with a normal
memory, anyone who will not just wander off after he has checked
the house, and so on. If the information needed includes the street
address, the pool of people competent to check it is slightly smaller,
but as in the case of checking the color, it seems to be possible to
ascertain the address with certainty, and again, anyone who knows
a simple convention can just look at the numbers attached to the
house and report back. Almost anyone whose eyes are pointed in
the right direction can certainly get it right. Let us consider a few
other bits of information that can be treated as routine to the point
of being universally accessible and certain even though each one
actually requires a slightly more specific competence based on a
human convention that must be learned. Finding a bibliographic
citation is like checking a special kind of address: anyone who
knows how to use a library and knows the conventional form of
a bibliographic entry can just look it up. Finding the citation for
a painting in a museum is slightly more specialized, but like the
previous examples, it is something that anyone who knows a few
simple conventions can certainly look up and get straight. None
of these tasks involves argument or reasoning, although they each
require something more than a universally shared natural endowment. It seems plausible that the correct color, the correct address,
the correct bibliographic citation, the correct catalogue number
for a painting can certainly be known by just about anyone in a
particular culture over the age of about ten who happens to be
standing in the right place.

It is common enough to simplify matters and treat these bits of
knowledge as if they were certainties equally accessible to anyone.
Classic style expands the domain of truth to include anything that
might require not merely the knowledge of a convention but even
the ability to make a judgment.

In classic style, opinions stated clearly and distinctly are treated
as if they can be verified by simple observation. The writer does
not typically attempt to persuade by argument. The writer merely

puts the reader in a position to see whatever is being presented and suggests that the reader will be able to verify it because the style treats whatever conventions or even prejudices it operates from as if these were, like natural reason, shared by everyone. It is a style of disguised assertion. A. J. Liebling writes, "The prize fighter is as reluctant as the next artist to recognize his disintegration." What is at stake here includes the claim that boxing is an art. The point is not argued or even asserted. It is referred to as if it were a fact that the reader, because she shares the competence that Liebling himself has, will recognize as true once it is presented. And that competence itself, Liebling implies, is a convention. The list of the arts, as we all know, includes music, painting, ballet, boxing.

If a writer in this style wants her readers to think that a certain restaurant has a great cellar, a certain book is beautifully written, or a certain time and place attained the summits of civilization, these complex matters of judgment, open to endless qualification and debate, are presented as if they were as obvious as the Library of Congress call number for the first edition of *War and Peace* in the Maude translation, and as easy to check as that number is for somebody who happens to be in the Library of Congress. The classic writer prototypically neither argues nor asserts what is true because it is part of the definition of the style that anybody in a position to see truth can recognize it for herself.

Truth Can Be Known

There is probably nothing more fundamental to the attitude that defines classic style than the enabling convention that truth can be known. People tend to deceive themselves; they want to make exceptions for reasons of sentimentality or friendship, vanity or interest. They want to avoid knowing truth when truth is painful, to distort truth when truth is inconvenient. But there is no doubt, in the classic attitude, that truth can be known. Knowing truth is as much a part of the equipment of a classic writer as knowing how to play the violin is part of the equipment of a concert violinist. Is it possible to play the violin? Can that question occur to a concert violinist? Could there be such a thing as a concert violinist if it were not possible to play the violin? Could there be such a thing as a classic writer if it were not possible to know truth?

Truth Is Not Contingent

The concept of truth that grounds classic style does not depend on what might be called "point of view" or "angle of vision." The truth of things can be perceived by attentive people of any age or condition. Human experience reveals the same conflicts, the same needs and desires, the same weaknesses and virtues. To pay close attention to personal experience is to see through it to truths that run through all such experience.

Thucydides, writing in Greece in the fifth century B.C., assumes that anything true he says about human conflicts and human institutions in *The Peloponnesian War* will be verified by the sense of recognition he will elicit from readers who will live through other wars in other times or other places because what is thoroughly local is thoroughly universal, if properly perceived. As Thucydides himself puts it, he seeks "an exact knowledge of the past as an aid to the interpretation of the future, which in the course of human things must resemble if it does not reflect it."

An experience that is uniquely personal and must therefore be accepted on faith is not a suitable subject for classic style. The reader cannot verify it from his own experience and cannot even check it against earlier testimonies of experience, such as Thucydides'. In the classic view, what cannot be universally verified cannot be true.

The classic attitude is thus both foundationalist and universalist—local events, properly observed, will always disclose universal truths as their foundations. This is an enabling convention. Just as the enabling convention "truth can be known" contradicts the view of the radical skeptic, so the enabling convention "truth is eternal" contradicts the views of the romantic, the relativist, and the ironist for whom truth is contingent. Classic style assumes that truths exist prior to an individual's experience but that knowledge of what is true is achieved through individual experience. Universal truths are eternal and will always be verified by normal experience. They are eternal in two senses: they are discovered, not created, and future experience will always corroborate past testimony. An individual discovers hypocrisy through his experience, but hypocrisy well observed and well described in one time and place will be recognized across cultures and across centuries, since to observe well and describe well in classic style is always to transcend contingent situations. Circumstances change; truth abides.

Truth Is Pure

Truth, in the classic attitude, is a standard for measuring human virtue. As such, it demonstrates an eternal human deficiency, since human virtue exists only in particular human actions, and human actions inevitably involve complex motives, contradictory emotions, and distracting sensations. These things are murky and fluid; they induce moral vertigo in all normal people. The resulting confusion can be temporarily and unsatisfactorily stabilized by deception, irony, and pretense. It can never be escaped.

Truth, on the other hand, has no feelings, no emotions, no motives. It exists always without seeking for anything. It is complete in a way that no person ever is. People feel their inadequacies and desires; they have ambitions. Their hungers cannot be permanently satisfied, merely temporarily assuaged. Truth, eternal and immutable, always remains available to the disciplined writer as a model and a standard, but classic prose is a refinement of human experience. It is what can be known; it is not what can be lived.

Alone with a piece of paper, a writer can submit to the discipline of classic style, prune away ambition and pretense, and achieve the clarity and suppleness that truth confers. But such moments are temporary accomplishments, not permanent possessions.

The classic attitude, especially in its origins, acknowledges human inadequacies: we are victims of our ambitions; fully accurate self-knowledge is unavailable; self-interest leads to self-deception; we are inconsistent, unreliable, impure. Yet the classic attitude is never despairing: these inadequacies are like an unfortunate layer of corruption over a fundamental soundness. We are not impotent, merely weak, and we can grow stronger. We recognize truth when we see it, even though the encounter with truth is brief and difficult to sustain. In the classic view, we can not only aspire to what is fundamentally true and valuable, we can even—and at the key moments—succeed in these aspirations. In Descartes, in parts of Pascal, and in certain American traditions influenced by classic style, encouragement constitutes the principal tone. For La Rochefoucauld, the classic attitude is a consolation for our failures. For Jefferson, it is rather more like the means to success.

The Motive Is Truth

The classic writer is licensed, so to speak, by the truth of what he says, not by his social position, political power, or technical knowledge. Classic writing is animated by a common motive, regardless of its local subject or local purpose

In classic style, the reader and writer are brought together by a common recognition of truth. The writer is never merely indulging personal interests. As a result, a complementary relationship is created between writer and reader: the writer presents truth, and the reader recognizes it. Of course, the classic writer may in fact serve personal interests through his writing, but the attitude adopted in classic prose is that the writer's governing motive is to present truth. To the extent that a work of classic prose has obvious practical purposes, the classic attitude takes the position that they are merely accidental.

One consequence of this attitude for classic prose is that the aphoristic quality of classic prose concerns observation ("No one is ever so happy or unhappy as he thinks"), not morality ("Those who live in glass houses should not throw stones"), or behavior ("Look before you leap"), although it tacitly conveys its expectations about both. The classic writer presents himself not as a guide to morals or behavior, but as an observer of truth.

Even when the classic writer's motive is persuasion, he is reluctant to admit it overtly, and even when he admits it, he does so conditionally, noting that persuasion can never take priority over the abiding motive of presenting truth. Local or practical motives are always constrained to respect this governing motive.

The classic writer presents truth, and typically takes the position that of course the reader will recognize truth. The classic writer rarely writes as if he is pressing claims and presenting arguments, but rather pretends that he is presenting subjects and conducting analyses. When, on rare occasions, the classic writer adopts the stance that the reader will not believe what is being presented, he never concedes that the reader's disposition should influence what he says. A writer who wishes to persuade is constrained from ever telling the audience something it is unwilling to believe, and this is a compromise unacceptable in the classic attitude. The classic attitude compels writers, in extreme cases, to express truth and leave the audience to its folly. In that case—as always—the writer's explicit motive is not hope of persuasion but rather respect for truth. It is the choice Socrates makes in the *Apology*.

Presentation

Prose Is a Window

In the classic attitude, writing serves to present something else: its subject. The subject is conceived of as a "thing" distinct from the writing, something that exists in the world and is independent of any presentation. Clarity is the central virtue of classic prose because the classic writer's defining task is to present something he has previously perceived. Self-evident truths, Madame de Chevreuse's character, the power of well-ordered thoughts, the food of France are conceived as "things" with their proper characteristics, existing "in the world" and completely independent of their presentation. The language of classic prose serves these things and should never draw attention to itself. Naturally, when we read La Rochefoucauld's passage on Madame de Chevreuse, we are looking at words; we cannot look through them to Madame de Chevreuse herself, nor could we possibly know what La Rochefoucauld wants to tell us even if we could see her. Nevertheless, classic style operates on the premise that La Rochefoucauld's experience of Madame de Chevreuse is a "thing" that he wants to present through a medium that will, at its best, be transparent, as if the reader were looking at something through a perfectly clean and undistorting window; the window should not draw attention to itself, and will not unless it is obviously defective in some way.

Classic writers speak with conviction. That conviction, they imply, comes from knowledge or experience of something that exists before the writing and is completely independent of it. Their prose is conceived of as a perfectly efficient instrument: it neither invents nor distorts. It is as if the language they use had no characteristics of its own and therefore could not be considered a "thing." Classic prose does not ask the reader to observe it as if it too is a thing; it invites the reader to look through it to what it presents. It draws attention to itself only when there is something wrong with it.

Consider Jefferson's phrase "that all men are created equal, that they are endowed by their Creator with certain unalienable rights, that among these are life, liberty, and the pursuit of happiness." Jefferson is an accomplished writer, but that is taken for granted and not something he wants his readers even to notice. If someone read the Declaration of Independence in 1776 and found the writing itself to be the most memorable thing about it, there would be something wrong with it.

Contrast Jefferson's style with that of Jeremy Bentham on the fallacy of begging the question:

> Having, without the form, the force of an assumption—and having for its object, and but too commonly for its effect, a like assumption on the part of the hearer or reader,—the sort of allegation in question, how ill-grounded soever, is, when thus masked, apt to be more persuasive than when expressed simply and in its own proper form: especially where, to the character of a censorial adding the quality and tendency of an impassioned allegation, it tends to propagate, as it were by contagion, the passion by which it was suggested.

Bentham is talking about a fallacy here; he has no reason to want to place his own writing in the foreground, but whatever he may be saying about begging the question, what is likely to make the strongest impression on anybody who reads him is his manner of presentation. It is as if we expect to find a window and encounter a fun-house mirror. Bentham's sentence can be puzzled out. We can determine what he means to say. We could rewrite it in classic style. But classic prose never has to be puzzled out. We never have to rework the expression in order to see what it means to present.

Classic Prose Is Perfect Performance

When a jazz master improvises, perhaps the most impressive aspect of the performance is its appearance of impromptu perfection. Although improvised, the performance has no mistake, false step, or deficiency. It looks inevitable, as if it could have been done in no other way, as if every stage were known to the performer from the beginning.

Paradoxically, we know that if the same jazz master performed the improvisation again, it would be entirely different, but it would still appear as if it could have been done in no other way, as if it were inevitable.

This same characterization might apply to a knock-out sequence in a boxing match, a lethal volley at Wimbledon, a winning stretch move in a horse race, or an ingenious screen pass in football. It is perfect, and we confront a paradox. We know that the performance is not just a rare example of everything going right, because the masters of these arts can give similar performances repeatedly. The performance therefore had to be prepared, because no performance can be routinely perfect without preparation. Yet it is difficult to imagine just what such preparation might have been. The performances are not canned. They are fresh and spontaneous even though we know that they are the result of practice and effort. The basketball player who sinks the ball amid a chaotic field of play without looking at the basket can do that because she has memorized a certain spot on the floor to the point where she no longer even needs to see the basket to hit it. But the preparation is hidden, and the performance looks like magic.

Classic style is perfect performance, with no hesitation, revision, or backtracking. Its essential fiction is that this perfection happens at the first try. Classic style does not acknowledge process or stages of discovery, does not acknowledge revision or successive refinements. The performance suggests that to write this way, one can never hesitate, grope, or struggle, whether in thought or in language. This is part of the performance, and when it succeeds it does not seem to be a performance at all. Its corollary fiction is that the performance cannot be prepared because it has no parts that could be worked on separately or in stages. It is seamless. The writer appears simply to have been born with an ability that the rest of us lack. To someone attempting to learn classic style, these fictions can be intimidating. In learning this style, it is helpful to remember that these are fictions.

Because classic style presents fully refined thought in inevitable prose, it is final. This finality excludes two kinds of hedges, which we will call hedges of process and hedges of liability. Hedges of process are hesitations and uncertainties that arise because one is in the middle of thought. For example, one may say something, then think better of it, and then add a disclaimer or a qualifier. But in the model of classic prose, the thought is final, so hedges of process are rare.

Hedges of liability are insurance against the possibility of having overlooked something or being ignorant of something that would change the writer's views or conclusions. For example, a writer may say that in her limited experience, such and such is true. This hedges the writer against contradiction by experience she has not had. But in the model of classic prose, the thought is fully refined, so hedges of liability are rare. The classic writer does not say, "As far as I know, there was never a more gallant court than that of Henri II," but rather, "There was never a more gallant court than that of Henri II."

There is a third sort of hedge that classic prose omits, which we will call hedges of worth. The classic writer spends no time justifying her project. The classic writer does not compare its worth to the worth of other projects. A classic writer will write about milk, for example, with no indication that there can be a question about the worth of writing about milk, no indication that the reader could entertain any doubt about the worth of writing about milk. A classic writer might begin an essay on milk with the claim, "In spite of its liquid state, milk must always be considered as a food and not as a beverage." A classic writer might begin an essay on a little-known species of bird with the observation, "Unusual among songbirds, shrikes prey on small birds and rodents, catching them with the bill and sometimes impaling them on thorns or barbed wire for storage." Classic writers do not distract readers with questions of the worth of the project. There is no hierarchy of importance of subjects in classic writing. Everything is in close focus.

Every Word Counts

It is possible to skim certain styles. Most after-dinner speeches are presented in styles that claim only part of our attention. Many textbooks and news articles are written in styles that allow us to bounce over words and phrases and still feel that we have extracted the sense accurately.

Browsing is different from skimming. In browsing, we look from thing to thing, deciding what to choose. Classic style allows browsing but not skimming. We may turn to just one paragraph, say, in an essay, or even to one sentence, and focus on just that. But once we focus on a unit in classic style, and intend to understand it, then we must pay attention to every detail. Writer and reader assume that every word counts. If the reader skips a single word or phrase or sentence, the sense of the unit may be lost. Classic style contains crucial nuances, which can be lost in skimming.

Clarity Everywhere Is Not Accuracy Everywhere

Fine, accurate distinctions and subtle nuance are among the most typical features of classic style. But classic style has a clear hierarchy of goals; what is subordinate to the main issue can never be allowed to obscure that issue or distract attention from it. When accuracy in the sense of being exhaustively correct involves complicated qualifications of no consequence to the main issue, classic writers do not hesitate to simplify. In this frame, accuracy becomes pedantry if it is indulged for its own sake. A classic writer will phrase a subordinate point precisely but without the promise that it is technically accurate. The convention between writer and reader is that the writer is not to be challenged on these points because they are merely scaffolding.

Waverley Root begins *The Food of France*, "As far back as the records go, the people of the land now known of as France have thought of food in terms of its taste more often than in terms of its nutritive qualities." Root wants to indicate that the culinary traditions he treats are immemorial, but the actual documentary history or demographic realities of France are not at issue. It would be silly to question whether Vercingetorix the Gaul really thought about food more often in terms of taste or nutritive qualities. The subordinate point is stated with care and precision, but without a tortured accuracy that would bury the essential distinction between nutrition and taste under a ton of scholarly documentation.

Scene

The Model Is One Person Speaking to Another

The idiom of classic style is the voice of conversation. The writer adopts the pose of a speaker of near-perfect efficiency whose sentences are the product of the voice rather than some instrument of writing. Johnson's sentence about Shakespeare is prototypically unclassic because it could never be taken for speech. Classic style models itself on speech and can be read aloud properly the first time.

In speech, an expression is gone the moment it is spoken, and has only that one instant to enter the mind and attain its place in memory. Since classic writing pretends to be speech, it never requires the reader to look forward or backward; it never admits that the reader is in a situation to do so. Each phrase is presented as if it has only one chance—now—to do its job. Of course, a reader may in fact go over a passage of classic prose many times. But the classic writer never acknowledges that possibility either explicitly or by implication.

The ideal speech of classic style appears to be spontaneous and motivated by the need to inform a listener about something. It has just occurred to the speaker to tell someone about this, and so he has begun to do so. Or perhaps he is talking to someone else and is overheard. What he has to say is not a set piece. He has not labored over it beforehand, systematically refining and arranging various thoughts, editing their expression, and then speaking the polished whole aloud. Something occurs to him and he says it. He takes another moment's brief but perfect thought and says the next thing. As a consequence, the rhythm of the writing is a series of movements, each one brief and crisp, with an obvious beginning and end. Of course, in retrospect, we may see that these movements are organized into a flawless global structure, but the pretense is that this global organization is the natural product of the writer's orderly mind. It comes out that way the first time without special effort. The global organization is never referred to; its existence is not even acknowledged. The classic writer thus banishes from his vocabulary phrases like "as we shall see," "three paragraphs ago," "before I move to my next point I must introduce a new term," "the third part of our four-part argument is," and all other "metadiscourse" that proclaims itself as writing rather than speech.

Pascal's *Lettres provinciales* are the prototype of this appearance. They are a defense of Jansenism, written in the form of letters from someone in Paris to someone in the provinces. The presentation is informal; the writer is just describing events in the capital. They do not suggest deliberate strategy. It is almost as if the writer had nothing better to do; it occurs to the writer to tell his provincial friend about something everyone in Paris is excited about. It could even be that the writer corresponds with this friend routinely, and that the controversy over Jansenism is merely this season's news. The letters give the appearance of spontaneity: the writer has not sketched out in advance how many letters there will be or what he will write about in each letter. He has not even sketched out the one letter he is writing. The letters do not suggest that they have been edited, either. In this way, classic style has something in common with dramatic performances of talk and conversation. The playwright or screenwriter has edited out everything that is dispensable, but the result is not supposed to sound edited.

The prototypical scene in classic writing is an individual speaking intimately to another individual. What the classic writer has to say is directed entirely to that one individual. But it can be over-heard. The reader is sometimes cast in the role of the individual addressed, sometimes cast in the role of eavesdropper. The role of the reader in the *Lettres provinciales*, for example, is someone who has come across these letters accidentally. These letters imply the participation of their original recipient in a conversation. There is even one short answering letter.

In fact, classic prose is meant to be overheard, because although it is directed entirely toward one individual it never needs to be bent to fit that individual. It is fine if it is overheard, because what it has to say and the way it says it are not contingent upon the audience. It is never dishonorable or problematic. The classic writer does not appear to have written things in a way she would not had she known others were listening.

Classic style is not a style for oratory—in the first place because its model scene is so different from the model scene of oratory. In oratory, the implied author is a rhetor, an actor, adopting a role to speak to an implied audience consisting of a group. The classic writer is not speaking to a group, and although she is of course also an actor, her act is to play at presenting herself. She takes the pose of authenticity. This acting, when good, makes the writer look vulnerable, in the sense that she is exposing what she cares about.

Paradoxically, classic style thus requires a strong revelation of personality even as it subordinates what is merely personal. The classic writer is not interested in mirroring the personal processes of her thought; certainly she is not interested in mirroring her personal sensations or emotions. Yet, since her only motive for speaking is the felt importance of what she has to say, she reveals herself through the topics she chooses and what she says about them.

The model scene of classic prose—an individual speaking to another individual—is not always followed literally from beginning to end. Some texts that appear ostensibly to be based on a different model turn out, on closer inspection, to have been based on the classic model. Let us take as an example the Declaration of Independence. Its beginning and end do not look classic. Its ending is a formulaic speech act, an official declaration of independence with all the appropriate legalistic phrases:

> We, therefore, the Representatives of the United States of America, in General Congress, Assembled, appealing to the Supreme Judge of the world for the rectitude of our intentions, do, in the Name, and by the Authority of the good People of these Colonies, solemnly publish and declare, That these United Colonies are, and of Right ought to be Free and Independent States; that they are Absolved from all Allegiance to the British Crown. . . .

Speech acts occur between two people informally and intimately all the time, as in "Can you open the door?," but formal versions of speech acts, like those in the Declaration or "I hereby promise to pay you the amount owed," are usually reserved for situations where the public audience serves as a witness that the act has been performed. There are no official witnesses to classic prose and no audience with institutional expectations, such as a theater audience, the audience at an inauguration, or the audience at the opening of a bridge.

The ending of the Declaration of Independence is unclassic in another way: its last sentence is a bit of inflated oratory:

> And for the support of this Declaration, with a firm reliance on the protection of Divine Providence, we mutually pledge to each other our Lives, our Fortunes and our sacred Honor.

The beginning of the Declaration of Independence is not classic, either. It announces a scene explicitly removed from the model scene of classic style: it pretends that it is an announcement from a people—the citizens of the colonies—to the whole world:

> When in the Course of human events it becomes necessary for one people to dissolve the political bands which have connected them with another, and to assume among

the powers of the earth, the separate and equal station to which the Laws of Nature and of Nature's God entitle them, a decent respect to the opinions of mankind requires that they should declare the causes which impel them to the separation.

But between the opening and the closing sections of the Declaration, its voice is the voice of one person talking, observing injuries. You can almost see the expression on the face of the speaker, and see his hand gestures as he speaks these words. The speaker wishes to present something to you: the state of things in the colonies, or more specifically in his own life, and why the colonies and he must go their own way. The language is clear and direct and memorable. It is written so as to be understood the first time it is heard. Here are a few examples:

The history of the present King of Great Britain is a history of repeated injuries and usurpations, all having in direct object the establishment of an absolute Tyranny over these States. . . .

He has called together legislative bodies at places unusual, uncomfortable, and distant from the depository of their Public Records, for the sole purpose of fatiguing them into compliance with his measures. . . .

He has plundered our seas, ravaged our Coasts, burnt our towns, and destroyed the lives of our people.

He has constrained our fellow Citizens taken Captive on the high Seas to bear Arms against their Country, to become the executioners of their friends and Brethren, or to fall themselves by their Hands.

The Declaration of Independence is not one person speaking to another, but in its body it never gets away from that model. The case is similar for sermons, technical reports, lectures, and business memos: the actual scene is not the model scene of classic style, but the writing can be formed upon the classic scene. In fact, not even the prototypical texts of classic style are literally one individual spontaneously speaking to another.

If classic prose is ideal speech, just between us, spontaneous, it follows that its occasions are informal. On the other hand, Johnson on Shakespeare assumes an imaginary protocol between writer and audience in which the occasion is the formal presentation of the writer's labors. It is something like the Mass, whose observers know that its occasion is formal and planned. The protocol of classic prose, by contrast, is spontaneity. It just occurred to the speaker to say this. The informality of the occasion overlaps with the pose of authenticity.

The sense of informality is truer of seventeenth-century French classic style than of its English or American versions. French classic style was at heart a style for memoirs or private reflections. Other occasions—governmental, military, religious, bureaucratic, political—already had their sophisticated protocols, which classic style could not supplant. To some extent in England and to a far greater extent in the United States in the seventeenth and eighteenth centuries, the styles of sermons, political speeches, and other formal presentations were not so immutably established. Classic style in America consequently had the opportunity to take on a use in formal presentations—such as the Declaration of Independence—that it could not have had in its French version.

We can contrast a political text like the Declaration of Independence—whose model scene though not its actual scene is one individual talking to another—with unclassic political speeches such as the typical State of the Union address to Congress or the typical inaugural speech by a governor. There is always a jolt of passion behind the real classic writer, a little excitement because there is a personal conviction and commitment that is often completely missing from a plain statement of what politicians say when they have no intention of acting on it. In the typical State of the Union address, the president of the United States not only can but must speak pieties clearly inconsistent with his actions. Who believes what he is saying? Who thinks he means anything related to action when he says it? In the course of reading the *Lettres provinciales*, it is possible to believe Pascal is wrong, but it is not possible to believe he is saying something he does not really believe, something he would not act on himself. The classic speaker of the Declaration of Independence is certainly going to act on what he is saying. In fact, his speech is an action, and he is putting his life and fortune at risk by that action. The classic writer is an individual, not the organ of a bureaucracy, and so he says what he believes rather than what a committee has decided it can live with. Classic writers are independent, not concerned to protect members of a bureaucracy. They are not controlled by policy, interests, or an organization, or at least they give no appearance of being controlled in such a fashion. Rid of this baggage, they have a freshness that no utterance cobbled together by committee can ever have. The typical political speech, such as a State of the Union address, cannot say much because it has so many constituencies to worry about. It cannot be written by any individual. It is always the product of a committee, so when it is said or read by the pope or the president or the secretary of lies, it does not sound like an individual speaking. It sounds like what it is: the rumble of bureaucracy.

The classic writer is an individual; his model audience is an individual. The classic writer, therefore, does not make distinctions between members of the audience, saying, for example, that some of them will be better prepared to understand what he has to say than will others, or that some will be interested in the first part and others in the second part. Of course, since he implicitly claims to be talking without having mapped out the global organization, he usually avoids any reference to parts. He also avoids raising any questions about whether the reader is interested in what he has to present, with the result that usually it does not occur to the reader to doubt his own interest.

Prose Is Efficient but Not Rushed

The efficiency of classic style is really a luxury. There are no pressures upon the classic writer. There is the absolute need to present truth about something, but that need, however strongly felt by the classic writer, is not an imposed need. Nothing external manipulates the classic writer, whose motive is neither gain nor reputation. Neither profit nor fear spurs the classic writer's efforts. Nor is there any internal anxiety or ambition. Certainly the clock has no effect upon the classic writer.

We think of efficiency as a weapon against time or as an instrument of productivity. The efficiency expert's job is conceived of as saving money by saving time. Efficiency in these contexts is a competitive trick.

The efficiency of the classic writer is purely a matter of mind. Efficiency in thought is the companion of grace and accuracy, indeed makes them possible. The efficiency of classic prose is the natural product of the classic writer's focused and orderly mind. The classic writer has the luxury of thinking without distraction or pressure. Nothing has the power to hurry the classic writer. Classic prose is thus free of disclaimers that the writer does not have time to do a proper job, or that abbreviations must be made in the interest of time, or that he must skip over something. Indeed, the classic writer seems almost to dwell over a sentence for the slightest moment after it ends, as if to savor it or allow its full impact, before going on to the next sentence.

Classic Style Is Energetic but Not Anxious

Students of martial arts explain that a muscle tensed before performance performs badly, because the tension interferes with the impulse to move. Classic style gives the impression that all of the writer's considerable energy is communicated directly to the writing, with none lost collaterally to anxiety or apprehension. The end of a particularly classic phrase seems to leave its writer in a state of repose out of which the next absolutely efficient movement will come.

If we think of a relaxed state as one free of needless tension but nonetheless fully attentive, then we can say that classic style is relaxed even as it performs, in the way a champion racehorse or sprinter is relaxed even at greatest speed. Inefficient effort is the mark of a neophyte.

Cast

Elite Is Not Exclusive

Classic style rests on an implied view of human nature that finds echoes in many religious traditions: left to themselves, people are sure to get things wrong; but with effort and discipline anyone can get the essential things right. Are the saints an elite? Of course. But sanctity, unlike, say, noble birth, is accessible to anyone who is willing to make the effort. So it is with classic style. The elitism of classic style is not the result of natural endowment. It is the result of effort and discipline ending in achievement. No one willing to make the effort is excluded from joining this elite.

The elitism of classic style has nothing to do with the object of presentation, which can range from fine wines to deep sewer tunnels. It has nothing to do with the connoisseurship of the writer either. The writer may speak with a technical mastery not possessed by the reader, but his attitude is always that the reader lacks this mastery only accidentally. You could know what he knows, and you would if you were standing where he stands, which is where the classic writer is trying to place you.

Classic Style Is for Everybody

Imagine someone sitting down to study the works of Marcel Proust, or Ezra Pound, or Walt Whitman with a view to learning to write as they did. It seems absurd, the ambition of a crackpot who does not have the first clue about style. Imagine trying to learn to write like Coleridge, Poe, Faulkner, or Baudelaire. These writers' styles are so suffused with their personalities and have been forged in pursuit of such specific and idiosyncratic goals that no one can acquire their styles short of becoming the writers in question and adopting their goals. The attempt obviously cannot succeed and if pursued to the end results in grotesque impersonation expressed as unconscious parody.

Classic style, by contrast, was assembled out of attitudes and techniques that are available to everybody and independent of any specific subject. There is a definite and knowable path to learning classic style, and you can acquire it fully. When you do, it is yours. The classic writer is impersonating no one. On the contrary, although the classic writer has learned a style instead of having invented one, his attitudes and techniques are authentic to himself. The writer is not appropriated by the style. It is possible to distinguish at a glance between Pascal, Descartes, and La Rochefoucauld. But unlike idiosyncratic styles, classic style is not shaped by the details of a writer's personality or the details of his subject. Neither is it a medium specifically designed to receive the imprint of a whole personality in all of its mysterious individuality. The project of a writer such as Proust, inseparable as it is from the details of his personality, is not a classic project. One consequence of his success in creating a style that answers his needs so well is that his style cannot usefully be adopted to anyone else's.

The Reader Is Competent

Classic style is modeled not merely on speech but on the core concept of conversation—conversation between equals. There is an implicit symmetry in the relationship between the writer and the reader. The model assumes that the reader could take the next turn in the conversation.

Those who have made the effort to acquire classic style comprise, then, a complementary cast of competent writers and competent readers. Becoming competent in this sense consists in being dispassionate enough to see things straight and to present what you have seen without the special pleading of someone whose interests affect her judgments. Such "competence" will seem illusory to many. Can anyone ever see things straight? Can anyone present what she has seen without her interests affecting her judgments? Classic style rests on the enabling assumption that the answers to these questions are yes and yes. When doubt about whether anyone can actually see anything straight and doubt about whether anyone can present what she sees without the distortion of special pleading suffuses a writer's style, that style cannot be classic.

The writer and the reader achieve their competence in the same way. The writer may know something that the reader does not, but the reader has access, in principle, to the same source of knowledge that serves the writer. There is a tacit reference to a shared standard that creates a symmetrical relationship between the writer and the reader. The duc de La Rochefoucauld's description of Madame de Chevreuse rests on this sort of tacit reference. La Rochefoucauld knew her; his readers do not, yet there is an almost irresistible conviction to his description. That conviction rests on the unspoken premise that if we knew her, we would notice what the writer noticed. The writer takes no credit for noticing just these things, and contrasting them in just this way. His unspoken claim is that it would be altogether peculiar not to notice these things and contrast them in this way.

We can see something of this deep conviction that all competent people observe the same things in a passage from *Pride and Prejudice*. Elizabeth Bennet and her sister Jane are discussing Charlotte Lucas's marriage to Mr. Collins. Elizabeth says that she is scandalized at her friend Charlotte's marriage to a man for whom no right-thinking woman could possibly have any regard. Jane replies that, in forming this judgment, Elizabeth has not "made allowance enough for difference in situation and temper." Here is part of Elizabeth's answer

> [W]ere I persuaded that Charlotte had any regard for him, I should only think worse of her understanding than I now do of her heart. My dear Jane, Mr. Collins is a conceited, pompous, narrow-minded, silly man; you know he is, as well as I do; and you must feel as well as I do, that the woman who marries him, cannot have a proper way of thinking. You shall not defend her, though it is Charlotte Lucas. You shall not, for the sake of one individual, change the meaning of principle and integrity, nor endeavour to persuade yourself or me, that selfishness is prudence, and insensibility of danger, security for happiness.

If Elizabeth thought that situation and temper could make a difference in how someone judges Mr. Collins, it would destroy her ability to talk freely to Jane. She would be obliged to hold back her judgments, and that would necessarily alter the whole style of their relationship. Charlotte's decision to marry Mr. Collins has altered forever her relationship to Elizabeth because they can no longer be open and truthful to one another. Jane has seen the same things Elizabeth has seen and they judge Mr. Collins by the same standards, so in the absence of incompetence or special pleading, they must reach the same conclusions.

This assumed symmetry between writer and reader saves the prototypical classic writer from appearing to stoop to mere grinding persuasion. The classic writer does not have to persuade the reader. All he has to do is offer the reader an unobstructed view, and of course the reader will see. This is the stance, for example, of the Declaration of Independence and of Pascal's *Lettres provinciales*: any reasonable person not corrupted by interest would have to agree; their writers are not arguing, they are presenting. As the Declaration puts it, "To prove [that the King is a Tyrant], let Facts be submitted to a candid world." The Declaration then lists facts, as if the conclusion to be drawn from them is evident to anyone who has "a proper way of thinking."

The relationship between writer and reader in classic style is based on an unspecified set of perceptions and values held in common. When a writer makes a decision, it is presented as if it is a decision that the reader is equally capable of making. The silent convention is that a competent reader who had seen the evidence would have made the same decision. The reader does not have to regard the writer as having superior judgment or having access to information not independently available to the reader.

Here is the New Testament scholar C. H. Dodd explaining why he has rejected the idea of rearranging the textual materials of the Fourth Gospel before undertaking a detailed interpretation of the text:

> Many attempts have been made to improve the work by re-arrangement of its material. Some of these have been (as it were) canonized by being adopted in large and important editions of the Fourth Gospel, and in modern translations. I have examined several of these rearrangements, and can-

not sufficiently admire the patience and endless ingenuity which have gone into their making. It is of course impossible to deny that the work may have suffered dislocation, and plausible grounds may be alleged for lifting certain passages out of their setting, where there seems to be some *prima facie* breach of continuity. Unfortunately, when once the gospel has been taken to pieces, its reassemblage is liable to be affected by individual preferences, preconceptions and even prejudices. Meanwhile the work lies before us in an order which (apart from insignificant details) does not vary in the textual tradition, traceable to an early period. I conceive it to be the duty of an interpreter at least to see what can be done with the document as it has come down to us before attempting to improve upon it. This is what I shall try to do. I shall assume as a provisional working hypothesis that the present order is not fortuitous, but deliberately devised by somebody—even if it were only a scribe doing his best—and that the person in question (whether the author or another) had some design in mind, and was not necessarily irresponsible or unintelligent. If the attempt to discover any intelligible thread of argument should fail, then we may be compelled to confess that we do not know how the work was originally intended to run. If on the other hand it should appear that the structure of the gospel as we have it has been shaped in most of its details by the ideas which seem to dominate the author's thoughts, then it would appear not improbable that we have his work before us substantially in the form which he designed.

In making his decision, Dodd takes the position that the reader, once the essential evidence has been assembled, will see precisely what he does. Even though scholarly editors of "large and important editions of the Fourth Gospel" have made a different decision, it requires only a disinterested review of evidence that is in principle accessible to anyone who might care to examine it to allow the reader to see not merely why Dodd has chosen not to rearrange the textual materials of the gospel but why anyone not positively perverse or whose judgment is not affected by personal preferences, preoccupations, or prejudice would do the same thing. In his presentation, his decision is not the product of his exceptional insight, or special knowledge, or personal experience. It has nothing to do with his situation or temper. Provided he is right when he says that the work "(apart from insignificant details) does not vary in the textual tradition, traceable to an early period"—something that can presumably be verified—his decision can be confirmed by anyone who wishes to undertake the investigation he has. There is a silent assumption that part of the reader's competence consists in his agreeing with the writer about what can serve as a proper investigation of this point. It does not affect this attitude in the least if the reader of this passage has, let us say, no knowledge of Hellenistic Greek, no experience with textual materials of this sort, and has never even heard of the large and important editions of the Fourth Gospel that have patiently and ingeniously rearranged the text. All this is merely information, which, in principle, anyone can acquire in just the same way Dodd himself acquired it.

This sense of shared competence is characteristic of the relationship between writer and reader in classic style. There is always a tacit appeal to a standard of perception and judgment that is assumed to be general, rather than special. There is no need for the writer to make appeals to his sincerity, for example, or to some special insight or competence, to arcane or technical knowledge, or to a lifetime of experience obviously not available to everyone else.

Consider how different this attitude is from one in which the author speaks to the reader from an assumed position of superiority. "Reader, you think that high unemployment is bad for an economy because you don't know the first thing about economics; you think that light makes the retina transmit signals because you can't tell the difference between old wives' tales and biochemistry; you think that authors write texts because you don't know the difference between literature and textual modes of domination; you think marriage is normal because you've been taken in by a repressive society. You're lucky you picked up this book, my friend, because you need help. You need it bad." The classic symmetry between writer and reader is broken whenever the writer presents distinctions as if they are the product of her own exceptional insight or temper, distinctions the reader could not have been trusted to see on his own in the right circumstances.

It is broken in a different but complementary way when the writer speaks as if from a knowledge of facts that is, in principle, private. The narrator of Proust's *A la recherche du temps perdu* breaks the classic symmetry between writer and reader in just this way. He dips a kind of cookie called a *madeleine* into a cup of tea, tastes it, and has his past come flooding into his memory in hallucinatory detail. The reader of this passage normally has no inclination to doubt the truth of what the narrator says, but neither can the reader verify it by furnishing himself with tea and *madeleines* of his own. There are all sorts of rhetorical inducements to believe the narrator, but then, you just have to believe him. You cannot see what he sees, and your exclusion is not accidental, as it is when a writer presents events he saw in the 1930s or conversation she heard at the court of Henri IV. Instead, you are in principle excluded from ever being able to verify the narrator's experience.

In "What Is an Author?" Michel Foucault defines a relationship between writer and reader that is asymmetric in both ways: he appeals tacitly to both his own superior judgment and private evidence. In his essay, Foucault observes that before Mallarmé, the concept "literary work" has a kind of validity that it does not have afterward because it is supplanted by "textual modes of domination." There may be reasons to accept what Foucault says, but it is not presented as the sort of observation that a reader can confirm by examining evidence that is, in principle, accessible to anyone who cares to look at it. It is extraordinary really that no one before Foucault seems to have noticed this remarkable rupture in the history of literature. Foucault does not address the point, but if a reader were to pursue it and ask how it came about that something so fundamental had never before been noticed, the answer has two related but distinct parts. First,

Foucault's ability to see what others have not is a consequence of his superior competence. Second, that superior competence defines the relevant evidence. That is why Foucault cannot point his reader to the evidence on which he has reached his conclusion in the way Dodd can. The competence needed to confirm Dodd by reviewing his evidence would take most of a lifetime to acquire—the linguistic, historical, and technical knowledge needed to conduct an investigation of the manuscript tradition of the Fourth Gospel and a critical review of the decisions made by its modern editors—but hundreds of people have acquired such competence and anyone who wants to is, in principle, free to do so. Foucault's evidence is difficult of access not merely because it requires competence that most people do not have and in practice cannot acquire; on the contrary, it is, in principle, private. You would need Foucault's superior insight even to realize that his evidence is evidence: it is, after all, exactly what everyone else since Mallarmé has been looking at without being able to realize that it is evidence for a historical discontinuity between literary works and textual modes of domination.

A reader can accept the idea that Foucault has superior competence, but the reader does not and cannot share that superior competence and, as a result, cannot share his perception either. He can merely be told about it. In classic prose, the relationship between writer and reader is never asymmetrical in this way because classic style appeals to a standard of perception and of judgment assumed to be general, rather than special.

The Writer Is Authentic

The classic writer stands fully behind what she has to say because she has thought it out independently. It may be that in thinking something out independently she has come to a common conclusion, but in expressing it she is neither joining a chorus nor embracing a platitude. Her conclusion is the product of her own thought. As a consequence, even when a classic writer reaches a common conclusion, it has the freshness of discovery. It does not come from camaraderie or conformity. She does not expect its common acceptance to be the evidence that causes it to be believed. It is possible to repeat clichés or say what you think you must to get people to believe you, but the classic stylist appears to have nothing to do with these activities.

It is not the accumulated acceptance of other people—even if these other people are right—that gives force to classic writing. It is the writer's conviction that she has earned a conclusion. To convince another competent person of what is being said does not involve appeals to authority or traditional wisdom or anything other than a simple presentation of the order of reason leading to that conclusion, so that someone else can also reach it independently.

This sort of thing happens every day. When a high school geometry student proves the Pythagorean theorem, she is not breaking new ground in mathematics. But if she has actually worked out the proof herself, she—not Pythagoras—stands behind the theorem. She can respond to any possible challenge by presenting her authentically personal—even if quite common—proof. Someone who copies the identical proof without understanding it cannot stand behind it. Under challenge, the inauthentic geometer has nothing better to offer than lame appeals to widespread acceptance: "Every geometry book since Euclid says this theorem is true, so it must be."

The Writer Is Sufficient

The classic writer perceives truth and, as a corollary, enjoys a uniquely open and incomparably full communication with the society of other people who perceive truth. It would be inaccurate to say that there is absolutely nothing the writer wants from the reader, because the writer does indeed want the reader to belong to that society as well, so much so that he treats the reader as someone who is already a member.

But there is nothing else the classic writer wants from the reader, and nothing at all that the classic writer needs from the reader: the classic writer will present truth without distortion or special pleading even if there is, in fact, no competent reader available.

Above all, the classic writer never appears to be pursuing self-interest. There is nothing the classic writer needs, and so there is nothing the classic writer is trying to get from the reader.

The Writer Is Competent

It is paralyzing to think of how many things can go wrong in an attempt to present something clearly and accurately. Perhaps you cannot see straight. Perhaps you cannot express what you see. Perhaps your conceptual instruments are dull. You might have disabling gaps in your knowledge. You might be lying to yourself.

The situation is not much better even if you have no fears about these potential sources of impotence, because the reader might have doubts, and then you have a different problem: how do you deal with the doubts of the reader?

It is enough to stop some people from writing. Even worse, from the classic point of view, it is enough to convince some people that they should allow their doubts about their own problematic situation as writers to supplant all other subjects, since these doubts are the only things that seem certain.

Classic style frees writers from anxiety or silence by making the enabling assumption that the writer is competent. Truth, which is available to all, can be seen and presented by this writer. Such a competence is no more impossible or problematic than the competence of quite ordinary high school students to prove the Pythagorean theorem. A writer does not have to be omniscient; he just needs an everyday form of competence—the competence of knowing what he needs to know for this talk. His mind is in order and his facts are straight.

The result of this enabling convention is prose that is unclotted and that stays on track. In reality, all the doubts surrounding any writer's situation remain. Both writer and reader know them, so it is merely tedious to rehearse them. There is something at least mildly fraudulent about offering to present a subject and then substituting for it the problematic nature of the presentation. "Let me tell you how to make bread pudding. My God, have you any idea of how impossible it is actually to explain how to cook in writing?

I can make bread pudding myself—done it a hundred times—but it's impossible to put into words how to know when you've got the right consistency. . . ."

The enabling convention that the writer is competent goes hand in hand with the absence of hedges in classic prose. There are styles of academic, legal, and business prose in which the motive is to ensure that no challenge can be raised that has not already been acknowledged by the writer, so that the writer is "covered." Some of these challenges concern the activities of thinking and presenting. Writers in these styles typically work hard to demonstrate that they have anticipated challenges: Could the writer have been deluded by his prejudices? Could there be crucial missing facts? Could the writer's language be radically and irresolvably ambiguous, even self-defeating?

These anticipations are largely pointless, because it is usually impossible to prove a negative ("No, it is in principle impossible that I could be deluded by prejudice," "No, there could be no crucial missing fact," "No, there could be no reader, however perverse, able to misunderstand what I am saying"). Classic style sees nothing to be accomplished by rehearsing these questions, and so eliminates them from the outset.

This enabling convention is made to save writer and reader from spinning their wheels on uncertain ground to no possible effect, but it is not made to constrain the reader's belief. The writer speaks with confidence, and this can be compelling; but the reader will bring his full competence to bear and will make his own judgment about whether the writer is right or wrong. The reader may conclude that a text is masterful, classic, and completely wrong. In classic prose, the writer takes the pose of competence so as not to waste our time with distractions as he presents those things that allow us to decide whether he really is competent.

The Writer Does All the Work Invisibly

Suggestion is powerful, since people believe a conclusion more readily if they think they have helped to reach it or have reached it themselves.

A catalogue of styles of suggestion would be long and varied. It would range from subliminal suggestion, in which the writer tries to give the reader all the credit by hiding the suggestion, to what we will call domestic moral suggestion, which consists of posing a problem, garnished with appropriate facts, as if you cannot see what to do, in the hope that the slow-witted spouse, sibling, child, or parent addressed will recognize his duty and get on with it. There are poetic styles of suggestion, as in haiku, in which luminous details are juxtaposed so as to launch the reader toward a perception that is never stated. There are mystic styles, which view truth as something that can be hinted at but never grasped intellectually or expressed accurately. There is participatory suggestion, in which the speaker as if by chance arrays all the right details and begins to grope toward a conclusion but has difficulty and turns to the reader to work out the rest. There is lotus-eater suggestion, which consists of some ill-formed attempts, combined with a few gestures, and closed off with the lame, "You know what I mean."

Classic style is not a style of suggestion. All necessary refinements have been made and are accurately expressed.

There are other styles in which the writer does all the work, but he does it under the reader's nose: "And now I think I need some decorative ornament with which to finish this off, a finial of some sort, so to make that I will have to fire up the lathe, and get the right piece of wood; let's see, this one won't do, it has a crack; we need one that has just the right grain; yes, here, now we mount this on the lathe. . . ." The classic writer, by contrast, does all the work invisibly. She pulls the finished finial out of her pocket. The classic writer is not like a television cook showing you how to mix mustard and balsamic vinegar. She is like a chef whose work is presented to you at table but whose labor you are never allowed to see, a labor the chef certainly does not expect you to share. There are no salt and pepper shakers on your table.

Thought and Language

The Thought Can Stand Alone

In the classic stand on the elements of style, writing is neither a way of thinking something out nor an art that exists for its own sake. Writing is an instrument for presenting what the writer has already thought. It is a record of that thought only to the extent that the intellectual experience is indistinguishable from the order of reason. The text is not a document that implies an individual process of thought; it is not a text that refers primarily to other texts; it is a transparent way of presenting a separate reality. Classic style always implies that there is value in what it presents. Characteristically this implied value is twofold: what is presented is important and it is independently intelligible rather than valuable as part of something larger. The independently intelligible thought often carries an implicit appeal to a refined and clarified version of common experience. Classic writing is never "notes toward" a thought that might, if developed further, stand on its own, nor is it the fifth part of a systematic inquiry that is unintelligible to someone unfamiliar with the previous four parts.

Classic expression cannot justify itself in advance. It presumes upon the reader's attention as its right. To justify its presumption, it must offer something important, complete, self-contained, and intelligible. Descartes's *Discourse*, for example, historically considered, is a response to Montaigne's skepticism. But Montaigne is never mentioned there. Descartes's thought is offered as a freestanding fable of the writer's own experience, not as a re-examination of philosophic issues full of cross-references to the history of philosophy. Such a citational presentation could only indicate to the nonprofessional that the book cannot be read independently. In Descartes, and in many other classic writers, the style implies that anything requiring erudition, anything intelligible only to a professional or an erudite is fundamentally unimportant. The importance and intelligibility of classic expression do not depend upon special knowledge; they depend upon the reader's clear and focused mind. There is a tacit contract between writer and reader: the reader's closely focused intelligence will be repaid with something valuable and self-contained. Classic expression has the distinctive character and the neat finality of a Bach partita, which begins by breaking a silence and ends by returning to silence, leaving nothing unresolved.

One of Wallace Stevens's poems is called "The Poem That Took the Place of the Mountain." The mountain existed before the poem and is independent of it. To a geologist, a mountain may be unintelligible by itself since it is an incident in the natural history of the earth, but it has a visual and nominal distinction and is, in common experience, an independent, distinct, and arresting object. The poem may require a dense network of concepts and conventions to be independently intelligible, but since these are widely shared within the culture in which it is written, the poem can be thought of as independently intelligible too. If we accept the idea that somehow a poem can "word for word" take the place of a mountain, we have a little emblem of classic style in which writing presents thought, nuance for nuance, in a distinct and intelligible frame.

Abstractions Can Be Clear and Exact

From the classic viewpoint, the distinction between abstract and concrete has no consequence. A writing instructor or consultant who advises us to write concretely and avoid abstractions offers shallow and impractical advice because the distinction is simpleminded. What matters is not the ontological category of the subject but rather the style in which it is conceived.

In romantic style, a tree could be conceived as if only the writer can see it for what it is. Its truth, then, has no existence independent of the writer; it depends upon the writer; to conceive of it as clear and exact would be to obliterate the writer's fragile and elusive insight, gained in a transporting moment of superior vision that language cannot express. In romantic style, there is no symmetry between writer and reader. That a tree itself is concrete does not impede a romantic writer from conceiving it in a manner unavailable to other observers, vaguely and indistinctly, as he might conceive the human soul.

By contrast, in classic style, the human soul can be conceived as clearly and exactly as the tree in front of your face. When a classic stylist presents an abstraction—cultural reality, heroism, historical causation, the nature of representation, taste—it is first conceived as independent of the writer, exhaustively definite at all levels of detail, visible to anyone competent who is standing in a position to see it, immediately recognizable, and capable of being expressed in direct and simple language.

Abstractions are not in themselves bad, vague, or inexact. They are only so in certain styles of conceiving them. When a classic writer deals in abstractions, it takes an effort to remind ourselves that she is not talking about a stone, a leaf, a statue. A classic writer presents the concrete diamond and its aesthetic beauty as if both are visible, clear, and exact.

Thought Precedes Speech

In the classic view, writing is not thinking. This runs counter to an extremely powerful and pervasive connection between a concept of writing and a concept of mind. Records are understood as a sort of external memory, and memory as internal records. Writing is thinking on paper, and thought is writing in the mind. The author's mind is an endless paper on which he writes, making mind internal writing; and the book he writes is external mind, the external form of that writing. The author is the self thinking. The self is the author writing in the mind. (Hamlet says, "Within the book and volume of my brain.") Sometimes, the self is an author who records the process of his thinking on paper.

Classic style takes an entirely different view. Since it is a presentational style, this kind of writing, at least, depends upon a prior process of thought. It is having a thought that is the very motive for writing. The kind of thinking a classic writer does, inasmuch as he is a writer, is limited to strategic thinking about presentation and is never explicit. Thinking is not writing; even more important, writing is not thinking. This does not mean that in classic style all of the thinking precedes all of the writing, but rather that the classic writer does not write as he is thinking something out and does not think by writing something out. Between the period of one sentence and the beginning of the next, there is space for the flash of perfect thought, which is all the classic writer needs. The sentence begins only after the thought it expresses has been completed. To the classic writer, the difference between thinking and writing is as wide as the difference between cooking and serving. In every great restaurant there is a kitchen, where the work is done, and a dining room, where the result is presented. The dining room is serene, and the presentation suggests that perfection is routine and effortless, no matter how hectic things get in the kitchen. Naturally the kitchen and the dining room are in constant and intimate contact, but it is part of the protocol of a great restaurant to treat them as if they existed on different planets. The cooks do not sit down and relax in the dining room and the guests do not observe the work of the kitchen.

Seeing something is not the same as presenting something. We can present only what we have already seen and recognized. In classic style, thinking is seeing, or more generally, recognizing; writing is presenting what the writer has seen so the reader can see it, too. The classic writer seems to be trying to place something before your eyes or trying to put you where he is so you can see what he sees.

The Language Is Sufficient

There are styles of writing that suggest that while words are inadequate, there is nothing else available, so writers do the best they can without expecting their language to do more than approximate their thought. Classic style takes the opposite stand. There are not merely better and worse ways of expressing particular thoughts, there is a best way. Everything that can be known can be said. Moreover, it is always possible to achieve a perfect fit between a thought and its expression just as it is always possible to achieve a perfect solution to a problem in elementary algebra.

A few years ago, *The Wall Street Journal* ran a short article about a dispute between a French government agency and a group of French research scientists. The scientists were publishing a journal in English; the government agency objected on the plausible grounds that the results of scientific research done by French scientists and supported by the French government ought to be published in French. The scientists retorted that English had become, for most purposes, the international language of science, so if scientists want their research reports to be read, they simply have to be published in English. The point was given summary expression in the following sentence: "To shun English is to court isolation."

This seven-word sentence has an economy, a symmetry, and a fit between thought and expression that suggest perfection, not compromise or approximation, and it is the sort of perfection that, once achieved, seems natural, not labored. It is something like tapping a golf ball with just enough force to sink it. It is a convention of classic style that every thought has a perfect expression; writers can fail to fit language to thought, but that is merely a failure of craftsmanship, not a limitation of the craftsman's material.

When we talk about a "way of putting" something, we suggest that there are many ways of expressing the same thought, each with its strengths and inescapable limitations. Any particular way of putting something is then just one way, necessarily incomplete and insufficient, so the price of putting a thought into any particular set of words is compromise.

The classic stand adopts as an enabling convention the opposite view: language is sufficient to any thought. Imperfect expression is the fault of limited writers, not limited language. It is not merely that the classic writer is a master of language; many writers in many styles are manifest masters of language. The classic writer works with the additional convention that the language he masters is sufficient to any thought. The classic writer must not make the language appear to struggle, giving the impression that the language is in over its head, fighting to survive. The classic writer does not use language to suggest a truth he cannot formulate. Suggestive language is merely imperfect use of language. Classic style avoids colloquialisms, neologisms, periphrases, and slang because it does not need them: the language is sufficient without them. New thoughts do not require new language.

Classic Thought and Classic Language Match

There are two kinds of fit between thought and language in classic style. The first—which makes the writer's language sufficient to his thought—is lexical: there are already expressions in the language to fit any thought.

The second—which makes the writer's language an image of his thought—is structural. Thought comes with a structure and a direction. Its structure is built upon skeletal images that underlie our everyday experience. We have a skeletal image, or image schema, of moving toward an object. We have an image schema of adding one thing to another. We have an image schema of a path that leads from a source to a goal. We have many image schemas, of hesitation and advance, of movement from a center to a periphery, of entering or leaving, of enclosing or extracting, of rising or falling, of stopping or penetrating. These image schemas are not exclusively visual. We have an image schema of a rising pitch, of increasing pressure, of a jab to the skin, and so on. Many of our most important and useful image schemas have to do with the way we structure space and interact with space. We use these spatial image schemas to make sense of abstract things that are not themselves spatial. We think of time as linear or circular. We think of solving a problem as "moving toward" a goal along a path. We think of the reasoning mind as a body moving in space, which "comes upon" ideas, "looks them over," "picks them up" for examination, "drops" them to look "further afield," and so on. A great deal of our reasoning consists of metaphoric projections of these bodily and spatial image schemas onto abstract concepts. We think of events, which have no shape, as having a shape: open ended or closed, discrete or continuous, cyclic or linear.

In the classic view, the prototype of truth is a thought that comes structured by one of these basic image schemas or some recognizable combination or extension of them.

But these same image schemas structure expression as well. Expressions are forms, and these forms can have image-schematic structure. A sentence, for example, can be thought of as linear, as moving, as approaching a point. A classic thought that has the image-schematic structure of moving along a path to stop sharply at an end for which the path exists will be mirrored in a sentence that has the image-schematic structure of moving along a path to stop smartly at an end for which the preceding part of the sentence exists. Here is an example from Clifford Geertz. "[I]f you want to understand what a science is, you should look in the first instance not at its theories or its findings, and certainly not at what its apologists say about it; you should look at what the practitioners of it do."

It is possible for thought and language to be misaligned in one of three ways. First, you can write a sentence that cannot be grasped through any basic image schema. This is unusual, since most writers align their sentences with basic image schemas automatically and unconsciously. Occasionally, however, writers with an advanced knowledge of prose style become self-conscious and defensive about their own writing and begin to misalign sentences. The result is both difficult to read and impossible to correct by making local revisions. Here is an example: "The fact is that the subtlety and control which philologists were willing to attribute to earlier writers' spellings and word-groupings as registers of distinctive features in phonology and morphology by and large stopped there."

Second, you can write a sentence that evokes an image schema but then fails to fulfill it or complete it. Suppose Geertz had written, "If you want to understand what a science is, you should look in the first instance not at its theories but you should instead, putting aside its findings, concentrate your attention on its practice entirely, taking care not to be distracted by anything its apologists might say about that." The first half of this sentence, to the word "theories," sets the reader to expect a crisp opposition. But the second half of the sentence frustrates the expectation.

Third, you can have a thought that is structured by an image schema but express it in a sentence structured by a different image schema. Suppose Geertz had written, "If you want to understand what a science is, and you look at its theories and its findings and its representations by apologists, you will find that you must set all this aside to look at what its practitioners do, which is where you should have directed your attention in the first instance." The image schema of Geertz's original thought consists of rejecting several things in order to select a different one. The image schema of his original sentence is compatible with the image schema of his thought. But the revision of his sentence is structured by an image schema of attending to various things and then returning to the beginning to attend to something different. The image schema that structures the revised sentence is common, but it is incompatible with the image schema that structured the thought it was meant to mirror.

Perhaps the most common image schema used in structuring expression is movement along a directed path from a source to a goal. In this image schema, the end of the sentence seems to be the goal of the sentence, what it is trying to get to. In consequence, there is a phenomenon in English known as the stress position: whatever you put at the end of the sentence will be taken, absent direction to the contrary, to be the most important part of the sentence, as it is in Geertz's sentence: "you should look at what the practitioners of [the science] do."

Classic style respects the stress position. La Rochefoucauld's classic sentence about Madame de Chevreuse—like Geertz's—puts the point of the thought at the end of the sentence: "and she almost always brought disaster to those she encountered on her way." The end of the sentence seems to be the reason the sentence is written; everything leads to it; and the sentence stops confidently when it reaches that end because the image schema of both thought and expression is complete. The use of the stress position in classic style is often quite subtle, but the classic writer frequently plays on it, as in this description of the northern shrike: "Unusual among songbirds, shrikes prey on small birds and rodents, catching them with the bill and sometimes impaling them on thorns or barbed wire for storage." Rearranging this sentence in any way diminishes it.

A common perceptual image schema is focusing-and-then-inspecting. First we locate the object or domain of interest, and then we inspect its details. This image schema is not restricted to visual perception; it operates equally well in tactile, auditory, and kinesthetic perception. Classic thought frequently follows this fundamental image schema, focusing on a subject and then inspecting its details, and classic expression of this thought shares the same image schema, first presenting the subject and then presenting details.

Many of the most familiar image schemas have to do with forces—impinging, pushing, pressuring, stopping, overcoming—especially when these forces are applied by agents in action. A classic thought is often structured by an image schema of action. Its classic expression mirrors this structure. The structure of the expression conforms to the structure of the action: the subject is an agent and the verb is the action performed by the agent.

Classic style is compelling often exactly because it exploits such common image schemas. Truth comes with basic image-schematic structure. We expect its expression to come with the same structure. Consequently, when a sentence has a clear image-schematic structure, it seems plausible that what the sentence expresses is true.

This is a psychological tactic of persuasion, founded upon our readiness to accept whatever has the same form as what we have already accepted. Consider *roles*, such as president, pope, professor, policeman. We accept new holders of these roles largely because they adopt an institutional form we have already accepted. The new president operates in known and accepted forms such as formal messages to Congress and press conferences in the Rose Garden. Presidential primaries are largely a test of who can best pick up the established forms. The new pope is accepted partly because he dresses in the same anachronistic fashion as the old pope, and uses the same ambiguous language of indirection. For centuries, visual representations of scholars have included a case of books in the background, and this form abides tenaciously even now, when scholarly work is as likely to involve brains in vats or electronic texts.

In the classic view, truth comes with a structure that we already know and accept. Adopting a new truth does not mean adopting a new form. In classic style, a new truth will be expressed in old words structured in a reassuringly familiar form.

The observation that expression mirrors thought by inheriting its image-schematic structure is both ancient and common in the history of rhetoric. Longinus views many rhetorical figures as linguistic instruments for achieving this alignment. For example, repeated physical striking has an image-schematic structure; it can be mirrored in expression through linguistic anaphora, as in: "By his manner, his looks, his voice, when he strikes you with insult, when he strikes you like an enemy, when he strikes you with his knuckles, when he strikes you like a slave." Demetrius talks of linguistic constructions being "rounded," "disjointed," "hastening towards a definite goal as runners do when they leave the starting-place," "circular," "tense," "periodic," and so on. He remarks that thought comes with part-whole structure that can be mirrored in the linguistic construction, and that we experience syntactic constructions image-schematically: "Long journeys are shortened by a succession of inns, while desolate paths, even when the distances are short, give the impression of length. Precisely the same principle will apply also in the case of members [linguistic constructions]."

Classic style typically aligns the image schemas structuring thought and its expression, but in a fashion that escapes notice. There are other, contrasting styles that intend to raise this correspondence to the level of the remarkable, to show the skillful labor of the writer, as does Longinus's example of anaphora. The role of image schemas in the alignment of thought and language, once treated in ancient rhetoric, has resurfaced as a topic in contemporary philosophy, cognitive science, and linguistics.

■ Other Stands, Other Styles

There is nothing new in the idea that a style is effectively a stand on a small number of central issues, and therefore that many different mature styles are possible. Classical rhetoricians analyzed contrasting styles from this perspective, and routinely demonstrated that what was good or appropriate to one style might be bad or inappropriate to another. By contrast, many modern books on "style" have, for one reason or another, suggested that there are only two styles: good and bad. On closer inspection, it becomes apparent that each of these modern books is actually about one style, not about style generally. For example, Strunk and White or Williams and Colomb work from an implicit model of writing as meant to be read by either (a) an indefinite audience not defined by working roles but having more-or-less common cultural and social standards; or (b) a somewhat more definite audience of working professionals with corporately defined roles. What Strunk and White recommend is meant as good advice for the one style they have in mind; what Williams and Colomb recommend is good advice for the one style they have in mind. Both assume a single cast and a single scene. But consider texts with quite a different cast or scene, such as a diplomatic address opening peace negotiations in the Middle East, or Pericles' Funeral Oration, or Samuel Johnson's "Preface to Shakespeare," or an address by Martin Luther King, Jr., to a large crowd of political activists. Were we to subject texts of this sort to editorial revision inspired by a careful study of Williams and Colomb or Strunk and White, the result would be simply the destruction of a style. These writers and speakers certainly break many of the "rules" to be found in *Style* and *The Elements of Style*, but that is because the styles discussed in those books are foreign to the styles chosen. It is unreasonable to expect that addressing a giant rally in Washington and writing a memo to the vice president for finance on the consequences of the new tax code should have lying behind them the same stylistic stand, or that either one of them should have the same stylistic stand as an article for *The New Yorker* or Johnson's explanation of Shakespeare's claim to our attention.

Classical textbooks such as Cicero's *Orator*, the pseudo-Ciceronian *Rhetorica ad Herennium*, and Demetrius's *On Style* list principal styles and explain their origins in different purposes, motives, or occasions. The standard list includes high, middle, and low style, otherwise called grand, middle, and simple. Demetrius gives instruction in restrained, elevated, elegant, and forcible style. Aristotle in the *Rhetoric* notes in passing that each kind of rhetoric has its own appropriate style: for example, the style of political speech cannot be the style of forensic speech because their originary purposes, scenes, and casts are opposed.

Classical rhetoricians routinely analyze the relationships between distinct styles. Elegant style, Demetrius explains, can unite with restrained style, but elevated style cannot, because elevated style and restrained style "stand in irreconcilable opposition and contrast": their fundamental decisions are consistently incompatible.

Certain failures to achieve a successful style are so predictable and common as to constitute styles of their own, which might be called styles that do not succeed. The *Rhetorica ad Herennium* explains how swollen style, slack style, and meager style arise as particular kinds of failure to achieve grand, middle, or simple style, suggesting that each good style has at least one deformed double. Longinus introduces us to two deformed versions of sublime style, each of which is a product of a particular kind of failure to achieve it. Bloated style "comes from trying to outdo the sublime." Adolescent style comes from puerility, "the opposite of greatness: abject, mean, smarmy, the lowest of faults. What is this puerility? Isn't it just obviously the academic attitude, where over-elaboration ends in frigid failure? Writers fall into this fault because they want to be uncommon and exquisite, and to impress everybody, and instead they founder upon the trash of affectation." Such failures all come "from the same cause, namely, today's crazy passion for novel ideas."

Surface marks of writing reflect the fundamental stands of individual styles, but surface marks do not constitute styles, and styles do not prescribe surface marks, even though styles can explain such marks. To Aristotle, excellence of style consists in being clear and not commonplace—this is a fundamental stand on the question of presentation. He then examines surface techniques that can help the writer to achieve clarity and distinction, and alerts us to typical errors at the surface level. Aristotle offers many examples, but the discussion of the surface in every case derives from an analysis of the base. Longinus does the same thing, walking us through a great range of surface marks appropriate to sublime style, and contrasting successful examples of the style with failed attempts, but he does not suggest that the style derives from surface marks appropriate to it.

The many such examples in classical rhetorical treatments, and the use of repeated examples as patterns on which students can model their own writing, should never be interpreted as suggesting that style consists of surface marks, or that if we imitate the surface marks, we achieve the style. This would be as foolish as imagining that by wearing the same kind of shoes as a great athlete and imitating the athlete's manner of tying the laces, we will become great athletes ourselves. Both Aristotle and Longinus recognize that without the fundamental stand, the surface marks form only a sorry and monstrous parody of the style. Neither of them would have endorsed the procedure of selecting one sentence for inspection and posing the question, "What is the style of this sentence?" For example, the sentence, "He died quietly" could occur with perfect appropriateness in a work whose style is plain, classic, romantic, contemplative, oratorical, sublime, prophetic, practical, or diplomatic. To recognize a style, one must recognize its fundamental stand on decisive questions, which will be reflected with greater or lesser skill in its level of expression.

The closest model in classical antiquity for our analysis of classic style is Longinus's analysis of "the sublime" in *On the Sublime*, perhaps the most brilliant treatment of a style ever written.

No reader can think that Longinus is trying to give a universal prescription for good writing; he analyzes the distinctive stand of one style, and is always aware that there are many others. Sublime style is distinct from other styles because it takes a distinct stand on the elements of style: truth, presentation, scene, cast, thought and language. Its cast, unlike the cast of classic style, does not involve a symmetric relationship between equals; its model scene is not conversation; the relationship of language to thought does not have the effect of either presentation or persuasion. "For the effect of genius is not to persuade the audience but rather to transport them out of themselves." Sublime writing, or writing at moments when it achieves the style of sublimity, consequently has a character entirely different from that of writing whose purpose is to persuade through detailed and systematic argument, for in linear argument, "inventive skill and the due disposal and marshalling of facts gradually emerge from the whole tissue of the composition, rather than showing themselves in one or two touches: on the other hand, a well-timed flash of sublimity scatters everything before it like a bolt of lightning and reveals the full power of the speaker at a single stroke."

Longinus situates the origin of sublime style fundamentally at the level of thought, not surface constructions: the prime and most powerful source of the sublime is "the command of full-blooded ideas." A natural faculty of expression is of course indispensable to sublime style, but cannot provide sublime style. Longinus's view of the source of sublime style depends upon a view of the relationship between writer and reader as fundamentally asymmetric: the writer is gifted with a fabulous mind and a natural talent for expression, which we admire, and the effect of which is to transport us out of ourselves in ways that otherwise are probably not available to us.

Yet for all the asymmetry between writers of the sublime and students of this writing, Longinus offers students a curriculum that might help them cultivate a capacity for the sublime. This curriculum consists not in mastering and parroting certain surface patterns, but rather in training the mind:

> Now, since the first, I mean natural genius, plays a greater part than all the others, here too, although it is rather a gift than an acquired quality, we should still do our best to train our minds into sympathy with what is noble and impregnate them again and again with high inspiration. "How?" you might ask. Well, elsewhere I have written something like this, "Sublimity is the true ring of a noble mind." And

so even without being spoken the bare idea often by itself wins admiration for its inherent genius. . . . In the first place, then, it is absolutely necessary to indicate the sources of the sublime and to show that the mind of the genuine orator must be neither small nor ignoble. For it is impossible that those whose thoughts and habits all their lives long are petty and servile should flash out anything wonderful, worthy of immortal life. No, a great style is the natural outcome of important thoughts, and sublime expressions naturally fall to people with spirit.

In the spirit of Longinus, we would like now to clarify the stand of classic style on the elements of style and to contrast classic style with a selection of other mature and consistent styles.

Classic Style Is Not Plain Style

Plain style is communal, its model scene a congregation in which speakers reaffirm for each other common truths that are the property of all. In the theology behind plain style, truth is always simple, and it is a common human possession. Individual revisions of this communal possession distort and dilute it. The wisdom of children can be the wisdom of adults, because knowing truth requires no special experience and no critical analysis. Sophisticated thought and conceptual refinement pervert truth. Any language that reaches beyond the simplest level is suspicious as the probable symptom of such a perversion. Simple language may not always be completely adequate to the expression of truth, but at least it is pure as far as it goes.

Classic style does not reject plain style, although it rejects the theology behind it and sees that theology as illegitimately elevating a necessary foundation into an achieved style. From the perspective of classic style, plain style is deficient because the theology behind plain style ignores the fact that, left to themselves, people are vulnerable to special interests and prone to special pleading. People are weak, and common wisdom is thus often self-serving. It is perfectly possible for common wisdom to be an anthology of a community's complacent errors, because common wisdom does not include any principle of critical validation. Without critical testing, common wisdom becomes received opinion.

Classic style views itself as repairing the deficiency of plain style by introducing sophistication and individual responsibility. First, classic writers and readers are an elite community, consisting of those who practice the critical discipline of its theology. Anyone can take up this practice and so join, but the style is aristocratic, not egalitarian. Second, classic wisdom cannot be the wisdom of children because it depends upon a wealth of adult experience. In plain style, everyone is equal; truth is everyone's birthright. It is seen by all; it is everyone's possession. It can come out of the mouths of babes. In classic style, truth is available to all who are willing to work to achieve it, but truth is certainly not commonly possessed by all and is no one's birthright. In the classic view, truth is the possession of individuals who have validated common wisdom; for them, truth has been achieved, and such achievement requires both experience and a critical intelligence beyond the range of babes.

Classic style remedies the deficiency of plain style by requiring the writer to stand entirely behind the thought she presents. Freshness is mandatory in classic style but freshness has nothing to do with novelty of ideas, on which classic style places no special premium. It is rather the requirement that the thinking behind the writing be the achievement of an individual. The classic writer has done the thinking, personally. Even when she accepts or uses a commonplace, she has thought it through herself and can stand behind it herself.

Classic style contains plain style concretely by incorporating it, but also by extending it, the way a Chinese ideogram contains a radical. A classic sentence is often a nuanced version of a sentence that otherwise might have been plain. "Grace is simple" is plain. "Grace, from the perspective of God, is simple" is classic, as is "The machinery of grace is always simple." Plain style values simplicity but shuns nuance. Classic style values both simplicity and nuance. "The truth is pure and simple" is plain. "The truth is rarely pure, and never simple" is classic. "Seeing is believing" is plain. "Seeing is believing only if you don't see too clearly" is classic.

Classic Style Is Not Reflexive Style

In the classic stand on presentation, writing is a perfectly transparent window through which a subject is presented; the ability of the writer and the sufficiency of the language to serve this presentation are never in doubt.

This fundamental stand opposes classic style irreconcilably to an entire family of styles in which the writing itself shares a focus with any other possible subject, and the difficulties of the writing are brought to the reader's attention.

Classic writing can present anything, but even when the subject presented is writing itself, the focus is not shared. La Bruyère talks about the conditions of good writing when he says, "It is necessary to express what is true in order to write naturally, powerfully, sensitively," but he does not call attention to his own writing as he is doing so. When Alexander Pope criticizes bad verse in *An Essay on Criticism*, the writing itself imitates the faults he discusses, becoming a focus of the reader's attention: "And ten low Words oft creep in one dull Line." Classic style is a performance style, and while classic writers can be skeptical about anything else, they cannot be skeptical about their own ability to perform when they are in the act of performing. The classic writer assumes that his subject can be known and can be expressed without distortion. These are enabling conventions of the style. The classic writer is not necessarily free of doubts about his enterprise, but as a performer he must appear to be. An acrobat, a concert pianist, an actor cannot simultaneously perform and question the possibility of performing. Classic style is a style for performance, not a style for questioning its own competence.

When we open a cookbook, we completely put aside—and expect the author to put aside—the kind of question that leads to the heart of certain philosophic and religious traditions. Is it possible to talk about cooking? Do eggs really exist? Is food something about which knowledge is possible? Can anyone else ever tell us anything true about cooking? These questions may lead to enlightenment or to satori; they do not lead to satisfying dinners. Readers of cookbooks expect to see cooking treated directly, as if such metaphysical and epistemological questions could never be entertained by anyone, even though we know they can be and have been entertained by saints and sages. We do not expect the writer to be immobilized by preliminary discussions of whether it is possible to talk about "cooking," if such a thing even exists. Classic style similarly puts aside as inappropriate philosophical questions about its enterprise. If it took those questions up, it could never get around to treating its subject, and its purpose is exclusively to treat its subject.

Raising skeptical doubts about the writer's own enterprise is a feature of nonclassic self-conscious styles. In such styles, the writer's chief, if unstated, concern is to escape being convicted of philosophical naïveté about his own enterprise. Such a writer is careful to gesture periodically toward the contingent frame of his own discourse, to disclaim any belief that his writing can treat any subject directly. The style stays in the foreground, inextricably mingled with its announced subject. It is marked with formulaic hedges concerning the possibility of knowledge, the contingency of knowledge, and the ability of language to express knowledge. "Impotence principles" such as the doctrine that discourse can never be about anything except itself share the focus of the writer's attention with any possible subject.

Classic prose does not discuss doubts or fears about its own enterprise, not because it is naïve, but because it has chosen something incompatible with reflexive inquiry. We can question the possibility of acting or we can act, but we cannot do both at once. Classic writers make an unspoken choice: they act. Rather than discuss the possibility of action, they put that possibility to the test, and let the reader be the judge.

Clifford Geertz, in *Works and Lives: The Anthropologist as Author*, quotes an example of such a self-referential and self-questioning style from the introduction, "Self and Other," to Loring Danforth's *The Death Rituals of Rural Greece*:

Anthropology inevitably involves an encounter with the Other. All too often, however, the ethnographic distance that separates the reader of anthropological texts and the anthropologist himself from the Other is rigidly maintained and at times even artificially exaggerated. In many cases this distancing leads to an exclusive focus on the Other as primitive, bizarre, and exotic. The gap between a familiar "we" and an exotic "they" is a major obstacle to a meaningful understanding of the Other, an obstacle that can only be overcome through some form of participation in the world of the Other.

Geertz comments:

The brooding note of Loring Danforth's "Introduction" (Who am I to be saying these things, by what right, and to what purpose, and how on earth can I manage honestly to say them?) is one now very widely heard, in various forms and with various intensities.

Clifford Geertz, an acute observer of style, calls attention here to one mark of reflexive style. Reflexive styles might consider classic style to be naïve or philistine; but there is nothing naïve in a tacit acceptance of incongruities in the nature of writing and nothing philistine in making unhedged choices.

Classic Style Is Not Practical Style

In the model scene behind practical style, the reader has a problem to solve, a decision to make, a ruling to hand down, an inquiry to conduct, a machine to design or repair—in short, a job to do. The reader's need, not the writer's desire to articulate something, initiates the writing. The writer's job is to serve the reader's immediate need by delivering timely materials. The motive can thus be almost anything productive of a need: greed, enterprise, competition, philanthropy. Since the reader is engaged in solving a problem, the reading is not an end in itself, it is instrumental to some other end. That is why, in this scene, the prime stylistic virtue is ease of parsing. In practical style, the best presentation will allow the reader to acquire timely information with a minimum of distraction because, in this scene, writing is an instrument for delivering information with maximum efficiency and in such a way as to place the smallest possible burden upon the reader, who has other—more important—burdens to bear.

In classic style, by contrast, neither writer nor reader has a job, the writing and reading do not serve a practical goal, and the writer has all the time in the world to present her subject as something interesting for its own sake. Her characteristic brevity comes from the elegance of her mind, never from pressures of time or employment. The writing is initiated by the writer, not the reader: the writer wants to present something not to a client, but to an indefinite audience, treated as if it were a single individual. Her motive is to present truth, not so that someone can use it to accomplish a practical goal, although someone might make use of it for such a purpose, but for its own sake.

Classic style and practical style have important areas of overlap; both styles place a high value on clarity and directness. Classic style values clarity because it sees itself as a transparent medium for the presentation of truth. Practical style values clarity because it places a premium on being easy to parse. Both styles can be described as precise and efficient, but for quite different reasons: practical style is precise and efficient because the reader wants to understand well and quickly for the purpose of making immediate use of what he is reading; classic style is precise and efficient because precision serves truth and because efficiency is a refinement. The efficiency of classic style is a sign of its having the leisure and luxury to afford refinement: the writer and reader have had all the time needed to train their minds to the requisite concert pitch.

Neither classic style nor practical style contains much of the sort of internal network of cross-references that linguists call "metadiscourse" ("I would like to tell you about x but first I have to tell you about y"). In classic style, such explicit acknowledgment of planning defeats the immediacy and spontaneity that mark the style's model scene, conversation. In practical style, a network of cross-references, clotting the text, is a poor substitute for less distracting indications of coherence.

There are a few recognizable prototypes of the model scene of practical style. The first, drawn from the world of corporate business or the legal profession, is a memorandum to a superior who has asked for information. The writer knows more about the subject than the reader, but it is the reader who will make a decision or take action, and so stands in need of some of the writer's knowledge. The reader's need is the motive for writing. A second prototype is a memorandum to a subordinate whose activities the superior is trying to direct and manage. In neither case does the reader want or expect to know everything the writer knows about the subject. Practical style is selective in a way that classic style is not. The cast is hierarchical, not symmetric. Clustered around these prototypes are recognizable extensions: the manual telling someone how to perform routine jobs; the manual telling someone how to use something; the how-to book instructing the CEO in the art of negotiation; the book about financial planning telling those with discretionary income how to invest it; the advisory from a manufacturer to owners of the manufactured product telling them that it has a defect and how to get it fixed.

Another prototype of this scene is the delivery of the results of research to fellow researchers, which is to say, fellow insiders. The writer knows more about his own research than the readers do, but they are fellow professionals who expect to know everything he knows as a result of reading his report, or know at least what they need to know for their own purposes. What is reported will affect their own independent activities in ways that they alone can judge. The writer is imparting information and does not want his writing, as such, to be noticed; it should fulfill every standard expectation and be as easy to parse as possible.

Most writing in schools and colleges is a perversion of practical style: the student pretends that he is writing a memorandum. He pretends that he knows more than the reader, that the reader needs this information, and that his job is to impart that information in a way that is easy for the reader to parse. This pretense is supposed to be practice for the real thing. Actually, the reader (the teacher) probably knows much more about the subject than the writer; the reader (the teacher) has no need whatever for the information; and the job of the writer is to cover himself from attack by his superior (the teacher). The actual scene interferes so much with the fantasy scene that the result is almost inevitably compromised, if not fraudulent.

The best-known teachers of practical style are Strunk and White, in their ubiquitous *Elements of Style*. The best teachers of practical style are Joseph Williams and Gregory Colomb, in Williams's *Style: Toward Clarity and Grace* and a series of academic articles and technical reports.

Strunk and White's disarming treatment of what everybody really needs to know about writing has been treasured by generations of people who are occasionally forced to write something and view the prospect with a sinking feeling of dread. As a guide to writing, *The Elements of Style*, being little more than an apparently arbitrary mixture of grammatical digest, handy list of common mistakes, and expert hand-holding, is drastically incomplete, but it is a masterpiece of psychological insight. Its attractions derive, we suspect, first, from its implicit, cheery, and optimistic promise that if you just read its few pages and work those few surface tricks it teaches you ("In summaries, keep to one tense," "*less* should not be used for *fewer*"), you will not embarrass yourself; second, from its exhortatory cheerleading that seems so assured and upbeat; and third, from its tone of common sense that masks, at key points, an essential vacuousness: "Choose a suitable design and hold to it."

Such advice has the same immemorial power of "Just use your head, and you'll be all right." Advice of this sort has the great merit of being brief and supportive. There is a welcome assurance that there is really nothing to it, except for those truly mysterious aspects of the subject that cannot be taught at all. "I can teach you where to put a comma in ten minutes, but don't expect me to teach you to write like Shakespeare."

Williams and Colomb present an incomparably deeper and more orderly treatment of practical style. The style they present is consistent and mature; it makes decisions about all the major questions that define a style, and is fully developed. The claim behind Williams and Colomb's treatment is large and theoretical: just as readers of an English sentence have expectations about word order and the distribution of information in a sentence, so readers of what Williams and Colomb call "pointed texts" have in their minds a grammar of such texts that tells them where to look for what. Readers will use that grammar. Writing that conforms to it will be easy for the reader to follow. Writing that resists it will be difficult for the reader to follow. For example, a reader looks for an opening section ("the issue") and a following section ("the discussion") within each unit of a pointed text. He looks for a rich lexical field, at the end of the issue, which will be used to weave the discussion together, to give it cohesion, as it progresses. He looks for a point at the end of the discussion. If there is a point at the end of the issue, it will be taken to be an adumbration of the point at the end of the discussion. Units of discourse nest, so that units within the discussion will themselves be composed of an issue and a discussion. These principles work themselves down to the level of the sentence, where the reader expects the first part of the sentence to present an issue (topic) and the second part of the sentence to present a discussion (comment). The reader expects old information in the sentence before new. The reader prefers to understand things in terms of actions and agents, so the backbone of a sentence should be a verb that conveys action, and the subject of such a verb should be one of the agents—perhaps metaphorical—in this action-story. Since readers link agents to actions in pairs, writers should try not to separate the subject (agent) from the verb (action) with distracting information. And so on.

Williams and Colomb's finely detailed treatment of practical style provides an indispensable guide impressive in its scope and intelligence. It is missing just one thing, namely, an explicit acknowledgment of its fundamental stand, and an acknowledgment that its fundamental stand is one of many alternatives. While their work is thorough, systematic, and theoretically sophisticated, and while they know that they are dealing with just one style, the work is misleading in its self-presentation: it pretends that the style it concerns, and about which it gives excellent advice, is universal and exclusive rather than merely ubiquitous. Practical style rests on a set of answers to basic questions; other styles rest on different answers to those same questions.

Practical style comes from deciding that what matters in style is the reader, and in particular the reader's ease in parsing features of the text, especially the discourse features of the text. Practical style is so firm in this decision that it treats it as no decision at all, but as a necessity: *of course* excellence of style consists in conforming to the reader's grammatical expectations in the act of reading. Why else would anyone presume to take up a reader's time than to solve a problem for the reader? Why then would anyone write except to inform the reader about a solution to that problem? How else can this be done aside from ordering the text so that readers can get the point before giving up in the face of the obvious difficulty? Williams and Colomb accordingly coach their students in a style of writing assimilated to a model of reading.

Classic style makes similar pretenses in adopting the rather different stand that the writer counts equally with the reader, that both are fully engaged by the subject, competent, and alert, that *of course* the reader will be interested in what the writer has to say, and that *of course* the reader will recognize truth once it has been clearly presented.

In the model scene of practical style, readers and writers hold standard job slots in existing institutions. The reader has no leisure and does not want surprises; the reader reads not for personal reasons but to accomplish a job. Accomplishing the job depends upon the communication of information, and practical style serves the purpose of keeping the information flowing efficiently through institutions. Since students will go on to such employment, they must be trained to write in practical style. The writer is not an individual writing to another individual but a job description writing to another job description. There is a job to do and practical style is the appropriate tool for doing it: the style is thus fundamentally optimistic, pragmatic, and utilitarian. The motive is the job; eternal and noncontingent truth is irrelevant except as it bears upon the performance of the job—even then its eternal and noncontingent nature is beside the point.

There is a surface mark of practical style as presented by Williams and Colomb that derives from its fundamental stand and distinguishes it sharply from classic style. If the reader always expects to find certain kinds of things in certain "discourse locations," and the writer submits uniformly to those expectations, then the style permits skimming, because the cream is always in the same place. This can be highly useful in certain practical situations: if you are sitting at a desk and need to plow through forty-three memos, most of whose substance you already know, it will be a great help if you can rely upon the memos to present their main points in the expected places; then you can simply glance through and extract what you want.

If you try to skim classic writing in this way, you run the risk of missing indispensable conceptual nuances or refinements. In the model scene of classic style, the classic reader is not pressed for time, distracted by jobs to do, or mired in routine. The classic reader is competent, sophisticated, quite able to handle surprises, and unimpressed with predictability. The surface mark of classic style that is most uncongenial to practical style can be picked out by what we will call the "last-third" test: once you have progressed a little way into a piece of writing, block out the last third of each sentence as you come to it, and imagine the standard things you might expect to occupy that position, based on what you have already read. If what in fact does occupy that position is routinely one of those standard and expected things, then the piece may be a paragon of practical writing but is unlikely to be classic. This is not because classic sentences reverse themselves at the end: once you see the end of a classic sentence, you will recognize that the sentence was true to its direction, but that does not make the sentence predictable, because it usually contains a conceptual refinement that is clear and simple as the truth but not a cliché and hence not predictable. Here are four passages that pass the last-third test beautifully; none of them is likely to occur in practical style:

> Although a dirty campaign was widely predicted, for the most part the politicians contented themselves with insults and lies. (Julian Barnes on the 1992 British parliamentary elections)

> With peer pressure and whippings at school and at home, we were soon completely socialized and as happy as children anywhere. (Ruth Baer Lambach)

> In the same year [1827] the United Kingdom, Russia and France decided to intervene to enforce an armistice "without however taking any part in the hostilities." The allied fleet went to parley with the Turkish fleet anchored in Navarino Bay (Pylos) and ended up destroying it. (*Greece* [Michelin Green Guide])

> It is from this weighing of delights against their cost that the student eater (particularly if he is a student at the University of Paris) erects the scale of values that will serve him until he dies or has to reside in the Middle West for a long period. (A. J. Liebling)

Classic Style Is Not Contemplative Style

Classic style implicitly defines itself as a normal, practically inevitable, perspective. It makes continual if tacit claims to transparency; it does not interpret; it merely presents. These claims are, of course, false. When the style succeeds, it simply obscures the distinction and manages to pass off interpretation as presentation.

In contemplative style, the distinction between presentation and interpretation is always observed: the writer sees something, presents it to the reader, and then interprets it. The stress is on the interpretation, but the transition is always explicitly marked. E. B.

White, a master of the contemplative essay, characteristically observes this sequence, as he does in "The Ring of Time," a dazzling piece of writing that is entirely unclassic. White describes himself casually observing a practice session of a circus, watching the lion tamer, a big, brown horse, and then a circus rider. He tells the reader precisely what he sees and how he sees it: "As she emerged in front of us, I saw that she was barefoot, her dirty little feet fighting the uneven ground. In most respects she was like any of two or three dozen showgirls you encounter if you wander about the winter quarters of Mr. John Ringling North's circus, in Sarasota—cleverly proportioned, deeply browned by the sun, dusty, eager, and almost naked." White describes what he sees and what anyone there with him might see. And then he contemplates what he sees and offers an interpretation: "I became painfully conscious of the element of time. Everything in the hideous old building seemed to take the shape of a circle, conforming to the course of the horse. The rider's gaze, as she peered straight ahead, seemed to be circular, as though bent by force of circumstance; then time itself began running in circles, and so the beginning was where the end was, and the two were the same, and one thing ran into the next and time went round and around and got nowhere." He then sees that the girl is deluded: "She is at that enviable moment in life [I thought] when she believes she can go once around the ring, make one complete circuit, and at the end be exactly the same age as at the start." The associations, the connections, the very way he turns a commonplace event into an allegory of time belong to him alone; contemplative style assumes that this is not what someone standing next to him would see. In contemplative style, the focus is on the interpretation and not on the event.

White stands in a tradition of American preachers who present a text and then interpret it. The common scene that White sees becomes, through his contemplation of it, an allegory of the world, which the reader is allowed to see because White offers his superior vision. He begins to discuss things that in principle the reader has no way of checking, and he does not hesitate to refer to himself as something like an authority. "The circus comes as close to being the world in microcosm as anything I know; in a way, it puts all the rest of show business in the shade. Its magic is universal and complex. Out of its wild disorder comes order; from its rank smell rises the good aroma of courage and daring; out of its preliminary shabbiness comes the final splendor." The asymmetry between writer and reader is profound. White takes the attitude that the reader could be perfectly competent and yet, in looking at this scene, see none of what he sees.

The first fundamental distinction between classic style and contemplative style is thus that classic style presents something but contemplative style presents an interpretation of something. This entails many different decisions concerning truth, presentation, cast, and scene.

The second fundamental distinction between classic style and contemplative style has to do with thought and language. Classic language is an instrument for presenting the product of thought according to the order of reason, not according to the sequence of experience. In contemplative style, writing is itself the engine of discovery: the writing is a record of the process of the writer's thinking, quite independent of its relation to the order of reason. In contemplative style, the touchstone of the writing is the process of the writer's contemplation. That process and the writer's engagement in it often become an explicit subject of the writing:

> In attempting to recapture this mild spectacle, I am merely acting as recording secretary for one of the oldest of societies—the society of those who, at one time or another, have surrendered, without even a show of resistance, to the bedazzlement of a circus rider. As a writing man, or secretary, I have always felt charged with the safekeeping of all unexpected items of worldly or unworldly enchantment, as though I might be held personally responsible if even a small one were to be lost. . . . The ten-minute ride the girl took achieved—as far as I was concerned, who wasn't looking for it, and quite unbeknownst to her, who wasn't even

striving for it—the thing that is sought by performers everywhere.... As I watched with the others, our jaws adroop, our eyes alight, I became painfully conscious of the element of time.... I thought: "She will never be as beautiful as this again"—a thought that made me acutely unhappy—and in a flash my mind (which is too much of a busybody to suit me) had projected her twenty-five years ahead.

Rather than presenting truth, White often quotes his own contemplation, giving its history:

"She is at that enviable moment in life [I thought] when she believes she can go once around the ring, make one complete circuit, and at the end be exactly the same age as at the start."... And then I slipped back into my trance, and time was circular again—time, pausing quietly with the rest of us, so as not to disturb the balance of a performer.

In these passages, White uses many of the surface marks of clarity, precision, and accurate vocabulary that are associated with classic style. But his fundamental stand on the elements of style is very far from the classic stand. Regardless of language or phrasing, none of these passages could fit comfortably in a classic text.

Because contemplation is a superior achievement by a superior individual who talks about the difficulties of contemplation, contemplative style splits into two modes that are not incompatible and that can be used alternately. Sometimes, the contemplative writer succeeds fully in his achievement: thought and language can be adequate. Thoreau frequently writes as if he has been successful in his contemplations. But sometimes, the contemplative writer fails in his achievement, and feels compelled to settle for what is merely his best effort. White often does this, as when he writes, "But it is not easy to communicate anything of this nature."

At other moments, White seems to take the extreme stand that language is always inadequate to the task: "It has been ambitious and plucky of me to attempt to describe what is indescribable, and I have failed, as I knew I would. But I have discharged my duty to my society; and besides, a writer, like an acrobat, must occasionally try a stunt that is too much for him."

Classic Style Is Not Romantic Style

Contemplative style is fundamentally about the writer's thought and often explicitly acknowledges this focus. Romantic style, although not necessarily focused on the writer's thought in the sense of his analysis or reflection, is always and inescapably about the writer. Romantic prose is a mirror, not a window.

Romantic style does not separate thought from sensation, memory, and emotion. All these things together are experience. Neither does romantic style distinguish the person who experiences from the experience. The romantic writer therefore cannot be an observer who sees something separate from himself; both the writer and his experience are inseparable elements of a perpetual dialectic in which the writer creates a world, which in its turn creates him. This process is something like the pulse of life. A writer can describe this dynamic relationship, but cannot "present" it and allow it to be verified.

If contemplative style views writing as an engine of discovery, romantic style looks upon it as an act of creation that both comes from the self and reveals the self.

The narrator of Proust's *A la recherche du temps perdu* offers a striking description of such an act of romantic creation in his account of his first direct encounter with the Duchesse de Guermantes, a woman who had a large place in his imagination before he had ever seen her. The image he cherished has little to do with her—no one but the narrator himself could validate it in a face-to-face encounter with her—but it reveals a great deal about the narrator:

> My disappointment was immense. It arose from my not having borne in mind, when I thought of Mme de Guermantes, that I was picturing her to myself in the colours of a tapestry or a stained-glass window, as living in another century, as being of another substance than the rest of the human race.

At this point, there is a kind of struggle between the classic outlook and the romantic.

> . . . I was endeavouring to apply . . . to this fresh and un-changing image, the idea: "It's Mme de Guermantes"; but I succeeded only in making the idea pass between me and the image, as though they were two discs moving in separate planes with a space between.

The Madame de Guermantes whose existence is independent of the narrator's idea of her does not, however, overcome the Madame de Guermantes who is a defining element of his mentality. He says these words to himself silently but distinctly:

> "Great and glorious before the days of Charlemagne, the Guermantes had the right of life and death over their vassals; the Duchesse de Guermantes descends from Geneviève de Brabant. She does not know, nor would she consent to know, any of the people who are here to-day."

His struggle ends with a creative act that allows the narrator to see the romantic truth, one unique to himself, one that could not be shared by anyone else present on the occasion he describes.

> . . . my eyes resting upon her fair hair, her blue eyes, the lines of her neck, and overlooking the features which might have reminded me of the faces of other women, I cried out within myself, as I admired this deliberately unfinished sketch: "How lovely she is! What true nobility! It is indeed a proud Guermantes, the descendant of Geneviève de Brabant, that I have before me!"

In contemplative style, which preserves a distinction between observation and the observer's reflections, it is possible to discover something that is outside of the self and not dependent on the writer for its existence. In romantic style, which observes no such distinction, creation replaces discovery and always depends on the writer for its existence.

Classic writing may present personal material as an instance of a more general truth, but it never presents something that is merely personal or in principle private. For romantic style to rule out personal experience or even experience that is in principle private would reduce the romantic writer to silence. In the theology of this style, the only things anyone can know are personal and in principle private.

Classic style never leaves the writer feeling incomplete, unfulfilled, or incompetent. Classic writers can know something, and once they know it, they can say it. Correction and revision are not infinite, because classic style is a craft that can effectively be learned by learning its parts, none of which is idiosyncratic. Thought and language fit, so it is possible to succeed completely in expressing truth. In romantic style, to separate thought and expression or thought and thinker as separate and fixed realities is to make a false division that leads to false conclusions. In the romantic perspective, writing is not a craft that can be learned, because it is an activity co-extensive with the writer's person; it cannot be reduced to discrete modules, separate writing jobs that can be completed one after another. There is no complete fit between thought and language because a writer's thought is not a formed and fixed reality independent of language and capable of being fitted into it.

It is a premise of classic style that truth has been perfectly perceived by the writer. The writer's problem is to articulate that truth perfectly, and in the theology of classic style this problem always has a solution. In romantic style, the writer can know truth romantically and whole, but truth cannot be conceived analytically without a loss of definition, and cannot be put into language without a further loss of definition. In classic style, truth is allied with clarity. In romantic style, clarity can be achieved only at the price of falsification.

Both the classic writer and the romantic writer are vulnerable but in entirely different ways. The classic writer is vulnerable because he speaks noncontingent truth to which everybody is vulnerable. The romantic writer is vulnerable because everybody is vulnerable to the conditions of life. The classic writer is always vulnerable to challenge; the romantic writer never. When the romantic writer says he dreams of Jeanie with the light brown hair, he yearns for her, he sighs for her, who can check to see whether it is true? He cannot be told he is wrong, for he stands in a special place, with incorrigible knowledge about his entirely private and personal subject matter. If he is wrong, his error is built into the human condition, so no human being can correct him. But the classic writer can be told that he is wrong, because the truth he presents is available to everyone, and can be tested by anyone.

Of the styles we have discussed, classic and romantic are furthest apart: they take strong fundamentally irreconcilable stands on every one of the elements of style. The distinction between them is as absolute as the distinction Demetrius saw between the restrained and the elevated. The classic stand on the elements of style is not always opposed in all particulars to the stands of other styles. Between classic style and practical style is an agreement that language is sufficient to express knowable truths. Between classic style and contemplative style is at least a channel for discussion: at least sometimes, truth can be known and language can express it. Between classic style and plain style is a gradient of conceptual refinement. But classic style and romantic style represent irreconcilable conceptual stands. There is no common ground between them, no gradient from one to the other; instead there is something like a permanent and impassable divide.

Classic Style Is Not Prophetic Style

Despite a shared affinity for unqualified assertion, classic style has little in common with prophetic or oracular style because prophetic style cannot place the reader where the writer is. The reader cannot verify through his own experience what the writer experiences. Classic style does not depend upon powers that are divine or that are available only to special people, or powers whose availability is subject to some agency that human beings do not control or understand. Prophetic style, on the other hand, depends entirely upon such powers. The ability of the prophetic writer to know truth has come through powers that are not part of the usual human complement. Even their possessor does not possess them reliably: these powers come and go in ways that he does not understand or control.

In Western culture, the best-known examples of prophetic style are in the Old Testament. When the sons of Jesse come before Samuel, the eldest, Eliab, makes an immediate impression on the aging judge, who concludes, "Here, before the Lord, is his anointed king." It is a response that stands for human insight and wisdom; it is the judgment of a wise and experienced person. Any reader who knows what Samuel knows would presumably share his view of Eliab. But in the model scene of the prophetic style, human judgment does not and cannot share the sacred perspective, even though it can, through a privileged channel, receive the fruit of divine wisdom. The Lord responds to Samuel: "Take no account of it if he is handsome and tall; I reject him. The Lord does not see as man sees; men judge by appearances but the Lord judges by the heart."

One of the most famous representations of the model scene of prophetic style occurs in the opening chapter of the Book of Jeremiah. The passage begins with the archetypical claim of the prophetic writer, that he is not speaking in his own voice and not conveying his own judgments. "The Word of the Lord came to me." It then passes on to a dialogue between the Word of God and the inarticulate Jeremiah.

> "Before I formed you in the womb . . . I appointed you a prophet to the nations."
> "Ah! Lord God," I answered, "I do not know how to speak; I am only a child." . . . Then the Lord stretched out his hand and touched my mouth, and said to me, "I put my words into your mouth. This day I give you authority over nations and over kingdoms, to pull down and to uproot, to destroy and to demolish, to build and to plant."

The equally famous representation of the calling of Isaiah establishes the same points although they run the risk of being lost in the fabulous vision in which they are embedded. The prophet inexplicably finds himself in the realm of the divine, where he does not belong. ("Woe is me! I am lost, for I am a man of unclean lips. . . .") But his deficiency is miraculously removed and "unclean lips" are made capable of speaking divine words. He volunteers his services as a messenger and receives his commission: "Go and tell this people. . . ."

The poet, painter, engraver, and printer William Blake is one of the few widely admired modern writers to make extensive use of prophetic style in something like its prototypical form. But prophetic style is not confined to the sacred literature of ancient Israel or an occasional genius-crackpot like Blake. It has its modern form on all those occasions in which a writer claims to be a channel for impersonal and normally inaccessible truth. The writer makes claims to authority, but not his own authority and not the kind of authority that is available to others. "History tells us" (and, tacitly, "I am history's spokesman") is a common anthem of politicians and of those mysterious channels of wisdom who write opinion columns in newspapers; prophetic style is used by jurists who on occasion claim to speak the judgment of principles or of long-dead foundation jurists; it is the style of all those innumerable spokesmen who tell us what "tradition," "common sense," or "common decency" demand and of those slightly less numerous spokesmen who tell us what fashions state or what eras or epochs tell us.

Classic Style Is Not Oratorical Style

The central model for most discussions of rhetoric in classical antiquity seems to be oratory. Even when something is written—rather than spoken—in an oratorical style and meant to be read silently by one individual, its effects are meant for the ear. The text may be written down formally in sentences, but its units are periods and are defined by sound.

The model scene of oratorical style is neither casual nor spontaneous. Its prototypical occasion is the assembly of a group of people faced by a public problem—like military invasion, the forming and maintenance of public values, or the judging of social offenders.

This scene creates a cast. Leadership is necessary, and the assembly's job is to respond to a candidate who puts himself forward. The orator assumes a role as leader of both the public moment and the setting of policy. He invites the audience to yield to his rhythms and to his views, which he typically presents as a version of common verities. The audience may coalesce and perhaps join in as his chorus, or remain splintered and perhaps heckle him randomly. The successful orator molds the audience into one body with one voice and one governing view. To the outsider, he may appear to be alternatively a demagogue with an echo or the selfless conductor of the common music.

In a slight variant of this model scene and cast, the audience has as its head a judge or perhaps a king who rules on policy under advice from the full audience. When Odysseus debates with Akhilleus over the best time for the Akhaians to engage the Trojans on the field of war, the judge is High King Agamemnon, but the entire council is the audience with Agamemnon at its head. Akhilleus, who wants to avenge immediately the slaying of Patroclos, vents his anger and represents his singularity:

> Let us recover joy of battle soon, that's all!
> No need to dither here and lose our time,
> our great work still undone. When each man sees
> Akhilleus in a charge, crumpling the ranks
> of Trojans with his bronze-shod spear, let each
> remember that is the way to fight his man!

Odysseus, by far the better orator, isolates Akhilleus by assuming for himself the role of defender and spokesman of the audience, thereby making it natural for the audience to identify with him and his views:

> Brave as you are, and like a god in looks,
> Akhilleus, do not send Akhaian soldiers
> into the fight unfed! Today's mêlée
> will not be brief, when rank meets rank, and heaven

breathes fighting spirit into both contenders.
No, tell all troops who are near the ships to take
roast meat and wine, for heart and staying power.
No soldier can fight hand to hand, in hunger,
all day long until the sun goes down!
Though in his heart he yearns for war, his legs
go slack before he knows it: thirst and famine
search him out, and his knees fail as he moves.
But that man stayed with victualing and wine
can fight his enemies all day: his heart
is bold and happy in his chest, his legs
hold out until both sides break off the battle!
Come, then, dismiss the ranks to make their breakfast.

Since oratory is designed to unite many listeners, whose attention may flag, it cannot be either very flexible or very subtle. Nuance is always risky with such an audience. Consequently, the surface of oratory usually looks like a few points with the help of a lot of music. Going along with the music helps the audience go along with the points, as Kenneth Burke has remarked in *A Rhetoric of Motives*:

[W]e know that many purely formal patterns can readily awaken an attitude of collaborative expectancy in us. For instance, imagine a passage built about a set of oppositions ("*we* do *this*, but *they* on the other hand do that; *we* stay *here*; but *they* go *there*; *we* look *up*, but *they* look *down*," etc.) Once you grasp the trend of the form, it invites participation regardless of the subject matter. Formally, you will find yourself swinging along with the succession of antitheses, even though you may not agree with the proposition that is being presented in this form. Or it may even be an opponent's proposition which you resent—yet for the duration of the statement itself you might "help him out" to the extent of yielding to the formal development, surrendering to its symmetry as such. Of course, the more violent your original resistance to the proposition, the weaker will be your degree of "surrender" by "collaborating" with the form. But in cases where a decision is still to be reached, a yielding to the form prepares for assent to the matter identified with it. Thus, you are drawn to the form, not in your capacity as a partisan, but because of some "universal" appeal in it. And this attitude of assent may then be transferred to the matter which happens to be associated with the form.

Burke, in writing this passage, surely had in mind Pericles' Funeral Oration, as reconstructed by Thucydides, in which Pericles attempts to guide the Athenians at a difficult historical moment in their sense of communal values by offering them an image of themselves that just happens coincidentally to serve Pericles' own purposes. In this oration, which takes place at the end of the first year of the Peloponnesian War, Pericles follows the model of Odysseus in the debate with Akhilleus. Like Odysseus, Pericles casts himself in the role of spokesman for the audience. His oration has as its most central and famous parts a series of explicit and implicit contrasts between the Athenians and citizens of rival cities:

> Our love of what is beautiful does not lead to extravagance; our love of the things of the mind does not make us soft. We regard wealth as something to be properly used, rather than as something to boast about. As for poverty, no one need be ashamed to admit it: the real shame is not taking practical measures to escape from it. Here each individual is interested not only in his own affairs but in the affairs of the state as well. . . . We are capable at the same time of taking risks and of estimating them beforehand. Others are brave out of ignorance; and, when they stop to think, they begin to fear. But the man who can most truly be accounted brave is he who best knows the meaning of what is sweet in life and of what is terrible, and then goes out undeterred to meet what is to come.

Later, after the plague and the second invasion of Athenian land by the Peloponnesians, the Athenians grow angry at Pericles. To defuse their anger, he summons them to Assembly and revives the oratorical theme of the previous Funeral Oration:

> No doubt all this will be disparaged by people who are politically apathetic; but those who, like us, prefer a life of action will try to imitate us, and, if they fail to secure what we have secured, they will envy us. All who have taken it upon themselves to rule over others have incurred hatred and unpopularity for a time; but if one has a great aim to pursue, this burden of envy must be accepted, and it is wise to accept it. Hatred does not last for long; but the brilliance of the present is the glory of the future stored up for ever in the memory of man. It is for you. . . . Do not send embassies to Sparta: do not give the impression that you are bowed down under your present sufferings! To face calamity with a mind as unclouded as may be, and quickly to react against it—that, in a city and in an individual, is real strength.

The contrasts between oratorical style and classic style can be illustrated right from this text of Thucydides. He comments on Pericles' oratory in a style whose impulses served as a prototype for the inventors of classic style:

> In this way Pericles attempted to stop the Athenians from being angry with him and to guide their thoughts in a direction away from their immediate sufferings. So far as public policy was concerned, they accepted his argument, sending no more embassies to Sparta and showing an increased energy in carrying on the war; yet as private individuals they still felt the weight of their misfortunes. The mass of the people had had little enough to start with and had now been deprived of even that; the richer classes had lost their fine estates with their rich and well-equipped houses in the country, and, which was the worst thing of all, they were at

war instead of living in peace. In fact, the general ill feeling against Pericles persisted, and was not satisfied until they had condemned him to pay a fine. Not long afterwards, however, as is the way with crowds, they re-elected him to the generalship and put all their affairs into his hands. By that time people felt their own private sufferings rather less acutely and, so far as the general needs of the state were concerned, they regarded Pericles as the best man they had. . . . He survived the outbreak of war by two years and six months, and after his death his foresight with regard to the war became even more evident. For Pericles had said that Athens would be victorious if she bided her time and took care of her navy, if she avoided trying to add to the empire during the course of the war, and if she did nothing to risk the safety of the city itself. But his successors did the exact opposite, and in other matters which apparently had no connection with the war private ambition and private profit led to policies which were bad both for the Athenians themselves and for their allies.

The roles adopted by Pericles the orator and Thucydides the classic writer differ sharply. Pericles leads a group but Thucydides merely presents something to the reader. Pericles is interested but Thucydides disinterested. Pericles is the conductor of the rhythm of the crowd but Thucydides is merely talking in his natural voice. Pericles wants something from his audience but Thucydides does not. Pericles asserts and advises but Thucydides merely observes. Pericles is formal, Thucydides casual. Pericles speaks in a public occasion but Thucydides is telling the reader something spontaneously. Pericles affirms common wisdom, but Thucydides operates at all moments as an independent thinker. Pericles expects his audience to notice his oratory while Thucydides pretends that his prose is transparent. Pericles asks his audience to look harder to see what needs seeing, while Thucydides is simply pointing out something that is obvious once presented. Of course, in fact, Thucydides' supposed historical account is a relentless argument about the nature of crowds and democracies, but he presents his conclusions the same way one might point out the first turning of the leaves in fall, as a fact, although a subtle fact. It is a characteristic strength of classic style to persuade by default. The classic writer offers no explicit argument at all. Ostensibly, he offers simply a presentation. If the reader fails to recognize that the ostensible presentation is a device of persuasion, then he is persuaded without ever realizing that an argument has occurred. It is always easier to persuade an audience unaware of the rhetorician's agenda.

The differences between the oratorical and classic models of speech are considerable because oratory and the writing styles based on it have a lot of practical work to do. These oratorical styles cannot concern themselves with thought exclusively or even mainly. They have not merely to keep an audience made up of many individuals attentive and alert but also to take a heterogeneous group of individuals and mold them into a unified body directed at action or the making of policy for action. They make use of what the audience already thinks much more than they introduce new observations or refine old ones.

■ **Trade Secrets**

Classic writers almost never discuss the classic stand on the elements of style, not because they want to keep secrets but rather because they take the classic stand to be obvious, needing neither explanation nor justification. But they have no axiomatic prejudice against investigating the classic stand, and there are classic works, such as Descartes's *Discourse on Method*, that explicitly lay out many of the principles behind it.

These principles constitute what we have called the theology behind the classic stand. The theology is acknowledged even if rarely discussed. But separate from the theology are a few trade secrets, acknowledged neither in the theology nor in the style. The theology can be learned by anyone, but only a classic writer is likely to come to an understanding of how the trade secrets of the style are related to its theology. There are two principal trade secrets: classic style's practical limitations and the ultimate incoherence of its theoretical perspective.

Classic Style Is Inadequate

There are theorems in mathematics—such as Gödel's Incompleteness Theorem, the Fundamental Theorem of Galois Theory, and Wedderburn's Theorem ("A finite division ring is a field")—that count as high art because of their elegance and purity. Their proofs move deftly and efficiently in clear and irrefutable steps through vast, seemingly incomprehensible landscapes of overwhelming complexity and detail, to bring out at a snap a crisp and powerful truth that is obvious once it is pointed out. As the absolute brilliance of the truth comes into focus, an absolute inevitability, completeness, and perfection accompany it, as if these proofs are not inventions of formal steps but rather the perfect discovery of the clear and simple truth they present. No one would have seen the truth without having seen it presented this way, but once seen, it is seen entirely and recognized absolutely. This is the stereotype of a mathematical proof: brief, efficient, clear, elegant, and pure. Classic style takes such elegance to be not merely normative but universal.

But there are problems in mathematics, like the four-color problem or the traveling salesman problem, that have been treated in a manner that is neither elegant nor pure. They are battles of attrition. The four-color problem, for example, was first solved by a computer program that spent night after night testing possibilities and ruling each out. The conception of this proof is of course extremely clever, but the proof itself, printed out, looks like what it is: the mechanical application of brute force. It is impossible to follow this proof, and no one could keep it all in mind. There is no clear and simple truth for anyone to see. The traveling salesman problem is still susceptible only to approximations and heuristics, again computer-assisted and very untidy. Many of the best mathematical minds of the last three centuries have sought an exact efficient solution to this and related problems, without success, leading to the current suspicion that there is no exact efficient solution. Worse, it is now widely suspected that there is not even an efficient approximate solution. If there is no efficient solution at all, the only approach to these problems is to work at this or that special case, and to leave off short of finality and perfection.

Mathematics acknowledges this situation and has invented many instruments, such as numerical methods, that do not fit the stereotype of brief, simple, and elegant proof. Classic style, on the other hand, acknowledges nothing that does not fit its model of elegance. The theology behind classic style does not admit that there is anything that counts as truth that cannot be presented briefly and memorably. In practice, this simply means that classic style prefers to limit its domain while tacitly claiming universal application.

Truth Is Not Mind-Independent

This, the most fundamental trade secret, concerns classic style's conception of truth. The classic stand on the elements of style depends upon a conception of a single objective state of affairs that is "the world" and a writer who sees that world without distortion. Of course, the classic writer has access to that world only through her own mind, but that mind has been cleared of all obstructions. In consequence, what it holds is a perfect and undistorted copy of objective truth.

Descartes formed the model for this view in saying that we can know there is God and that God would not have provided us with minds that are fundamentally deceptive. All error must therefore come from such perversions of our fundamental mental endowment as received opinion and prejudice. What is seen clearly and distinctly by a mind cleansed of perversions must necessarily be true.

The theology behind classic style has at its base this model: truth cannot be known independently of thought, but the thought through which it is known can be perfect. Although truth is never independent of mind, the classic writer can know a truth that can be conceived of as independent of mind, as purely "objective," because the mind of the classic writer has introduced no distortion. There is no difference, then, between the truth the classic writer knows and the "objective" truth as seen from a God's-eye view, external to any particular mind.

The contemporary philosopher Hilary Putnam describes the view that there is an objective state of affairs that can be known objectively as an externalist perspective "because its favorite point of view is a God's Eye point of view."

The trade secret, to put it bluntly, is that there is no such perspective available to anyone who is part of the human world. As Putnam says, "There is no God's Eye point of view that we can know or usefully imagine; there are only the various points of view of actual persons reflecting various interests and purposes that their descriptions and theories subserve." Classic style always assumes that it might as well be standing outside the world of actual persons because the classic writer is above mere personal interest; he has no motive but truth, or at least, his highest and governing motive is truth. The classic perception of truth is a perfect copy of truth.

The trade secret can be expressed as two qualifications to the classic conception of truth. The first qualification is a practical limit: no writer can maintain for long the discipline needed to transcend personal interests and personal situations. The second qualification is an absolute limit: there is in fact no way at all even for the briefest space to know truth or the existence of truth independent of thought. All conceptions of truth and all supposedly true concepts are exactly that—conceptions and concepts.

The conception of truth assumed by classic style is based on what Putnam calls the "copy" theory: what is true corresponds to the mind-independent facts. Classic style cannot be described without recourse to this conception of truth, but the copy theory itself rests on a fundamentally impossible premise. How can we compare what we have thought and expressed in language to a mind-independent reality? How can we be independent of our own minds or have any access to what stands apart from mind? There have been many solutions proposed—they include Descartes's plan of cleansing the rational mind through applying judiciously the instrument of doubt, and the positivist plan of using the scientific method to factor out of theories any merely subjective components. But all such plans still involve human thought as the engine of escape, and it is not possible to escape the human mind through the faculties of the human mind.

It requires only a moment's thought to realize that any writer who claims that his writing is "clear and simple as the truth" is claiming that his access to the truth is essentially independent of his thought. It is a claim that can never be known to be true since, as Putnam says, it is impossible to verify a perfect correspondence (or any correspondence) between two things if we have access to just one of them. The classic writer actually has access only to his own thought. How can someone who has access only to thought check that his thought corresponds to mind-independent truth? It is like expecting someone who knows English but no Chinese to be able to claim that an English translation of a Chinese text is accurate. But the classic stand on the elements of style is always in the position of claiming that the translation is accurate with no access to the original except through the translation. The classic claim rests on impossible conditions—as do all the mature and consistent styles of which we are aware—but despite its internal incoherence, it has enjoyed an exceptionally important role in the way people think.

While it is beyond the scope of this book to consider in detail why such an incoherent view has had such a prominent place in the history of thought—much less to consider sophisticated alternatives to the copy theory—it is worth noting that the copy theory has an unparalleled two-thousand-year career in Western philosophy and has come to seem natural. Putnam thinks that "perhaps most philosophers hold some version of the 'copy' theory of truth today" and furthermore that before Kant it may be impossible to find even one philosopher who did not hold such a theory. Even for Kant, the existence of some mind-independent reality is in Putnam's phrase "virtually a postulate of reason."

"It's not what I think, it's what I know." "See for yourself." "Ask anyone." "I would not have believed it if I hadn't seen it for myself."

"This shipment has been checked and verified by trained inspectors." All of these common expressions are normally understood with the help of a tacit reference to the copy theory. This is one way of suggesting what we think to be the case: classic style is not "classic" for no reason. It is so deeply entrenched in our normal way of looking at the world that the only commonsense alternative seems to be that we just make up the world we see, and every claim is as "true" as every other. Although this dichotomy is naïve, it is commonly accepted as inevitable. On that view, there is only one alternative to the copy theory, and it is so generally unacceptable that the copy theory, warts and all, has been embraced as the only possible protection from chaos.

■ Envoi: Style Is Not Etiquette

This book is meant to be a guide to learning classic style and approaches its subject from the inside out, so to speak. Although it takes for granted that its audience writes in English, the style it discusses is not confined to any particular language. It is a style used by ancient Greek writers such as Thucydides, and it is a style used by a distinguished group of seventeenth-century French writers, most of whom knew no Greek; it is a style used by the French chemist Lavoisier in the eighteenth century, and by the American reporter and press critic A. J. Liebling in the twentieth. The principles this book discusses are a stand on the elements of style, not the foundation of a usage manual of one or more varieties of English. Anyone who has attained competence in any language can learn classic style because the principles of the style are as applicable to Japanese or Bengali as they are to English.

We have tried to distinguish the concept of style from the much broader concept of writing, but it is not easy to prevent two commonplace American conflations: style with writing, and writing with English. Most Americans learn to write in English courses, and surveys have shown that what most people mean by English is, first, spelling and then, usage ("can and may," "affect and effect," "imply and infer," and so on through a list of indefinite length).

In addition to books treating fundamental aspects of writing, there is a large and ever-growing number of what amount to etiquette books on conventions of usage and other surface features that proceed from the tacit assumption that someone who masters all these points of etiquette will be able to write "English." This assumption is a corollary of the thesis that knowing something consists of knowing surface details.

Consider a couple of almost universally effective put-downs based on this assumption. "How on earth can X know anything about epistemology? He can't even spell it!" The equivalent dismissal for spoken language is: "What can Y possibly know about Degas? She can't even pronounce his name!" These are almost invariably effective lines, even though neither has any merit. It is perfectly possible to know a great deal about anything anyone cares to name without being able to spell it or pronounce it according to a prevailing convention.

We will not say it is absolutely impossible to learn to write what will pass for standard English by learning everything in an etiquette book about current conventions in spelling and by consistently distinguishing "allusion" from "illusion" and making similar distinctions between all the other sets of terms frequently confused. But it is a most unlikely procedure, being something like Malcolm X's attempt to attain literacy by memorizing a dictionary. The problem is that anyone seeking to learn something about writing from an etiquette book—and dictionaries are one kind of linguistic etiquette book—remains forever passive to its advice; there is no set of principles to grasp that can ever make such a person independent of the etiquette book. Consider that a competent speaker of English will *never* make a mistake about fundamental word order: it really is impossible for such a speaker to be uncertain about whether to say "Pass me the molasses" or "Me molasses pass the," but the same speaker may never be confident of spelling "molasses" correctly even if he becomes editor in chief of a newspaper or a professor of English.

What gives a writer command of a style is not mere correctness; even if an essay, a letter, a report, or a book is completely "correct," it may also be completely incoherent; it may entirely fail to accomplish what its writer has set out to do. The performance, if merely correct, even should it work, can never be more than an isolated success that leaves no permanent trace. Charles de Gaulle once startled his hosts on a state visit to Moscow by delivering a speech in quite correct and intelligible Russian. Until then, he had not been known to speak the language. Intelligence services in several countries were embarrassed by their apparent lapse in gathering information about his linguistic range, until they found out that they had been right all along. He really did not speak Russian; he merely had been coached to pronounce the Russian words correctly, group them in an apparently thoughtful way by memorizing a tape, and deliver them with appropriate inflection through the same device. It was an actor's trick skillfully carried off. The performance was sensational, but it did not make de Gaulle a Russophone; he remained completely incompetent in the language.

This little book does not offer itself as a short cut to the impossible goal of learning to write English or any other language. It does not aim for something as vague as excellence in a skill as indefinite as writing English. It aims for the eminently possible goal of perfect understanding in a much more definite domain: classic style, with a local application to English. The first goal, "writing English," is as much a mirage as perfect spelling; the second goal, writing classic prose, is as attainable as correct word order. If you cannot remember the difference between "effect" and "affect," this book will not help you, and neither of its authors will ever win a spelling bee, but then no one can ever become a competent writer if we consider mastery of the indefinite list of accidentals at the surface of any language to be competence in writing. Is there any competent speaker of English anywhere who can pronounce, spell, and use every word in the *OED* or *Webster's*? Does that mean there are no competent speakers of English? What a competent writer can know perfectly are the principles of a style, and no style is an inert set of rules. Once the principles are grasped and the writer begins to use the style from a position of command, the writer becomes active in that style, and the style becomes part of the writer's active competence as surely and perfectly as word order. There is unlimited room for invention and discovery within the constraints of the style just as there is unlimited room for meaning and expression within the constraints of the word order of English, for the mastery of a style, like the underlying linguistic competence, is a living activity, not a rote performance.

T W O

The Museum

> "Tufted Titmouse, including Black-crested Titmouse"
> (*Parus bicolor*)
>
> Titmice are social birds and, especially in winter, join with small mixed flocks of chickadees, nuthatches, kinglets, creepers, and the smaller woodpeckers. Although a frequent visitor at feeders, it is not as tame or confiding as the chickadees. It often clings to the bark of trees and turns upside down to pick spiders and insects from the underside of a twig or leaf. The "Black-crested Titmouse" of Texas was until recently considered a separate species.
>
> VOICE: Its commonest call, sung year-round and carrying a considerable distance, is a whistled series of four to eight notes sounding like Peter-Peter repeated over and over.
>
> "Northern Shrike"
> (*Lanius excubitor*)
>
> Unusual among songbirds, shrikes prey on small birds and rodents, catching them with the bill and sometimes impaling them on thorns or barbed wire for storage. Like other northern birds that depend on rodent populations, the Northern Shrike movements are cyclical, becoming more abundant in the South when northern rodent populations are low. At times they hunt from an open perch, where they sit motionless until prey appears; at other times they hover in the air ready to pounce on anything that moves.
>
> —John Bull and John Farrand, Jr., *The Audubon Society Field Guide to North American Birds, Eastern Region*

A field guide, in its stand on truth, presentation, scene, cast, thought, and language, fits the classic stand on the elements of style perfectly. Its implied model is one person presenting observations to another, who is in a position to verify them by direct observation.

The reader is not in a library doing research, but in the field looking and listening. Since the field guide assumes a scene in which the reader is in the field, it cannot be written in a style that requires study or rereading. It strives to be brief and efficient. It seeks to present the birds it describes specifically and precisely enough for the reader to recognize them.

The writing in a good field guide is certainly the product of deliberation and revision but sounds like ideal spontaneous speech, as if an accomplished companion in the field wanted to tell you something. There is a symmetry between writer and reader: although the writer knows more about the subject than the reader, the reader would know exactly what the writer knows had he seen what the writer has seen in the past. And the guide's purpose is to put the reader in a position to achieve that parity.

The writer needs nothing from the reader. The writer's purpose is purely the presentation of truth. Neither writer nor reader has a job to do. The writer writes and the reader reads not for the sake of some external task—solving a problem, making money, winning a case, getting a rebate, selling insurance, fixing a machine—but rather for the sake of the subject—in this case, the birds—and for the sake of being united in recognizing the truth of this subject. The writer takes the pose of full knowledge, since nothing could be more irksome to someone in the field than a passage clotted with hedges about the writer's impotence.

The entries in the *Audubon Society Field Guide to North American Birds, Eastern Region*, come as close to classic style in its pure form as anything we have found. In classic style, the model is one person talking to another to present something they both can perceive. A field guide does not perfectly coincide with that model since it is writing, not speech, and the two people are not literally together, but otherwise it fits the classic model closely. Field guides are particularly remarkable for their unfailing refusal to draw attention to their prose. A phrase such as "not as tame or confiding" in the presentation of the tufted titmouse or a sentence like "Unusual among songbirds, shrikes prey on small birds and rodents, catching them with the bill and sometimes impaling them on thorns or barbed wire for storage" in the presentation of the northern shrike is a masterpiece of expression, but refuses to acknowledge that it is anything other than the one inevitable way to present the subject. The prose suggests the same clarity and inevitability as the complex and wonderful but unambiguous and uncontrived presence of the species it describes. There is no more suggestion of deliberation or effort in writing about the tufted titmouse or the northern shrike than there is in seeing one. Writing is assimilated to seeing. There is no more struggle in writing than there is in seeing.

The passages in the *Audubon Field Guide* assume without hesitation that *of course* the reader is interested in birds. All details are presented at an equal level of importance. The entire passage is in close focus. The entry for the hairy woodpecker notes that it destroys insects such as wood-boring beetles, "which it extracts from holes with its barbed tongue. Like other woodpeckers, it hammers on a dead limb as part of its courtship ceremony and to proclaim its territory." The speaker shows not the slightest diffidence or embarrassment about reporting that the call note of the hairy woodpecker "is a sharp, distinctive *peek*," or that the western meadowlark and the eastern meadowlark "are so similar that it was not until 1844 that Audubon noticed the difference and named the western bird *neglecta* because it had been overlooked for so long." The writer takes the stand that he is simply presenting truth and is being neither cute nor partisan when he reports that "The song of the Western Meadowlark is often heard on Hollywood sound tracks even when the movie setting is far from the bird's range." There is nothing self-conscious in his matching of language to thought, so there is no hint of fear or shyness in the way he puts his vocabulary to work in descriptions, such as the following account of the western meadowlark's call: "rich, flute-like jumble of gurgling notes, usually descending the scale; very different from the Eastern Meadowlark's series of simple, plaintive whistles." The speaker never overshoots or undershoots, but always hits his mark. The tone is as it must be. There is nothing for the writer to be defensive about.

"Dragoon Tie"

In the late 16th century, a European mounted soldier who fought as a light cavalryman on attack and as a dismounted infantryman on defense was called a "dragoon." The term was derived from his weapon, a type of carbine or short musket called the "dragoon." In the early wars of Frederick II the Great of Prussia in the 18th century, "dragoon" referred to the medium cavalry. The light cavalry of the British army, for the most part, was called "light dragoon" in the 18th and 19th centuries. The term and function disappeared, as did the cavalry, in the 20th century.

The dragoon image used on our exclusive silk twill tie is taken from a design on a 17th-century pewter cap ornament in the Military History exhibit in the National Museum of American History.

—The text of a small card presenting the dragoon tie in the gift shop of the National Museum of American History, 1991

An actual scene is unclassic when the writer wants or needs something from the reader. The classic writer never explicitly argues for the reader's agreement, never overtly solicits a reader's vote or ostensibly engages in salesmanship at any level. He does not write to convince his reader of anything or to lead his reader to any action; he does not write for any practical purpose at all. He is simply presenting an interesting truth. It may be that certain judgments or actions must fall out as a natural consequence of this truth, but in such cases, truth alone is sufficient to ensure the judgment or the action.

Writers in professional or business worlds who want something from readers normally use practical style. Technical manuals, sales pitches, political arguments, undergraduate essays, computer instructions, op-ed pieces, and the great range of prose that attempts to get our attention so it can push us and pull us is typically written in at least an attempt at practical style.

There are reasons for this. When someone wants something from us, we are not necessarily disposed to listen, and certainly not disposed to listen to every detail. Practical style is designed to allow skimming and to excuse the reader as much as possible from having to make an effort. If the writer knows that the reader is plowing through hundreds of similar documents, is weary and perhaps even bored, is skimming the writing and for reasons of either incapacity or disposition simply cannot be made to pay attention to the details of the writing, practical style is almost a necessity.

Yet classic style can be extraordinarily effective in cases where the actual scene conflicts with the model scene of classic style. Classic style is a general style of presentation and can present absolutely anything. Adopting the model scene of classic style can have the effect of distracting the reader from the actual scene by suggesting the much more pleasant and distinguished model scene assumed by classic style. This substitution, all alone, can accomplish the writer's actual purposes at one stroke. In the model scene of classic style, someone is simply presenting truth spontaneously, succinctly, and informally. If this model scene can hide the actual scene—which involves some potential conflict of interest between writer and reader, or some reason the reader might not care to give her full attention voluntarily, or some effort by the writer to apply pressure to the reader, or indeed anything other than full disinterested participation by writer and reader in the truth of what is being presented—then the writer has accomplished his goals not by achieving them but rather by assuming a scene in which they are already achieved.

The most persuasive of all rhetorical stances is to write as if one is not trying to persuade at all but simply presenting truth. The most seductive of all rhetorical stances is to write as if *of course* the reader is interested in what is being presented, as if the issue could never possibly arise. In general, the best rhetorical stance, if one can get away with it, is to speak as if no rhetorical purposes are involved. Properly adopted, this stance accomplishes at the outset the actual rhetorical goals: the reader is interested and persuaded without ever stopping to realize that any effort has been made to interest or persuade her. This rhetorical strategy can be remarkably effective in situations where practical style or oratorical style is more common. It is also much more pleasant than the labor of practical or oratorical style. It flatters the reader by making her an equal, and relaxes the reader by making her part of a disinterested conversation about something really interesting.

Classic style judiciously used to mask practical goals can bring distinction to its subject, its writer, and its reader. The reader plowing through one hundred memos written in practical style may welcome being addressed in classic style, which adopts the stance that reading it is not part of anybody's actual *job*, but rather something that the reader is interested in and would have no reason to resist.

The exhibit presenting the Smithsonian dragoon tie is an example of classic style used to sell something, but it has one glaring flaw that shows the difference between classic style and practical advertising style. The phrase "our exclusive" is wrong on two counts. First, the classic writer speaks for himself. He does not acknowledge that he is speaking as the mouthpiece of an institution. Instead, he is having a conversation with an equal. Second, the word "exclusive," although it technically means that the tie can be bought only from the Smithsonian, comes from the lexicon of sales, and calls up immediately in full force the model scene in which a seller is trying to sell something to a customer.

However, if the phrase "our exclusive" were simply replaced with the word "this," the result would be a passage in classic style. It pretends to be speech. Its purpose is to present an interesting truth. It takes the pose of full knowledge. Someone is simply telling you something interesting about what you are looking at. Everything is in close focus. It assumes a symmetry between writer and reader. Although skillfully written, it refuses to draw attention to the prose. A phrase like "as did the cavalry," which is an extremely felicitous and understated way of presenting the historical situation in a brief and unforgettable parenthesis, is used as if it came to the writer without deliberation. Of course the reader is interested in the tie, its details, the image on the tie, the materials out of which it is made, the history surrounding it. It follows naturally that the reader might want to have this tie. That the writer is actually trying to get the reader to do something as vulgar as *buy* the tie is never allowed to surface.

A single revision, substituting "this" for "our exclusive," turns this passage into classic style. "This" and "our exclusive" are both instances of what syntacticians call "determiner phrases." The substitution changes nothing at the "phrase-grammatical" or "text-grammatical" level but changes the style, demonstrating that classic style cannot be defined, or distinguished from other styles, by listing its "phrase-grammatical" or "text-grammatical" features. Consequently, a writer cannot be taught classic style by being taught to follow certain patterns of "phrase grammar" or "text grammar." That is why this book is not an instruction manual in such grammatical procedures. Rather, it is a presentation of the concept of style, the elements of style, and the classic stand on the elements of style. The reader who considers the classic stand will come to see, for himself and through the demonstrations of this museum, that some surface features may derive in certain cases from the classic stand on the elements of style. But these surface features do not constitute the style.

Known locally as Acadiana and more widely as Cajun country, this isolated, dank area is dominated by descendants of French refugees and freed slaves.

—*Los Angeles Times*, 28 August 1992

Hemorrhoids are actually varicose veins in the rectum.

—First sentence of an anonymous brochure in a medical clinic, 1992

We include this exhibit to suggest the ease with which classic style can be used to present anything. Because classic style is a style of distinction and was used by its seventeenth-century French masters usually for aristocratic concerns, it might mistakenly be thought of as somehow reserved for aristocratic subjects. Quite the contrary. The first exhibit is a front-page report about a current event, the landing of Hurricane Andrew on the Louisiana Gulf Coast. The writer takes the pose of full knowledge and assumes that of course the reader is interested in the subject. All details are in close focus: "Known locally as Acadiana."

The second exhibit is the opening sentence of an anonymous brochure about everyday medical problems. The writer writes as if his subject must manifestly be important to the reader, as if he is talking about the mystery of the Holy Ghost or the irregular evolution of great wine. "Actually" presupposes that the reader is of course already interested in this subject.

The ancients wished to explain away the scandal of Homer's gods.

—Michael Murrin, *The Allegorical Epic: Essays in Its Rise and Decline*

Physics has a history of synthesizing many phenomena into a few theories.

—Richard P. Feynman, QED: *The Strange Theory of Light and Matter*

Reflexive principles are sought by analyzing a problem or a subject into a whole sufficiently homogeneous and independent to permit solution of the problem or statement of the subject.

—Richard McKeon, "Philosophy and Method"

Perception has some basic patterns. In one of the most fundamental, we orient to a stimulus and then inspect its finer details. The eye is structured to serve this pattern: our peripheral vision is not very sharp, but it allows us to pick out what we want to pay attention to; we then orient our heads so as to bring the stimulus into the central area of the retina, or fovea, which is a more sensitive receptor, suited to inspecting fine details.

This perceptual pattern is basic not only to all our senses but also to our understanding of abstract concepts. We think of conceptual inspection as structured by it: we pick out a concept, orient to it, then inspect its finer details. This is why we routinely say things like, "Let us now *turn* our attention to the bond market," or "He would have *seen* what was going on if he had bothered *to look around*."

Since classic style presents a subject to its reader, it is not surprising that it has an affinity for basic patterns of perception and inspection. Often, the classic writer will view her task as getting the reader to pick out a particular abstract subject, orient to it, and then pay attention to its finer details. It is not uncommon for a classic passage or sentence to mirror this pattern at the grammatical level. When a classic passage gives us a title—The Tufted Titmouse, The Northern Shrike, The Dragoon Tie—followed by text, we can understand it immediately through this image schema: the title lets us pick something out and orient to it; the text will present the fine points.

The first two sentences in this exhibit are structured by this basic image schema of presentation. Conceptually, each wishes to present a subject—the ancients or physics—and then to make a fine observation about that subject. Grammatically, each sentence first refers to the subject and then makes a predication specific to that subject.

The use of this image schema will not ensure a classic style. Suppose these sentences were, "The ancients wished to acquire glory" and "Physics has a history of trying to explain reality." Both of these sentences orient the reader to a subject and then try to pick out a detail. Both take a pose of full knowledge and avoid distracting hedges. Both have as their model scene one person talking to another. Both are patterned on voice rather than writing. And so on. But they are deficient as classic prose, because classic predication involves fine conceptual distinctions, articulated in a precise vocabulary.

Classic presentation lives and dies by fine conceptual distinctions. The distinctions drawn in our first two exhibits, by Michael Murrin and Richard Feynman, appear to have been carefully chosen. Both convey the impression that to be able to make these fine choices and careful conceptual distinctions, the writer must have acquired a vast wealth of knowledge. They do not draw attention to the learning of the writer, and they do not assume that the reader would have failed to see these truths if he had the writer's experience, but they do convey the impression that these presentations can only be made after a great deal of personal experience, although only the appropriate truth, not the experience, is presented.

The first two sentences of this exhibit risk trying to state the essence of something immensely complicated. Each needs its refined observation. Lacking it, they would be no different from such sentences as "In the ancient world, everybody believed the gods decided everything," or "Sex has a way of making you feel good": texts that express shallow knowledge or repeat clichés without authority.

The third selection, from Richard McKeon, is disorienting even though, using conventional stylistic checklists, it is not easy to see why. Manuals of usage usually discourage the passive voice, but putting this sentence into active voice will not make it easier to read. McKeon, the model for the Chairman in Robert Pirsig's *Zen and the Art of Motorcycle Maintenance*, often wrote prose that, like Jeremy Bentham's, had to be solved rather than read. Some people thought the quality of his writing helped to create his reputation—narrowly based but tenaciously held—for profundity. When a philosopher is difficult to read, some readers ascribe the difficulty of his literary style to the difficulty of the subject. They expect to encounter thoughts inaccessible to ordinary thinkers in language inaccessible to ordinary readers. Feynman thought he could make quantum mechanics accessible to general audiences; McKeon could make *The Hound of the Baskervilles* as inaccessible as quantum mechanics. But whatever readers may think about the quality of his thought, reading a few pages of McKeon generally leaves them feeling as if they have been caught in a whirlpool. The reason for this feeling of vertigo is that McKeon was one of those rare writers whose sentences do not respect normal patterns of human perception. This one seems to invite us to understand it through the normal perceptual and conceptual pattern of orientation to a clear subject and then investigation of its fine details, but the reader who tries to understand it in this fashion will find that the subject of presentation never seems to settle down. The sentence seems to ask for repeated orientation with no inspection of detail, giving it a peculiarly confusing circular figure.

Marquette had solemnly contracted, on the feast of the Immaculate Conception, that if the Virgin would permit him to discover the great river, he would name it Conception, in her honor. He kept his word. In that day, all explorers travelled with an outfit of priests. De Soto had twenty-four with him. La Salle had several, also. The expeditions were often out of meat, and scant of clothes, but they always had the furniture and other requisites for the mass; they were always prepared, as one of the quaint chroniclers of the time phrased it, to "explain hell to the salvages."

When I was a boy, there was but one permanent ambition among my comrades in our village on the west bank of the Mississippi River. That was, to be a steamboatman. We had transient ambitions of other sorts, but they were only transient. When a circus came and went, it left us all burning to become clowns; the first negro minstral show that came to our section left us all suffering to try that kind of life; now and then we had a hope that if we lived and were good, God would permit us to be pirates. These ambitions faded out, each in its turn; but the ambition to be a steamboatman always remained.

—Mark Twain, *Life on the Mississippi*

Classic prose is a window to its subject. This subject is never displaced by the writer. When the subject is a tufted titmouse, a dragoon tie, Hurricane Andrew, physics, the ancients, or anything that could not possibly be mistaken for the writer, the distinction is simple. When the subject is an event in which the writer has had a part, the distinction is subtler. This distinction is standard in classic literary journalism, in which the writer often reports a scene he experienced: presenting his own role may be part of presenting the scene. When A. J. Liebling writes about learning to eat in *Between*

Meals, he does so from the experiences of a young American university student sampling Paris restaurants instead of going to class. When Twain writes about life on the Mississippi, he does so from the experiences of a boy raised on the Mississippi who imagined becoming a pilot on the Mississippi and who in fact became a pilot on the Mississippi.

Twain the boy and Twain the cub pilot are part of the subject; they are not displaced by Twain the writer. We do not start reading a book that purports to present life on the Mississippi and soon find ourselves mired in a discussion of the psychological turmoil undergone by the writer as he tries to recollect his youth before the Civil War.

When a classic writer presents his own experience, it is neither private nor merely personal. The experiences Twain presents are not private: had you been there, you would have seen what he saw, and his purpose is to put you in a position to see exactly that. It is only accidental that you cannot now visit antebellum Hannibal, Missouri to see for yourself. Similarly, these experiences are not merely personal. You are expected to recognize the truth of childhood ambition he presents and to confirm it from your own experience, or from other people's reports.

In this way, Twain the writer and Twain the possessor of entirely personal experiences are never allowed to displace the subject—life on the Mississippi. Twain the boy and Twain the steamboatman are part of that subject and are presented as such.

Twain was a deeply opinionated man, and in some of his books he argues with an unclassic interest or aggression, but *Life on the Mississippi* is a work of classic disinterest and disguised assertion. The writer takes the pose that life on the Mississippi is interesting and it occurs to him to tell you about it, spontaneously. He writes as if there is nothing to argue about, only truth that the reader will of course recognize once put in a position to see it. In the wicked little history about explorers and priests, Twain passes off his assertions as mere observations. At his best, Twain is a complete master of such disguise, as in the following passage, which actually argues that those who send an invading army cannot understand at a distance what it is like to be invaded. Twain neither asserts nor doubts his central thesis. He simply presents the manifest differences in outlook between Northerners and Southerners:

> In the North one hears the war mentioned, in social conversation, once a month; sometimes as often as once a week; but as a distinct subject for talk, it has long ago been relieved of duty. There are sufficient reasons for this. Given a dinner company of six gentlemen today, it can easily happen that four of them—and possibly five—were not in the field at all. So the chances are four to two, or five to one, that the war will at no time during the evening become the topic of conversation; and the chances are still greater that if it become the topic it will remain so but a little while. If you add six ladies to the company, you have added six people who saw so little of the dread realities of the war that they ran out of talk concerning them years ago, and now would soon weary of the war topic if you brought it up.
>
> The case is very different in the South. There, every man you meet was in the war; and every lady you meet saw the war. The war is the great chief topic of conversation. The interest in it is vivid and constant; the interest in other topics is fleeting. Mention of the war will wake up a dull company and set their tongues going, when nearly any other topic would fail. In the South, the war is what A.D. is elsewhere: they date from it. All day long you hear things "placed" as having happened since the waw; or du'in' the waw; or befo' the waw; or right aftah the waw. It shows how intimately every individual was visited, in his own person, by that tremendous episode. It gives the inexperienced stranger a better idea of what a vast and comprehensive calamity invasion is than he can ever get by reading books at the fireside.

A portrait now in the possession of the descendants of the
Kiryū clan shows Terukatsu sitting cross-legged on a tiger
skin, fully clad in armor with a European breastplate, black-
braided shoulder plates, taces and fur boots. His helmet is
surmounted by enormous, sweeping horns, like a water buf-
falo's. He holds a tasseled baton of command in his right hand;
his left hand is spread so wide on his thigh that the thumb
reaches the scabbard of his sword. If he were not wearing armor, one could get some idea of his physique; dressed as he is,
only the face is visible. It is not uncommon to see likenesses of
heroes from the Period of Civil Wars clad in full armor, and
Terukatsu's is very similar to those of Honda Heihachirō and
Sakakibara Yasumasa that so often appear in history books.
They all give an impression of great dignity and severity, but at
the same time there is an uncomfortable stiffness and formality in the way they square their shoulders.

—Junichirō Tanizaki, *The Secret History of the Lord of
Musashi*, translated by Anthony H. Chambers

The classic writer is distinguished by the fineness and accuracy of
his sight. Often this sight is literally visual—as when Tanizaki picks
out the detail of the left hand in the portrait of Terukatsu. Classic style extends the domain of sight to include all things that are
perceptible through the senses or through reason. Tanizaki moves
seamlessly from observing the visual details of the helmet, breastplate, and tasseled baton of command to observing the invisible:
dignity, severity, formality, and uncomfortable stiffness; conven-
tionally heroic posture; and the cultural and historical frame. We
cannot see heroism, cultural moments, or severity in the same way
we can see a hand, but classic writers assume that we see them in
the same way. The truth Tanizaki recognizes and presents is conceived as public: anyone not blind looking at the painting can see
the hand and its unusual distension, once it is pointed out. Sim-

ilarly, anyone not mentally blind can see the cultural frame, the heroism, the stiffness, and the severity, once they are pointed out. Truth is self-evident; the classic writer need only present it accurately for the reader to recognize and verify it.

We hold these truths to be self-evident, that all men are created equal; that they are endowed by their Creator with certain unalienable rights; that among these are life, liberty, and the pursuit of happiness.

—Thomas Jefferson, Declaration of Independence

Ceux qui ont le raisonnement le plus fort, et qui digèrent le mieux leurs pensées, afin de les rendre claires et intelligibles, peuvent toujours le mieux persuader ce qu'ils proposent, encore qu'ils ne parlassent que bas-breton, et qu'ils n'eussent jamais appris de rhétorique.

[Those who have the best reasoning power, and who order their thoughts best in order to make them clear and intelligible, can always argue most persuasively for what they propose, even if they speak nothing but low Breton and have never learned rhetoric.]

—René Descartes, *Discours de la méthode*

Truth is pure, eternal, not contingent. Jefferson's sentence hangs there like a star. It is true that his sentence is a response to a particular occasion, but he chooses to meet that occasion with something that does not depend upon occasion. What he expresses is grounded in something that was always there and that will always abide: we are endowed with it by the Creator. It is bedrock, not the result of a process. It is not achieved. It is unalienable and so cannot change.

According to Descartes, truth is not only eternal and independent of any occasion, but also potentially available to anyone—
there is no principle of exclusion from knowing truth; there is only
natural defect, the mental equivalent of being born blind. Being
persuasive does not depend upon special techniques available only
to an elite, such as the literate, the educated, the urban, the wealthy,
the French. Jefferson agrees that truth is democratic. That is why
he can view these truths as "self-evident," able to be seen by all. A
Breton farmer who never went to school and cannot even speak
French can be more persuasive than a Parisian professor of rhetoric if his thinking is in better order.

Both sentences express a global optimism. Truth will triumph
ultimately and for the most part locally. This optimism is typical of
American classic style, as an American cultural attitude.

En montrant la vérité, on la fait croire.

[To present truth is to have it believed.]

—Blaise Pascal, *Pensées*

Truth can never be told so as to be understood, and not be
believ'd.

—William Blake, *The Marriage of Heaven and Hell*

Pascal, like Jefferson and Descartes, implies that truth is universally accessible: to see it is to recognize it. Who is it that is made to
believe truth in Pascal's sentence? The answer is anybody to whom
it has been shown, anybody at all, provided that person has a full
human endowment. As in Jefferson and Descartes, the perception
of truth is independent of social status, education, wealth, or any
other qualification. It is not exclusive. What are the local occasions
upon which truth can be shown so as to be perceived? What are the

particular circumstances under which it can be shown so as to be perceived? The answer is any occasion at all and under any circumstances whatsoever: truth and its perception are not contingent.

The perception of truth is immediately and completely convincing. A trick can be seen with your own eyes and still not be believed. You can see some things that you are convinced cannot possibly be true, a mirage in the desert, for example. There are many things one can see while still being suspicious of sham. But truth is not like this. To see it is to know that it is truth.

To show truth is automatically to persuade. Truth carries its own sufficient force. In this way, truth is inhuman: it is absolutely self-sufficient; it cuts through all human deficiencies; it needs no help from human beings. All it needs to be perceived is an unadulterated human presentation. As in Jefferson, truth is self-evident once shown.

Truth is perfect. It can gain nothing by being perceived. It is therefore disinterested. It has no motive for deception. It cannot present itself falsely because it does not present itself at all. Self-presentation is for human beings. Human beings are not completely visible; we come with packaging. The package is always shaped by human contingencies, temporary interests, and personal desires, and is therefore suspicious. But truth has no package. Any package given to it is false.

What underlies Pascal's statement is the notion that appropriate prose or appropriate presentation is a window: one can see right through it to truth. It is possible to get the presentation wrong, so that truth is not shown, and therefore people do not see it. The window can be warped or dirty or smoked or blocked and thus be a kind of false package. This is a failure of presentation, not a failure of truth. Truth is never deficient in force or power.

Truth cannot fail any test. It can only be misperceived and mishandled. But nothing is lethal to it. It is immortal. It survives any attempt to deface it. The instruments of perception can be perverted, as can the means of presentation, but truth cannot be perverted or even touched by such corruption. It is independent of human purpose. No one can be so perverse as not to recognize truth once it is shown, though anyone can refuse to look at it or refuse to present it.

It requires discipline, but anyone can present truth, and it often is presented. When it is presented, its effect is complete.

Blake's sentence seems a good deal like Pascal's. Stylistically, it introduces a small unexpected sophistication: truth can never be told *so as to be understood* and not be believed. A plain style version of this sentence is "Truth can never be told and not be believed."

Blake's sentence introduces a refinement, a qualification, a meditation on the plain version. It introduces a pivotal conceptual refinement in simple words, transporting the assertion to a level of sophistication that the plain style shuns. Such an introduction of simply expressed conceptual refinement is characteristically classic, so Blake's sentence looks classic.

It is not. In fact, it is stylistically ambiguous. The case is complex and unresolvable. Upon consideration, Blake's sentence can be seen to wobble, but the channel between writer and reader is incomplete; the reader cannot even be sure that Blake meant it to wobble. Ostensibly, it seems to present truth as eternal, knowable, not contingent, of no particular occasion. But if we look closely, it might appear to express something quite different. It never says that it is *possible* to tell truth so that it can be understood at all. Such a view undercuts the classic premise. Blake's sentence makes the premise contingent upon a precondition that might or might not be fulfilled. The sentence is unclassic not because it contradicts the classic view about truth, but rather because what it presents is fluid. It can alternate between the classic and an unclassic view. What is unresolved in this fashion cannot be classic.

Blake's sentence is like a Necker cube: it contains two different figures, and we can watch it shift back and forth under inspection. It is not eternal. It is not stable. It cannot be stabilized. It looks classic, but that appearance is deceptive.

Il faut exprimer le vrai pour écrire naturellement, fortement, délicatement.

[It is necessary to express what is true in order to write naturally, powerfully, sensitively.]

—Jean de La Bruyère, *Les Caractères*

En vérité [le roi] est admirable et mériterait bien d'avoir d'autres historiens que deux *poètes:* vous savez aussi bien que moi ce qu'on dit en disant *des poètes:* il n'en aurait nul besoin. Il ne faudrait ni fable, ni fiction pour le mettre au-dessus des autres; il ne faudrait qu'un style droit, pur, et net. . . .

[The truth is that {the king} is admirable and would certainly merit having historians other than two poets. You know as well as I do what we mean in saying *poets*. He would have no need of them whatever; it would require no invention, no fiction to place him above the others; it would require only a pure style, clean and straightforward. . . .]

—Madame de Sévigné, letter to Bussy-Rabutin, 18 March 1678

These two passages, by two of the founders of French classic style, are complementary expressions of the prototypical classic stand on truth, which, in this tradition, is more compelling than any invention and is the natural object of unobstructed human intelligence. Invention requires artifice. Truth, which carries its own conviction, can dispense with sophisticated rhetorical or poetic artifice; it needs only to be presented clearly. Human intelligence recognizes truth naturally. Artifice misleads—that is its purpose. It does so by blunting the natural human sensitivity to truth, and in doing so weakens our natural capacity to perceive what is true.

Truth, then, is natural, powerful, and sensitive; the language that presents it best draws no attention to itself. When we talk about someone's personal style, or the style of someone's prose, we often refer to conspicuous attributes. When La Bruyère talks about writing "naturally," he is thinking about a style that is anonymous in the way nature is anonymous. The format of a modern book is more natural in this sense than a codex, because, when open, a book is bilaterally symmetrical, as is the human body. A duodecimo book "fits" the hands, and while the modern book is a style of setting out a written text, it is so "natural, powerful, sensitive" that only a textual bibliographer, a binder, or an archivist is likely to be aware of it *as* a style of presenting a written text.

Classic style is like the form of a book; it can be noticed, but it is not conspicuous. It fits truth the way a book fits the hand. If we can imagine a machine or an extraterrestrial, with no knowledge of the human body, trying to design a format for presenting written prose to human readers, we have an image of La Bruyère's concept of the writer trying to be natural, powerful, and sensitive in the absence of truth. The mechanical or extraterrestial design will be no more natural, powerful, or sensitive to a human reader than a duodecimo volume would be to an intelligent creature with the body of an oyster.

Madame de Sévigné, one of the supreme French masters of classic style, had an exceptional literary education. She read Latin and Italian in addition to French and admired many styles of writing. She loved the allegorical epics of Tasso and Ariosto, as well as the classic prose of Pascal, La Rochefoucauld, Retz, and her close friend Madame de Lafayette. But poetry, in her view, is not a good model for the portrayal of the real virtues of a real king, because poetry "improves" the truth. In seventeenth-century French usage, *poésie* meant "invented story" as opposed to "true story": its distinguishing characteristics were artificial ornament and exceptional invention. She therefore deplores the fact that Louis XIV has no one to record his victories except two poets who acted as historiographers royal in 1678 when he took Ghent, even though one of them was Racine and the other was Boileau. Madame de Sévigné is not rejecting figural forms of thought and language—metaphor, metonymy, simile, narrative, symbol, various forms of condensing and crystallizing—which are generally indispensable in thought and language and have a central role in classic style when they serve the presentation of truth. She is rejecting rather their use as embellishment, adornment, and artifice meant to "improve" truth. For Madame de Sévigné, poetic ornaments are appropriate for talking about Roland or other heroes of epic and romance, but contemporary reality needs nothing more than a pure, clean, straightforward style. Any ornament would just distract attention from truth, which needs no help, just an unimpeded view.

Three days after the first allied landing in France, I was in the wardroom of an LCIL (Landing Craft, Infantry, Large) that was bobbing in the lee of the French cruiser Montcalm off the Normandy coast. The word "large" in landing-craft designation is purely relative; the wardroom of the one I was on is seven by seven feet and contains two officers' bunks and a table with four places at it. She carries a complement of four officers, but since one of them must always be on watch there is room for a guest at the wardroom table, which is how I fitted in. The Montcalm was loosing salvos, each of which rocked our ship; she was firing at a German pocket of resistance a couple of miles from the shoreline. The suave voice of a B.B.C. announcer came over the wardroom radio: "Next in our series of impressions from the front will be a recording of an artillery barrage." The French ship loosed off again, drowning out the recording. It was this same announcer, I think—I'm not sure, because all B.B.C. announcers sound alike—who said, a little while later, "We are now in a position to say the landings came off with surprising ease.

The Air Force and the big guns of the Navy smashed coastal defenses, and the Army occupied them." Lieutenant Henry Rigg, United States Coast Guard Reserve, the skipper of our landing craft, looked at Long, her engineering officer, and they both began to laugh. Kavanaugh, the ship's communication officer, said, "Now what do you think of that?" I called briefly upon God. Aboard the LCIL, D Day hadn't seemed like that to us. There is nothing like a broadcasting studio in London to give a chap perspective.

—A. J. Liebling, "Cross-Channel Trip"

Although I have used the testimony of Elyot's letters and writings to document his encounter with the resurgent Scripturalism of the 1530s and 1540s, the context in which he worked was clearly energized by cultural and historical currents that encompassed considerably more than the issues of doctrine, religious practices, and ecclesiastical sovereignty dividing Protestants from Catholics, exacerbated as these issues were. Elyot himself identified the challenges which he faced and met with his literary enterprise as questions about his commitment to the king's and Cromwell's reforming measures or to the "savor" of "holy scripture." Yet the successful popularizing and secularizing measures which Elyot took in jointly pursuing his course as a vernacular writer and bypassing religious issues are, I think, to be construed as evidence running with rather than against the momentum of a larger ideological movement—in the first place because popularizing and secularizing were real options for Elyot, and in the second place because he was able to make them work. Given our present state of knowledge, even as advanced by Elizabeth Eisenstein's study of the printing press as an agent of cultural change, we are constrained to deal symptomatically and speculatively for the most part with the complex of energizing developments—in which printing, humanism, and the Reformation figured prominently with social and economic changes—that ushered in the modern era of the book.

—Janel Mueller, *The Native Tongue and the Word: Developments in English Prose Style, 1380–1580*

The passage from A. J. Liebling follows his account of the Allied invasion of Normandy on 6 June 1944 as he experienced it from an infantry landing craft. The style is recognizably classic. Its model is conversation, its occasion is informal, its tone is relaxed, confident, and unhedged, and it takes the pose that it is presentational rather than argumentative. It actually makes many strong assertions, concerning what D-Day was really like, the nature of institutional reporting, and the reliability of interchangeable mouthpieces who speak from something other than local knowledge and according to the agenda of their institutions. But these assertions are disguised as mere presentations of what would have been evident to anyone present on the little craft.

The passage supplies the accidental information that a reader cannot be expected to have: what "large" means in measuring an infantry landing craft, the number of the crew, the way Liebling was accommodated on board. But there is no gratuitous display of arcane military knowledge unnecessary to the narrative. Nothing is merely the product of the observer; nothing depends on being able to share the writer's personal construal of the evidence; everything depends on being able to share the writer's position.

The anecdote is a reporter's reflection on reporting and rests on a contrast between a description without authority and an experience that Liebling can stand behind. Just as the real artillery salvo drowns out the recording of one on the radio, so Liebling's experience, which he shares with the officers on board the landing craft, drowns out the account of the Normandy invasion as related from a radio studio in London. The force of the anecdote depends upon the position of the writer; the details are marshaled to put the reader in the same position, so he can see for himself what the writer relates.

As befits conversation, the sentences follow one another in a sequence that seems natural and inevitable, but this is a very efficient narrative. On reflection, it is a miniature masterpiece of construction. The complete narrative is a figural argument for Liebling's view of news reporting as set against the B.B.C's. It contains within it, perfectly positioned, a miniature version of the same figural argument—the drowning out of the B.B.C's canned account by the real thing. The global figure of the passage and the local figure of the salvos mirror each other like macrocosm and microcosm. Both figures work by giving the reader a highly imagistic narrative from which he will certainly draw the obvious point. Yet the entire passage sounds spontaneous and conversational. The writer has done all the work invisibly, and the prose does not draw attention to itself or to the writer's work.

Classic style used in this way is not in the least restricted to eyewitness reporting. The passage from Dodd we treated in "The Reader Is Competent" works in just this way. It includes a wealth of facts and scholarly machinery, but it presents them as accidental information that merely needs to be supplied to the reader in a sufficiently clear fashion: the reader will then make, with Dodd, the inevitable observations. Dodd's passage, like Liebling's, sounds conversational, confident, unhedged. This appearance of confidence comes largely from the way the writer introduces facts and citations with perfect clarity: neither the facts nor their relations to each other are fuzzy. The way the components stand together is fully formed: the writer knows exactly the relationships he means to present.

Janel Mueller's passage on Sir Thomas Elyot appears in her book on late medieval and renaissance English prose style. The passage is unclassic, not principally for local reasons—the side issues that bury in obscurity the figure structuring the passage, for example—but in its conception of scene, cast, and subject. It is a summary of evidence, but assertive and defensive rather than disinterested. The writer presses for agreement while defending from objection and attack, as if the scene and cast were adversarial, not conversational. If the writer obscures what she has to say as she goes along, it serves a strategic purpose: in the end there will be no clear interpretation to which the reader might respond. This style is best suited to juridical scenes and casts, where winning is everything; it is normally incompatible with the obligations of scholarship. The confusion of scene in Mueller induces an obvious strain, resulting in a conflicted form in which bits of scholarly evidence, vague in themselves, are imprecisely connected to each other, and sometimes not connected at all: "Given our present state of knowledge, even as advanced by Elizabeth Eisenstein's study of the printing press as an agent of cultural change . . ." Scholarly asides are scattered at random, offering the decor of erudition without the justification of scholarly argument.

Liebling, who writes about what you can see and hear, and Dodd, who writes about the most abstract concerns of textual editing and historical interpretation, both write as if the subject they are presenting has a clear existence independent of the writer or the writing. Mueller, on the other hand, writes as if her subjects depend upon the writer for their very existence: Elyot's encounter with "the resurgent Scripturalism of the 1530s and 1540s," "the context in which he worked," the nature of the "cultural and historical currents" that "energized" that context. That may be why the word "clearly" in the phrase "the context in which he worked was clearly energized by cultural and historical currents that encompassed considerably more than the issues of doctrine, religious practices, and ecclesiastical sovereignty dividing Protestants from Catholics, exacerbated as these issues were" rings false. Clearly? To whom? Could it be clear to just anyone who reads Elyot's "letters and writings"? Could it be clear to Elyot himself? Apparently not. For the author appears to be disagreeing with Elyot's claims. What he did should be construed, she says, in a certain way, namely "as evidence running with rather than against the momentum of a larger ideological movement." And it should be construed this way, she claims, tautologically, because it is precisely what he did. The "evidence" she offers is "presented" as dependent upon her "point of view," and the particular view of the evidence that gives it force is not described in a way that would allow the reader to adopt the writer's perspective. Only the conclusions from that perspective are offered, in a manner so obscure as to place them beyond challenge.

Even though there is an ostensible presentation of evidence in the passage on Elyot, the evidence depends entirely upon the writer's disposition. A skillful practitioner in this style can deflect questions about the validity of such evidence, but in this case, there is a marked strain in trying to establish with precision relationships among abstractions that are themselves shapeless and indefinite. In consequence, the whole passage betrays an understandable anxiety that even the writer might lose sight of her own subject. She must reassure herself that what she is talking about is real, that it matters, that her understanding of it is both defensible and significant, and that the reader is interested. It is not surprising that her anxiety is communicated to the reader.

In mathematics, whose normal subject is precise relationships between abstractions, such problems are rare. The objects, while they are abstract, are as definite as infantry-landing boats, and the evidence for the relationships is precise and publicly accessible in a way that the direction of "the momentum of a larger ideological movement" never can be. The borders of such an ideological movement are not public and definite the way the borders of an isosceles triangle—or the dimensions of the wardroom on an infantry landing craft—are. The strain evident in the passage on Sir Thomas Elyot's career as a vernacular writer is the strain of attempting to talk about imperfectly formed conceptions of invented relationships between indefinite abstractions as if they had the precision and public accessibility of square roots or the complement of officers on a Landing Craft, Infantry, Large. Dodd, because he has thought through thoroughly and precisely the relationships and abstractions he wishes to present, can do so as if he were Liebling writing about one boat bobbing in the lee of another. Classic style is perfectly suited to presenting abstractions, but the classic writer, having thought out the features and borders of abstractions, presents them confidently, without recourse to hedges, contortions, and obscurities that undercut a reader's ability to judge the writer's conclusions for himself.

La grande nouveauté technique de l'artillerie a mis quelque temps à faire sentir toutes ses conséquences. La dotation de l'armée de Charles VIII a suffi à lui ouvrir Milan, Florence, Rome et Naples. Cette «invention diabolique», que devaient stigmatiser l'Arioste et Rabelais après lui, condamnait les méthodes traditionnelles, les parades et les offensives de belles armures. Elle rendait, à long terme, inutile la classe aristocratique dont la guerre était la raison d'être, à moins d'une adaptation qu'il lui fallut cruellement accomplir pendant quarante ans de batailles en Italie et ailleurs. Surtout, l'artillerie va amener une révision complète de la fortification et des systèmes défensifs. Les plus grands architectes-ingénieurs, Francesco di Giorgio, Giuliano da Sangallo, étudient les plans à redents et des bastions articulés qui modifient la physionomie des murailles et par là assez directement celle des villes. Les études les plus saisissantes seront celles de Michel-Ange pour la défense de Florence en 1529–1530. C'est comme ingénieur que César Borgia eut un moment Léonard à son service. On n'a pas encore complètement mesuré toutes les conséquences de l'évolution de l'art de la guerre à la Renaissance.

[The great novelty of Renaissance warfare, the use of artillery, took some time to make its full effect. Thanks to it Charles VIII had Milan, Florence, Rome and Naples at his mercy. This "diabolical invention" as Ariosto called it (and Rabelais was to denounce it after him) put an end to the traditional mode of warfare, to the dashing charges of knights in armor. And in the end it rendered useless the aristocratic class whose *raison d'être* was warfare—until it had undergone the re-education provided by four gruelling decades of fighting in Italy and elsewhere. The increased use of artillery led to drastic modifications of the fortifications and defensive outworks of towns, and the greatest experts in this field,

Francesco di Giorgio and Giuliano da Sangallo, invented a system of indented traces and articulated bastions which radically changed the aspect of the walls and even the layout of fortified cities. The most remarkable plans were those which Michelangelo made for the defense of Florence (1529–1530), and it was in the capacity of engineer that Cesare Borgia called in Leonardo. The extent to which the evolution of the art of war affected the Renaissance has yet to be fully assessed.]

—André Chastel, *Le Mythe de la Renaissance 1420–1520*

This passage on the introduction of artillery in sixteenth-century warfare and its effect both on large abstractions such as "the traditional mode of warfare" and on tangible things such as walls and fortifications, in addition to its social consequences—things that in other hands might become "the direction of cultural and social trends energized by the complex of military developments"—is organized by one short point at the beginning and a complementary one at the end. Everything between them is a careful expansion of the first point, at once supporting it with illustrations and examples and preparing the way for the concluding point. Although this passage of just two hundred words contains references to eight people and four cities, as well as allusions to actual fortifications, to plans for new defenses, and to four decades of fighting in two places (one specified, the other not), in addition to the citation of one epithet and an aside on its later repetition, each of these elements occupies a well-conceived place in the discussion. None of them seems awkward or arbitrary. The erudition does not seem gratuitous or strained; it does not obscure the figure that organizes the passage or obstruct its easy flow. The complexity and obscurity of the subject are not offered as a tacit justification for a complex and obscure presentation.

Palabra por palabra, la versión de Galland es la peor escrita de todas, la más embustera y más débil, pero fue la mejor leída. Quienes intimaron con ella, conocieron la felicidad y el asombro. Su orientalismo, que ahora nos parece frugal, encandiló a cuantos aspiraban rapé y complotaban una tragedia en cinco actos. Doce primorosos volúmenes aparecieron de 1707 a 1717, doce volúmenes innumerablemente leídos y que pasaron a diversos idiomas, incluso el hindustani y el árabe. Nosotros, meros lectores anacrónicos del siglo veinte, percibimos en ellos el sabor dulzarrón del siglo dieciocho y no el desvanecido aroma oriental, que hace doscientos años determinó su innovación y su gloria. Nadie tiene la culpa del desencuentro y menos que nadie, Galland.

[Word for word, Galland's version is the worst written, the most fraudulent and the weakest, but it was the most widely read. Readers who grew intimate with it experienced happiness and amazement. Its orientalism, which we now find tame, dazzled the sort of person who inhaled snuff and plotted tragedies in five acts. Twelve exquisite volumes appeared from 1707 to 1717, twelve volumes innumerably read, which passed into many languages, including Hindustani and Arabic. We, mere anachronistic readers of the twentieth century, perceive in these volumes the cloyingly sweet taste of the eighteenth century and not the evanescent oriental aroma that two hundred years ago was their innovation and their glory. No one is to blame for this missed encounter, least of all Galland.]

—Jorge Luis Borges, "Los traductores de las 1001 noches"

The story of the story of the thousand and one nights is perhaps untellable. The cultural provenance of the tales—Indian, Persian, and Arabic—is perhaps irrecoverable. The manuscript traditions of the originals are a nightmare that makes the legendary textual problems of Marlowe's *Doctor Faustus* look trivial. The constitution of the work—which tales belong to it, or at least which tales belong to which versions of it, and in what order—is fundamentally unsettled. It was disseminated through Europe in the eighteenth century through a series of famous translations whose history is at best complex and subtle, at worst unknown.

These impediments to knowledge might paralyze any writer who allowed his style to be influenced by doubts about his capacity to perform. Additional impediments could plausibly be found in the cultural and personal situation of the writer. Jorge Luis Borges was an elite twentieth-century Latin American classic writer, a librarian, a famous erudite, and male. *The Thousand and One Nights*, by contrast, comes from traditions that are not elite, not privileged, not scholarly, not twentieth-century, not white, not European or Latin American, and not male: the transmission and perhaps creation of the tales were largely in the hands of women. They were subversive tales recognized as such in their own time, intentionally politically incorrect not just for our age but for their own: they present an onslaught against the very notion of ideological engineering as an effective response to the complexity of human affairs. These tales were introduced to Europeans by English and French men of the eighteenth and nineteenth centuries.

Borges, confronted with this sea of difficulty and separated culturally and personally from the origins of the tales and their translators, nonetheless adopts the classic pose. He presents truth that is generally available. In principle, it could be confirmed by anybody, regardless of cultural identity. He conceives of and presents his subject as existing independently of the writer. He presents it to a competent audience in prose that itself is never allowed to become a subject of the writing. There is a symmetry between writer and reader: like Dodd in considering the textual history of the Fourth Gospel, Borges assumes that in principle anybody could learn what he has learned, and would then see just what he sees. Although Borges is dealing with large abstractions—orientalism, quality in writing, the reception of a text, happiness, the flavor of the eighteenth century, innovation and glory, blame, and extraordinarily complex cultural patterns—he conceives of them as clear and exact. They are as highly defined and visible as cut crystal. None of them depends upon the writer for its existence.

Anything can be presented in classic style, including the cultural and historical situation of the writer and reader, when these are part of the intended subject. Borges presents our situation as twentieth-century readers as part of presenting the truth of these translations and their history. But such matters never *displace* the chosen subject and never *interfere* with the performance. Although a classic writer could take as his subject ways in which cultural, historical, and personal situation might make writing impossible, or at least hard, his actual writing would never betray any evidence of the difficulty of which he speaks. He would present clearly, simply, intelligibly, and assuredly the truth that it is impossible to write clearly, simply, intelligibly, and assuredly. He would take the pose that the reader will share his recognition of the truth that it is impossible for the reader to share his recognition of anything.

The Touraine is the heartland of France. It was here, as much as in any other single locality, that the subtle, clear, precise language of modern France developed, and here also, fittingly, that the subtle, fine, expert cooking of modern France developed.

—Waverley Root, *The Food of France*

Man kann etwas finden, ohne es gesucht zu haben, ja jeder Kunstforscher weiß aus Erfahrung, daß man fast stets etwas anderes findet, als was man sucht. Wer Erdbeeren sucht, weiß, wie eine Erdbeere aussieht, wer aber den Zusammenhang sucht, weiß nicht, wie dieser Zusammenhang aussieht. Die allgemeine Gefahr besteht nun darin, daß Wunsch und Wille, etwas zu finden, vorzeitig im Geiste des Suchenden ein Bild des Zusammenhangs und zwar ein falsches hervorbringen.

[One can find something without having sought it—indeed, every connoisseur knows from experience that one nearly always finds something other than what one seeks. When you go looking for strawberries, you know what a strawberry looks like—but when you go looking for interrelationships, you do not know what they will look like. The ever-present danger is precisely that the desire and the will to find something may, in the mind of the seeker, precociously project a connection—one that does not exist.]

—Max J. Friedländer, *Die Altniederländische Malerei*

The imperfect structural correspondence of painting to literature does not in fact preclude or even severely limit the comparison of the arts. What it does is permit an ever changing set of correlations by painters and writers, who are free to stress different elements of the structures of their art in order to achieve this correspondence. An interartistic parallel thus is not dictated by the preexistent structures of the arts involved; instead, it is an exploration of how these two structures can be aligned. This alignment is part of the overall essential homonymity and synonymity of semiosis by which sign systems and their texts approximate one another and then diverge.

—Wendy Steiner, *The Colors of Rhetoric: Problems in the Relation between Modern Literature and Painting*

The passages by Root and Friedländer are classic; the passage by Steiner is not. The difference has nothing to do with the nature of the subjects they treat, but with how those subjects are conceived. Root and Friedländer treat their subjects with a clarity and exactness that makes them appear to be entirely independent of the writers. Steiner treats her subject in a way that makes it dependent upon her for its existence as well as for its expression.

Root treats food and language while Friedländer treats "inter-relationships": food is available to the senses, "interrelationships" to abstract thought, and language to both, demonstrating that classic style is not determined by the nature of its subject. Root says something absurd while Friedländer says something we can all confirm, demonstrating that classic style is not determined by whether what it says is actually true.

What Root says is assured, relaxed, conversational, and classic. It is no less classic for being wrong. The supposed aboriginal "purity" of French in the Touraine is an enduring fairy tale that withstands all contradiction—the shop sign in Tours, for example, that announces "Le Fast-Foud"—and any claim that modern French cuisine has its roots in the Touraine will provoke outrage from approximately Sens to the southern limit of the Lyonnais. The claim of a relationship between the qualities of a cuisine and the qualities of a language—and, of course, the linguistic qualities Root refers to are qualities of a style, not of a language—must be regarded as doubtful. Many great chefs whose dishes are subtle, clear, and precise speak in a style far removed from that of Pascal and Madame de Sévigné. But Root is not seriously making claims about a relationship between cuisine and language. He is rather offering the disguised assertion that cuisine—as well as literary style—is an important mark of a culture.

Language and cuisine, even if both are limited to their modern French varieties, are large and indefinite domains here confidently subsumed under a deeply entrenched ontological metaphor and so treated as "things" more or less on the order of Friedländer's strawberries. Friedländer, the third director of the great Kaiser Friedrich Museum in Berlin, liked to start with evidence of a primary sort—actual pictures—and subsumed his abstractions to this model, treating them as "things" so clear and exact that it is almost impossible to remember that they are abstractions. He noticed, with characteristic mordancy, that a theorist whose abstractions could not clearly and in detail be separated from his discourse produced students who, like their teacher, invariably saw only what they expected to see, whereas connoisseurs like himself whose abstractions were conceptually independent of their discourse regularly encountered pictures that contradicted all their expectations about the painting of particular times and places.

Steiner's procedure is just the sort of thing that raised his skeptical doubts. Her passage, as it reaches its crescendo, is more and more speculative and impossible to verify by looking at what Friedländer would have regarded as common evidence, particular literary texts and paintings. The classic writer, no matter how abstract his subject, will present it as so sharply defined in itself and so independent of the writer as to count for all of us as a "thing," with the implication that any one of us will see the evidence for it if only we are placed in the appropriate position. Steiner's passage, by contrast, is fundamentally unclassic because it rejects any responsibility on the writer's part to present its subject as a "thing" independent of the writer. On the contrary, the amorphousness of her subject, its dependence upon her for its existence, and the lack of a symmetry between what she and her reader might be able to see as evidence are valued in her writing as marks of the writer's brilliance instead of the writer's incompetence. The final dance of abstractions between "sign systems and their texts" and "the overall essential homonymity and synonymity of semiosis" that contains the "structures" of literature and painting has lost contact so completely with anything available to classic style as to suggest that Steiner's gifts are at least partly oracular. Root is vulnerable exactly because he has presented something so precise and open to our own verification that anyone who has the good fortune to learn both French and French cuisine can challenge him. Steiner, wrapping her speculations in a rhetorical mantle whose most conspicuous colors are those of jargon, suggests she knows things that the rest of us do not, and so avoids Root's vulnerability, but at the risk of claiming for herself a kind of supernatural sight and insight. She suggests she has entered into deep mysteries unavailable to the sort of person who might observe that while painting and literature are not in all respects similar, they can be compared, and that a general inquiry into the subject will yield the not surprising result that painting and literature are similar in some ways and different in others.

[I]l est impossible qu'avec tant de vérité, je ne vous persuade mon innocence.

[It is impossible that with such truth I should fail to persuade you of my innocence.]

Elle lui parla avec tant d'assurance, et la vérité se persuade si aisément lors même qu'elle n'est pas vraisemblable, que M. de Clèves fut presque convaincu de son innocence.

[She spoke to him with such assurance, and truth so easily persuades even where it is improbable, that Monsieur de Clèves was nearly convinced of her innocence.]

—Madame de Lafayette, *La princesse de Clèves*

Both of the selections from *La princesse de Clèves* come from a scene in which the princess is attempting to persuade her husband on his deathbed that she has not been unfaithful to him. Although she is not disinterested, the scene remains classic because the princess—an exceptional character with a disciplined and religious devotion to truth—is governed by a respect for truth and not by her interests. We include these passages because they illustrate the classic conception of truth and because they explicitly connect that conception of truth to persuasion.

The conviction that truth persuades easily even when it contradicts appearances almost certainly belongs to Madame de Lafayette herself, not just to the narrator of her most famous novel. It is not a view idly held by a naïve person. Madame de Lafayette was an intimate of Henrietta of England, Louis XIV's sister-in-law, and enjoyed exceptional access to the king. Although the details remain obscure, she was actively involved in political questions—exceptionally so for a woman. She lobbied the French court on behalf of the dowager duchess of Savoy and, through her, kept the French informed of Duke Amadeus's secret policy decisions. After the death of Henrietta in 1670, she retired from court citing ill health, but powerful members of the court continued to visit her in Paris for years afterward. She dined at the king's table in 1672 to celebrate the treaty of Versailles, and retained a strong influence with his minister Louvois. She had seen dozens of reputations made and destroyed by intrigue and had an extraordinary sense of how powerful an apparently disinterested presentation could be. She had a reputation for respecting truth and for despising people who, from weakness, tried to evade unpleasant truths.

The kind of persuasion that interested her most was the persuasion of private conversation. It happens, as in the passages cited here from her novel, that prejudice, interest, or passion may prevent truth from being accepted. But in her conception, as in the princess's, truth is naturally persuasive, so much so that even against appearances, it will carry conviction with any unbiased listener. It was this principle upon which she built a career that any modern political lawyer or lobbyist could envy.

We would naturally suspect the scene of being unclassic, because the princess is clearly interested, but she takes the classic pose that the highest and governing motive is truth, whatever immediate pressures she may feel. As she says, "J'avoue que les passions peuvent me conduire; mais elles ne sauraient m'aveugler." 'I admit that passions can lead me, but they do not have the power to blind me.' We cannot control our interests—we lack the power always to be in a situation of disinterest—but those interests do not have to govern our actions, even if it takes an extraordinary discipline to discount them. Ordinarily, we do not trust someone who claims to be acting apart from his interests. It is for this reason that Madame de Lafayette has taken such pains to establish the exceptional fidelity to discipline in the princess as a character. Once the character has been established both by summary and by event, it is possible to believe that despite the pressures of interest, her actions are governed by the classic motive of truth. This motive, despite the temptations of self-interest, can govern the actions of anyone willing to submit to exceptional discipline. When a reader is persuaded that someone who could be affected by self-interest is in fact acting on truth, the classic concept that truth, no matter how unlikely, carries its own persuasive force can have an overwhelming effect.

Persuasion in the classic conception is the mere establishment of a classic scene in which truth definitively supersedes all actual or possible motives of interest. A speaker in a situation of interest who can establish this scene through whatever means has overcome the countervailing presumption that people are always governed by interest.

In general, it may be true that people are governed by interest, but it does not follow that everyone in all cases is governed by interest. The classic writer governed by truth belongs then to an aristocracy—an aristocracy open to anyone willing to submit to the discipline of classic style.

Hardy was something of a Turing of an earlier generation; he was another ordinary English homosexual atheist, who just happened to be one of the best mathematicians in the world.

—Andrew Hodges, *Alan Turing: The Enigma*

The study of history would be unnecessary for political education if the lessons to be drawn from great historic events could be summed up in a few trenchant sentences. We would then need no more than these final sentences. But political prudence does not consist in recipes which can be conveyed: it is a virtue which has to be acquired the hard way. The greatest possible economy of effort is achieved if a very competent guide takes you through the important experiences of others. He tells you just enough and not too much: why this step was taken and how it turned out to be disastrous. It is for you to think out why it turned out to be disastrous and how it might have been avoided: it is only by such personal speculation that one gains political education; in that realm, as in all others, one only learns by thinking for oneself.

—Bertrand de Jouvenel, "Introduction" to the Thomas Hobbes translation of Thucydides, *The Peloponnesian War*

There is an unargued assertion within Hodges's sentence, although one that is not controversial: in his lifetime G. H. Hardy was one of the best mathematicians in the world. There is also a tacit claim here that is a little more pointed: great mathematicians may be quite ordinary in other respects. Finally there is a disguised assertion that neither homosexuality nor atheism is an abnormality, either in such special populations as great mathematicians or in the population at large.

Both Hardy, Sadleirian Professor of Pure Mathematics at Cambridge, who died at seventy—a year after a botched suicide attempt—in 1947, and Alan Turing, convicted sex criminal sentenced to a hormonal "cure," who committed suicide at forty-two in 1954, lived in a time and place that regarded both homosexuality and atheism as shocking abnormalities, neither of which ordinarily was associated with any form of eminence.

Hodges, who is both a mathematician and an active critic of the medical model of homosexuality, gives a devastating selection of examples illustrating British concepts of homosexuality in Turing's lifetime and the effects they had on the lives of homosexuals. His book certainly encourages some ways of thinking about the subject and discourages others, but it does so by using resources of classic style. The power of the book derives not mainly from overt argument, but from the invisible argument of presentation.

This sort of invisible argument attempts neither to show the inadequacies of other opinions nor to offer explicit support for its own. It depends almost exclusively on showing the reader where to look. Hodges, in this passage, seeks to place his readers in a certain perspective; he asks them to line up "homosexual atheist" with "great mathematician." There are people who might be so horrified by "homosexual atheist" that the last thing they would think to associate with such a description is "great mathematician." But Hodges neither pontificates nor condescends. He speaks as if, of course, his reader knows, as well as he does, that an atheist homosexual can be an ordinary Englishman as well as a great mathematician.

At first the passage from Bertrand de Jouvenel may seem to be similar to the passage from Hodges. Jouvenel, like Hodges, asserts rather than engaging in grinding step-by-step argument, but the assertions are not just presented as truths that the reader will recognize as a matter of course. Jouvenel's writing is not tortured, but it does not have the ring of spontaneous speech, either. His assertions are made as if they were the beginning of an argument, even though no argument follows. The passage departs from the model scene and cast of classic style. The scene is not a conversation between equals; it is the scene of professor to sophomore. The writer prides himself on having come through difficulties to the wisdom he has earned and asks his readers to accept what he says because he knows more than they do, not because they can verify what he says by sharing his perspective. What he says is plausible and well expressed, but it is really a form of pontificating. The style is not classic, although the sentences are fine, and lead to a nice, if unearned, generalization.

The truth is rarely pure, and never simple.

—Oscar Wilde, *The Importance of Being Earnest*

Understanding a people's culture exposes their normalness without reducing their particularity.

—Clifford Geertz, "Thick Description" in *The Interpretation of Cultures*

Pour s'établir dans le monde, on fait tout ce que l'on peut
pour y paraître établi.

[To establish oneself in the world, one does everything one
can to appear to be established there.]

—François VI, duc de La Rochefoucauld, *Maximes*

[N]othing is more certain, than that much of the *force* as
well as *grace* of arguments or instructions, depends on their
conciseness.

—Alexander Pope, "Design" for *An Essay on Man*

There is nothing immediate or "natural" in contrast to
what is mediate or sophisticated; there are only degrees of
sophistication.

—Michael Oakeshott, *Experience and Its Modes*

The chronologically earliest of the five brief texts in this exhibit
was written in the seventeenth century, the latest in the twentieth.
Written in different cultures, for different purposes, even in different languages, they appear in quite different sorts of works, yet
they share a family resemblance. Each is built around a fine but
"simple" and—once formulated—inevitable distinction.

They all take the stand of noticing, as if casually, something
that the reader too can notice, once his attention is properly directed. The reader has the pleasure of being able to "verify" what
each writer claims, although in each case there is a refinement of
commonplace observation that amounts to novelty.

Wilde suffuses his most famous play, *The Importance of Being
Earnest*, with the attitude that plain style's conception of truth is
fundamentally wrong. He takes the central verbal cliché of plain
style—truth is pure and simple—and refines it. Oakeshott, although
not working from a specific verbal cliché, similarly introduces a

conceptual refinement, one transforming crude polar categories into degrees along a gradient. Geertz takes two clichés of ethnography—to expose is to reduce; to see normality is to miss particularity—and recasts their terms into a specific and refined four-way balance. La Rochefoucauld takes conditions normally conceived of as distinct—belonging to a category versus striving to belong—and observes their inseparability in the case of becoming established in "the world," where appearance is so nearly everything that careful imitation of a social state is an effective way of achieving it. Pope, a master of the phrase that illustrates its own meaning, reconsiders the crude opposition of force to grace and makes the fine observation that they share a common source in conciseness.

Neither Geertz nor Pope explicitly rejects an established verbal cliché, but each tacitly rejects a conceptual commonplace without making a fuss about it. Geertz implicitly rejects the notion that to expose a culture is to make it like all the rest, and Pope actually demonstrates that grace and force are not mutually exclusive.

In each case, the effect is something like that of a brilliant move in chess; it was there all along and seems inevitable once made, but to see it in the first instance requires an uncommon refinement of perception.

> You imagine what you desire; you will what you imagine; and at last, you create what you will.
>
> —Bernard Shaw, the serpent speaking to Eve in *Back to Methuselah*

The thought expressed in this passage has three steps. They are schematically identical. In each, an activity is located and then linked to its source in a different activity. There is a sentence expressing each step. Each of these sentences inherits the schematic structure of the thought, as in "You imagine what you desire." Paired activities are expressed as paired clauses—"you imagine" and "you desire"—and the conceptual link between paired activities is mirrored in the linguistic link between paired clauses.

These three steps are not independent, but are ordered as a temporal sequence in which the product of one step serves as the source of the next. The grammatical structure mirrors this conceptual sequence: three sentences of the same grammatical form occur in linear order; the clause referring to the product in one sentence serves to refer to the source in the next.

Shaw's passage—with its precise and detailed combination of schematic images—is the result of conceptual and linguistic work, but the work is not exhibited. Reading the sentence is like watching a champion gymnast perform a routine on the parallel bars. Obviously the gymnastic performance is the result of previous work, but only the achievement is exhibited.

The achievement is final. In the classic view, thought comes first and language is sufficient to express it. Any problem of expression has an exact solution in the language, and this solution, once found, will appear to be obvious, perfect, and definitive. The writer knows when he has finished revising.

Perfection of phrasing in classic style is assumed to follow from precision of preceding thought. The classic writer draws precise conceptual distinctions and locates exact conceptual relations until the analysis is finished. He then expresses the result of this analysis. Its schematic conceptual structure is mirrored in the schematic linguistic structure. Often, the result appears to be something like a mathematical formulation.

In classic style, the goal of analysis is truth in its most efficient form consistent with accuracy. Expression, carrying the elegance that comes from compressed energy, is like a perfectly tuned stringed instrument: the strings are taut to exact degrees to correspond to exact pitches that stand in exact relations to one another. The pitches and their relations exist before the strings are tuned. Each string is tuned to a pitch and the results are judged by comparison to this pre-existing reality. A musician tuning an instrument is not finished until everything is exactly right, but once it is exactly right, there is simply nothing left to do.

Similarly, in the classic view, the thought exists before the expression, and the expression is judged by comparing it with the pre-existing thought. In writing a sentence, a writer knows when he has it exactly right, after which there is nothing left to do.

Shaw's sentence knows when to stop because it expresses a complete analysis. It might be contrasted with the following passage—written by an editor for the influential journal he edits—which isn't over even when it *is* over.

> The concept of spatial form has unquestionably been central to modern criticism not only of literature but of the fine arts and of language and of culture in general. Indeed, the consistent goal of the natural and human sciences in the twentieth century has been the discovery and/or construction of synchronic structural models to account for concrete phenomena.

Classic style is not exclusive. A writer's position or status cannot make her a classic writer, or bar her from becoming a classic writer. An undergraduate at a junior college wrote the following classic passage in her discussion of the spatial form of Rembrandt's *Old Man with a Gold Chain*:

> Rembrandt was a very young man when he painted this picture, but it is a work demonstrating the insight and wisdom of an older man. It is a poignant picture and painful to look upon because it is not just a painting of a man, but an expression of mortality.

. . . l'amour-propre & la confiance en nous-mêmes, qu'il sait si bien nous inspirer, nous sollicitent à tirer des conséquences qui ne dérivent pas immédiatement des faits; en sorte que nous sommes en quelque façon intéressés à nous séduire nous-mêmes.

[. . . self-love and self-confidence (which so easily inspires us) tempt us to draw consequences that do not derive immediately from facts; so that we become in a fashion interested in deceiving ourselves.]

—Antoine Laurent Lavoisier, "Discours préliminaire" to
  Traité élémentaire de chimie

On n'est jamais si heureux ni si malheureux qu'on s'imagine.

[One is never so happy or unhappy as one thinks.]

—François VI, duc de La Rochefoucauld, *Maximes*

Car il me semblait que je pourrais rencontrer beaucoup plus de vérité dans les raisonnements que chacun fait touchant les affaires qui lui importent, et dont l'événement le doit punir bientôt après s'il a mal jugé, que dans ceux que fait un homme de lettres dans son cabinet, touchant des spéculations qui ne produisent aucun effect, et qui ne lui sont d'autre conséquence, sinon que peut-être il en tirera d'autant plus de vanité qu'elles seront plus éloignées du sens commun. . . .

[For it seemed to me that I could find a great deal more truth in the reasonings everyone makes concerning his own affairs, and whose consequences will quickly make him suffer if he has made a mistake, than in those made by a man of letters in his study, concerning speculations that have no effect whatever, and no consequence for him except perhaps to allow him to feel prouder according as they are further from common sense. . . .]

—René Descartes, *Discours de la méthode*

. . . la puissance de bien juger et distinguer le vrai d'avec le faux, qui est proprement ce qu'on nomme le bon sens ou la raison, est naturellement égale en tous les hommes; et ainsi, que la diversité de nos opinions ne vient pas de ce que les uns sont plus raisonnable que les autres, mais seulement de ce que nous conduisons nos pensées par diverses voies, et ne considérons pas les mêmes choses. Car ce n'est pas assez d'avoir l'esprit bon, mais le principal est de l'appliquer bien. Les plus grandes âmes sont capables des plus grands vices aussi bien que des plus grandes vertus, et ceux qui ne marchent que fort lentement peuvent avancer beaucoup d'avantage, s'ils suivent toujours le droit chemin, que ne font ceux qui courent, et qui s'en éloignent.

[. . . the power to judge well and to distinguish the true from the false, which is properly what one calls common sense or reason, is naturally equal in everyone; and thus the diversity of our opinions does not come from some of us being more reasonable than others, but only from our conducting our thoughts in different ways and not considering the same things. For it is not enough to have a sound mind but the principal point is to apply it well. The greatest souls are capable of the greatest vices as well as the greatest virtues, and those who walk only very slowly can get much further ahead if they always keep to the right way than those who run in another direction.]

—René Descartes, *Discours de la méthode*

This juxtaposition of classic French texts—from chemistry, philosophy, and the observation of human behavior—very nearly speaks for itself. While everyone is endowed with reason, everyone's reason is compromised by self-deception and self-interest. Classic thought depends upon finding a way, through discipline, of avoiding these frailties and avoiding, too, pride at having avoided them. This is of course impossible.

> The self cannot be escaped, but it can be, with ingenuity and hard work, distracted.
>
> —Donald Barthelme, "Daumier"

Classic style lends itself to the expression of a complete temperament in a single statement. People who do not like this style think of this feature as a narrowness, a sameness that falls into routine or self-parody; people who admire the style think of its aphoristic character as a consistency that is something like integrity. Barthelme's sentence is much more than a statement or an observation. It is the expression of an attitude toward life. It is like the autobiography of a temperament in miniature. Its subject is central to the temperament in question—the self, conceived as a sort of cage. Naturally, someone in a cage would like to get out, but the first clause assures us there is no escape. Curiously, this situation leads neither to despair nor to passivity but to action. For, "with hard work and ingenuity," the victim of selfhood can achieve if not the ideal goal then the most desirable practical alternative. It is a rather bleak picture of the world, but one in which there is a surprising reason to value effort and skill.

This temperament is at odds with the temperament found in Jefferson or Descartes, neither of whom begins with a restriction on basic human possibilities. Temperaments of resignation similar to Barthelme's can be found, however, in a few notable classic French writers of the seventeenth century. La Rochefoucauld, for example, assumes that there are fundamental restrictions on basic human possibilities: self-knowledge is unavailable and the knowledge one has of others, if correct, always reveals them to be acting from self-interest. La Rochefoucauld's maxim "On n'est jamais si heureux ni si malheureux qu'on s'imagine" (One is never as happy or as unhappy as one imagines) expresses a temperament resigned to unalterable restrictions on human possibilities.

Barthelme's thought is globally structured by a schematic movement to a goal, in two impulses: a failed step toward an ideal goal—marked as impossible—and a subsequent step to a substitute. The first impulse is desire, the second, acceptance. The second impulse is interrupted right before it comes to its expected end by a consideration of the unanticipated and quite difficult requirements for attaining this inferior but possible goal.

The sentence imitates the schematic form of the thought it expresses: it moves directly toward a goal to be rejected (escape) and then moves from the rejected goal toward the available goal (distraction). Grammatically, we expect a participle to follow "can be."

But the sentence takes an unexpected grammatical detour, through a parenthesis. This grammatical detour creates a sense of the distraction to which the end of the sentence refers.

Inserting the parenthesis "with ingenuity and hard work" into the final verb phrase destroys the symmetry of a radical version of this sentence: "The self cannot be escaped, but it can be distracted." Adding this nuance suggests a distinction between the fantasy of escape and the arduous work of distraction. Escape, because it is impossible, is not burdened with conditions. Distraction belongs to a different order of things, an order neither so desirable nor so uncomplicated as the order of fantasy.

In the classic view, truth comes with structure that is part of its meaning and is preferably to be inherited by its expression. The structure of expression is therefore, by this inheritance, meaningful—two grammatically equivalent expressions can have different meanings. Let us consider two such expressions:

The self cannot be escaped, but it can be, with ingenuity and hard work, distracted.

The self cannot be escaped, but with ingenuity and hard work it can be distracted.

The first has a schematic structure of derailment, delay, distraction, and arduousness in reaching a goal. It inherits this structure from the thought it expresses. The second does not have this schematic structure. The difference is only a nuance, but the nuance is indispensable.

Classic style is highly attentive to nuance, and as a consequence is highly sensitive to the schematic structure of expression. In the classic view, nuance is neither arbitrary nor decorative; it *is* meaning. Nuance is recognized through discipline and precision and can be lost sight of through carelessness. Classic style lives on fine distinctions. However fine they may be, their significance is absolute. Two things that are almost the same are in fact different, and classic style was invented as an instrument for presenting such careful discriminations.

Classic expression presents the simplest accurate result of analysis. It presupposes that an analysis has been completed, and it is distinguished by expressing the result *in the simplest accurate form*. The thought locates exact distinctions, exact relations, exact objects and forms; the expression presents this analyzed array. The expression is clear and simple as the truth, but no clearer or simpler. Barthelme's sentence is classic in expressing a precise analysis. It does this clearly and simply without blurring the fine distinctions indispensable to the thought.

They fuck you up, your mum and dad. They may not mean to, but they do.

—Philip Larkin, from "This Be The Verse" in *High Windows*

These two sentences, here set out as prose, are the first two lines of a twelve-line poem. Although Larkin uses conventional poetic forms of meter and rhyme, he imparts to his poetry the sound of talk—casual, spontaneous, conversational. His best poetry not only aspires to, but achieves the condition of classic prose.

His first line, "They fuck you up, your mum and dad," sounds like a conversational observation; the words seem to be as commonplace as the thought, but they unobtrusively give vitality back to the cliché they express. The observation crystallizes a vast and indefinite history of personal experience without incorporating any of it, and the reader is expected to be able to confirm the truth immediately from her own experience.

His next line, "They may not mean to, but they do," sounds like an afterthought. In fact, it is an example of the writer doing all the work invisibly. Larkin deliberately avoids the surface brilliance of classic writers such as La Rochefoucauld, or Shaw, or Wilde, preferring instead the maximum understatement of his capacity and labor—on a casual reading, their very existence can go unsuspected. These lines are however a deliberate presentation after the writer has done quite a lot of invisible work. Try any alternative—"your mum and dad fuck you up even if they don't mean to," for example—and see how flat and unmemorable this unforgettable little text becomes.

We can begin to see how careful and studied this passage actually is, despite its deceptively casual presentation, if we consider Larkin's choice of words. A moment's reflection will establish that your mum and dad are not the same as your mother and father or your mommy and daddy or dad and mom. The phrase "mum and dad" is a set phrase used to refer to parents as they inhabit a particular role with respect to their children. A native speaker of English, particularly British English, knows exactly when and under what circumstances to use this phrase, but the amount and variety of this knowledge is vast. It is the perfect phrase for referring to parents in Larkin's text because it is precisely in their capacity as "mum and dad" that they "fuck you up." The language has supplied a perfect phrase for crystallizing the extraordinarily complicated normal history wherein parents not deficient as parents nonetheless routinely, predictably, and inevitably debilitate their children. "They may not mean to, but they do."

Profanity is almost never encountered in classic prose, exactly because the usual reasons for using it are unclassic. It is rarely a precise instrument of presentation and often has the effect of slurring or smudging an observation. The nonstandard "mum and dad," the vulgar "fuck you up" exceptionally in this text fit their subject precisely. As a result, the expression itself, while disguised as commonplace, is unstridently memorable and undeniably certified by the culture whose artifacts are these phrases.

The novels of Theodore Dreiser, Marxist political rhetoric, the landscape of northern New Jersey, souvenir shops in airports—these have the special qualities of an ugly which is at once settled into itself, varied in its particulars, yet bound to go on and on interminably.

—Robert Martin Adams, *Bad Mouth*

Mme de Chevreuse avait beaucoup d'esprit, d'ambition et de beauté; elle était galante, vive, hardie, entreprenante; elle se servait de tous ses charmes pour réussir dans ses desseins, et elle a presque toujours porté malheur aux personnes qu'elle y a engagées.

[Madame de Chevreuse had sparkling intelligence, ambition, and beauty in plenty; she was flirtatious, lively, bold, enterprising; she used all her charms to push her projects to success, and she almost always brought disaster to those she encountered on her way.]

—La Rochefoucauld, *Mémoires*

When La Rochefoucauld wrote his description of Madame de Chevreuse, Theodore Dreiser had written no novels, there was no Marxist political rhetoric, the landscapes of northern New Jersey were unexplored by English professors, there were no souvenir shops in airports, there were no airports. He and Robert Martin Adams are each saturated in local knowledge of a certain kind, but they live in different worlds and speak of different things. Yet their observations share a great deal if we consider not what they have to say but how they arrange what they say.

Each of them builds carefully to a point, a point known from the beginning but reserved and prepared for so that it will achieve its maximum effect without seeming to be forced. Each of them assumes a pose of abundant and assured experience from which he speaks. They succeed in turning away the normal temptation to question their unargued judgments because they do not betray any anxiety by overstatement. Adams is disarming in suggesting that he is familiar with not just *this* kind of ugly but other varieties as well. It is as if the question of these things being ugly is settled; he is concerned only to make sure he has placed them in the right category of ugly.

La Rochefoucauld succeeds in suggesting that he has a wide acquaintance among women, some of them attractive, others talented or ambitious, none of them quite like Madame de Chevreuse. Both La Rochefoucauld and Adams speak from a secure haven. Adams is not threatened by the bleak and eternal ugly he delineates; La Rochefoucauld will not be enlisted in any of Madame de Chevreuse's projects. Their position of safety suggests that they have no urgent interest in getting their readers to believe what they say, and this implicit claim is supported by the structure and tone of the sentences themselves.

Adams's sentence has a musing tone to it and certainly his own expression has not been invaded by any variety of the ugly. La Rochefoucauld is not eager to say anything negative about Madame de Chevreuse; there is a tone of appreciation and equity to his description. The proven danger of associating with her does not subtract from her attractive qualities, which are abundant and not commonly united in a single person. Consider how different the effect would be if he had said, "Even though Madame de Chevreuse was beautiful, intelligent, . . ."

While neither of these sentences expresses the least doubt and both make positive, unshaded judgments that might court a reader's resistance, they distract resistance by making the sort of fine distinctions that are the expression of serene, unrushed judgment. Such distinctions cannot be made casually; they are the result of work, observation, testing—something like research. None of this effort is allowed to show, however, in the expression; even the writing is made to sound easy. Neither writer suggests that he has considered ways of disarming a reader's impulse to question, although each of them has anticipated problems and devised solutions.

Although each word has been carefully weighed and carefully placed, the finished sentences suggest spontaneous speech. It is only on reflection that we see how impossible it would be for someone spontaneously to say something so complex and perfect. (Almost any change in either sentence would be a change for the worse.) Neither writer wants to suggest that what he is doing is *work*. That is why so much work has gone into getting this writing to suggest speech; writing suggests effort and work, persuasive writing suggests strategy. To make writing imitate speech is a great deal of work and yet the happy phrase that is just right and suggests that it *is* just right simply because it is true can happen in conversation—usually after a lot of forgotten false starts.

All these shared characteristics are what makes it possible to see these sentences as *stylistically* similar, even though they do not share a subject or even a language.

A heroic, photographically literal statue of [Huey Long] stands on a high pedestal above his grave in the Capitol grounds. The face impudent, porcine and juvenal, is turned toward the building he put up—all thirty-four stories of it—

in slightly more than a year, mostly with Federal money. The bronze double-breasted jacket, tight over the plump belly, has already attained the dignity of a period costume, like Lincoln's frock coat. In bronze, Huey looks like all the waggish fellows from Asheville and Nashville, South Bend and Topeka, who used to fill our costlier speakeasies in the late twenties and early thirties. He looks like a golf-score-and-dirty-joke man, anxious for the good opinion of everybody he encounters. Seeing him there made me feel sad and old. A marble Pegasus carved in bas-relief below his feet bears a scroll that says, "Share Our Wealth." That was one of Huey's slogans; another was "Every Man a King."

—A. J. Liebling, *The Earl of Louisiana*

In this last chapter I wish to observe and trace the transformation of American Africanism from its simplistic, though menacing, purposes of establishing hierarchic difference to its surrogate properties as self-reflexive meditations on the loss of the difference, to its lush and fully blossomed existence in the rhetoric of dread and desire.

—Toni Morrison, *Playing in the Dark: Whiteness and the Literary Imagination*

Christopher Lehmann-Haupt, in a *New York Times* review of Toni Morrison's essay *Playing in the Dark* and her novel *Jazz*, cited this sentence as an example of the essay's style, which he contrasted with what he called the poetry of her novel. He expressed disapproval of "the style she employs to make her points." His tacit and conventional assumption, almost an enabling convention in journalism, is that style is completely separable from thought. Morrison, accordingly, should have presented her thought in a more immediately intelligible style. This is the same assumption that underwrites the many programs for correcting prose by giving its surface a final jiggle to shake out blemishes and clots.

The difficulty in Morrison's sentence lies not in its surface but in its thought. The image-schematic structure of the sentence—spatial movement along a path from location to location—is basic and classic. Here is an immediately intelligible sentence formed on that image schema:

> I want to observe and trace the history of Christianity as it moved from its origin as a Jewish heresy, to the state religion of the Roman Empire, to the high religion of medieval Europe.

Combined with this image schema is a basic metaphor: ideas, beliefs, and institutions—which are not physical objects and which do not move—can be understood metaphorically as physical objects that do move; different states are metaphorically different locations; transformation is metaphorically movement from one spatial location to another; the history of an idea, a belief, or an institution can be "followed" by "tracing" visually the "path" "traced" by its "movement" in historical time. Morrison's sentence and the sentence about Christianity are equally built upon this union of metaphor and image schema. But the sentence about Christianity is immediately intelligible while Morrison's is not. The difference lies in the conception of subject.

Classic style conceives of its subject, whether concrete or abstract, as a publicly available "thing" clear and distinct at all levels—from anatomy to fine detail. This cultural "thing" can be acknowledged by any competent observer who looks at it. Its existence is independent of the writer's conception and certainly independent of the writer's prose. A subject conceived of in this way as a "thing" fits nicely the image schema of spatial movement and the metaphor of change as spatial movement.

Even if a reader cannot offer any precise description of Christianity, and may be barely able to distinguish it from Buddhism, it will be acknowledged by most likely readers of *The New York Times*—and certainly by Christopher Lehmann-Haupt—as if it were observable in the same sense that the statue of Huey Long on the Capitol grounds in Baton Rouge is observable. "American Africanism," unlike Christianity, calls attention to itself as an abstraction precisely because it does not have the sort of agreed-about borders, however imprecise, that a concept needs before it leaves the status of special conception intelligible to special audiences and becomes a vulgar cliché indistinguishable for rhetorical purposes from a planet whose path can be traced.

A similar difficulty attaches to the three stages of American Africanism's history, all of which are unfamiliar abstractions, none of which has general currency in contemporary American culture. "Medieval Europe" is also an abstraction, but it has general currency; a reader of *The New York Times* can be expected to accept such an abstraction as definite and legitimate even if that reader's image of medieval Europe is completely featureless, since such a reader will believe he could, so to speak, look it up. "The rhetoric of dread and desire" does not enjoy a similar standing, so that the lush and fully blossomed existence of American Africanism in the rhetoric of dread and desire is an existence that cannot be accepted as a matter of course.

Morrison is not offering arbitrarily difficult descriptions of what can be described in "another style," that is, more accessible language. She is talking about special concepts without common currency whose very existence depends on her thought. As a result, the passage features an asymmetry between writer and reader that marks her style as unclassic. A writer presenting such a subject in classic style could not trace a movement before establishing the reality of American Africanism down to quite fine details, so that the reader can accept it as a "thing" he can experience. The model scene would have to be substituted unobtrusively for an actual scene of persuasion, and the classic writer would have to persuade his reader that she can accept American Africanism the way she can accept the planet Venus, and that the path of American Africanism can be traced the way an astronomer can trace the planet's path. The abstract nature of the subject is no impediment to such a conception: a cultural historian like Chastel, a connoisseur of old painting like Friedländer, a New Testament interpreter like Dodd, a mathematical physicist like Feynman, an observer of the emotions like Madame de Lafayette, and an observer of society like Madame de Sévigné can present the most abstract matters in the most abstract fields as if they were talking about statues, strawberries, or the evening star.

The passage from A. J. Liebling describing the statue of Huey Long may seem at first glance to have nothing in common with the passage from Toni Morrison. Morrison is talking about a cultural abstraction and its sequence of change; Liebling is talking about a static statue that anyone standing at Huey Long's grave can see. The juxtaposition of these passages may suggest an attempt to illustrate the advice of so many writing manuals to be "concrete," and to avoid abstractions. It is, of course, impossible either to think or write without using abstractions, so like most scattershot advice, the mantra "be concrete, avoid abstractions" is generally useless in practice. The mantra is nevertheless at least remotely related to a sound observation about style, in the way, for example, that the phrase "you can't be certain of anything" is related to Heisenberg's Uncertainty Principle.

Liebling's description of Huey Long's statue turns on concepts about American culture in the 1920s and 1930s that are as abstract as anything in Toni Morrison's passage and are at least as personal to Liebling as anything Morrison says about the movement of American Africanism is personal to her. The stylistic difference between them rests on how they treat those abstractions. It is easy to feel excluded from Morrison's vision of American Africanism because she does not choose to conceive of her subject as a "thing" that anyone can verify. As a result, the abstract nature of her concepts is put into relief, and she leaves the reader with the choice of either accepting what she says or considering it, to a greater or lesser degree, an arbitrarily personal vision.

Liebling demonstrates a typical classic elision from what is easy for any reader to see for herself—the statue—to his highly personal interpretation, based on abstract cultural and ethical concepts. He never says that anyone else can see the cultural matrix into which he places the statue; he treats that matrix as a matter of course and suggests that its finest details can be delineated by anyone who was there. As a result, it requires deliberate analysis to realize that while anyone can verify the existence of the statue and the inscription on the scroll ("Share Our Wealth"), the interpretation that has been slipped between the description of the statue and the description of the scroll can be seen by no one who does not agree to accept Liebling's reflection as a thing. This agreement, Liebling recognizes, requires persuasion, but he never explicitly acknowledges a need to persuade. Instead, he addresses his problem by artful juxtaposition and tacit assurances that what he supplies (whether fact or interpretation) is as reliable as what is right there in front of him and—accidents of time and place aside—can be right there in front of you. Consider the comparison between "Share Our Wealth," the slogan actually carved on the scroll, and "Every Man a King," which Liebling cites as another of Huey Long's slogans. The second slogan is nowhere to be seen at the gravesite, but it is one of Huey Long's best-known lines. Liebling's claim can be verified by anyone who checks the relevant sources. It is only an invisible step to treat the interpretation as something that can be verified in the relevant sources too, and it is a classic technique to distract the reader from observing that the relevant source in this case is the writer's imagination.

When that was once begun, it was as little in my fear, that what words of complaint I heard among lerned men of other parts utter'd against the Inquisition, the same I should hear by as lerned men at home utterd in time of Parlament against an order of licencing; and that so generally, that when I had disclos'd my self a companion of their discontent, I might say, if without envy, that he whom an honest *quæstorship* had indear'd to the *Sicilians*, was not more by them importun'd against *Verres*, then the favourable opinion which I had among many who honour ye, and are known and respected by ye, loaded me with entreaties and perswasions; that I would not despair to lay together that which just reason should bring into my mind, toward the removal of an undeserved thraldom upon lerning.

—John Milton, *Areopagitica*

This passage, a single sentence of 142 words, is almost impossible to understand at one reading. Although it comes from an essay ostensibly meant to be a speech to Parliament, it does not model itself on speech and distances itself self-consciously from any possible model of conversation. It has no image schema indicating a clear direction or a goal. It is in every way unclassic and offers a striking contrast to the most conspicuous style of French prose contemporary with it.

It would be tempting for any contemporary writing consultant to offer a sort of over-the-counter prescription for improving this sentence if it were not for the fact that it occurs in a major seventeenth-century prose text that has been studied and admired around the world for over three centuries. Such a writing consultant would place a premium on clarity and would suggest effective means of rewriting the entire *Areopagitica* so as to make it easier to parse. But Milton would have viewed these revisions as a complete destruction of his mature and accomplished style, and he would have been right.

Clarity is a prime virtue within classic style or practical style, and it is easy to begin judging other styles by the standards of one of these general styles, especially for writers who actually use one of them on a regular basis. Classic style, like practical style, encourages such judgments by making a tacit claim to being a universal style. But this claim is deceptive. Neither classic style nor practical style can suit Milton's purposes because his model scene is not the scene essential to either classic or practical style. In this way, this passage resembles Samuel Johnson's opening comments in his "Preface to Shakespeare": both Milton and Johnson write in mature and consistent styles completely incompatible with either classic or practical style. The model scene behind classic style is conversation, with the result that it tends to come in discrete units, intelligible when excerpted. The model scene behind the *Areopagitica* requires a display of ostentatiously orchestrated erudition. This scene places the highest premium on gravity and allusion—not on clarity. Far from depending on a model of conversation, it is not even modeled on English speech; it is modeled on written Latin. The influence of Milton's model scene upon his style is such that an excerpted passage may be nearly unintelligible, but there is no reason for Milton to view this as a fault. He does not mean the *Areopagitica* to live through pithy excerpts, and he most certainly would suffer from using a style that looks as if it is easy to parse or conveniently packaged into easily digested bites. To rewrite the *Areopagitica* in the style of La Rochefoucauld or A. J. Liebling would be to ensure that the reader Milton is addressing would immediately brand it as trivial.

Socrates in the *Apology* expresses a touchstone of classic style, as if it were a fundamental priority of all style: "If you hear me defending myself in the same language which it has been my habit to use, both in the open spaces of this city (where many of you have heard me) and elsewhere, do not be surprised."

He explicitly refuses to adopt the mannered style of the courtroom, and he implies that there is something artificial and dishonest in that style. He adopts as his model scene conversation, voice, spontaneity. As a result, it is easy to excerpt from his speech discrete, intelligible units of discourse. The *Apology* is, after all, with a very minimum of glossing, perfectly intelligible today in translation to audiences in Oregon or Ohio or Hong Kong, audiences who know absolutely nothing about the conventions of Athenian courtrooms at the beginning of the fourth century B.C.

By contrast, imagine a speech by an Athenian orator whose main goal, unlike Socrates', is to win his case. Contemporary readers in Hong Kong or Ohio cannot, of course, imagine any such thing in detail. The specific good moves in such a speech would go unnoticed or function as barriers to understanding in much the fashion that Milton's elaborate syntax and classical allusions do in the passage from the *Areopagitica*. It would be impossible to "correct" Milton's style (or the Athenian orator's) without understanding the scene that helps define his style as well as he does. Only a few specialists in seventeenth-century English parliamentary history have any such knowledge today, and it is not obvious that any of them now knows how to address the Parliament that Milton wished to address as well as Milton did himself. No general principle ("Omit needless words," for example) can ever supersede a specific knowledge of such elements of style as the scene and cast that help define a style, for only they can indicate which words are needless.

> While I've indicated to you previously that we may well have, probably do have, enough monetary stimulus in the system to create that [economic recovery], I'm not sure that we will not need some insurance or to revisit this issue, and all I can say to you is that we're all looking at the same set of data, the same economy, the same sense of confidence which pervades it. We're all making our judgments with respect to how that is evolving with respect to economic activity and where the risks of various different actions are. And there will be differences inevitably.
>
> —Alan Greenspan, chairman of the Federal Reserve Board, responding to senators at a congressional hearing, who were trying to get him to cut interest rates in order to speed economic recovery (March 1992)

This passage from Alan Greenspan, as reported by *The New York Times* of 20 April 1992, is certainly not an example of classic style, but it is a definite style and a cultivated one. Since it is above all a spoken style (meant, however, to be read in newspaper accounts), Mr. Greenspan refers to it as "an incoherent mumble." Its virtues are just the opposite of classic style's virtues, and performances in this style should not be confused with the speaker's general level of articulateness. It is not a style of obfuscation as it is sometimes claimed to be, for its speaker is not hiding a conclusion or a point that he actually expresses buried in all that confusing verbiage. It is rather a style of gridlock, expressed in a manner that is built around images of contradictory and asymmetrical motion and a shifting kaleidoscope of qualifications. It is not, like classic style, a general style; it is a special style deliberately deployed by the relatively few people in positions like that of the chairman of the Federal Reserve Board, whose powers are vast and whose words are carefully studied for hints of what they are likely to do. If the passage is pored over carefully, it gives no hint about whether Greenspan will or will not lower interest rates, whether he has made up his mind on the subject, or even whether he agrees that lowering interest rates will have the effect that the senators think it will have.

For powerful directors of policy forced to testify in public, the virtues of classic style can be disastrous. The protocol of congressional hearings requires that the respondents appear to respect the committee, so people like Alan Greenspan cannot say, "I'm here because I have to be here, but I'm not telling you anything." The unusual circumstances of this scene require the successful practitioner to give the impression that he or she actually may have said something of substance, and to avoid at all costs inviting any further clarifying questions of an obvious sort. If Greenspan had said, "I think we've already lowered interest rates enough, but we are monitoring the situation continually and it may be that at some point it will make sense to lower them further. I will do what I think is indicated at the appropriate time, and that may not be what you think is indicated," he would have made his essential points much more clearly, but at an unacceptable cost. It is unwise for him to indicate to the senators in a clear fashion that he will do what he thinks best and will be unaffected by anything they think, nor does he wish clearly to rule out what they suggest since it is against his interests to indicate either that he will or will not lower the interest rates and equally against his interests to give any indication about when he will make up his mind. The hypothetical revision is clearer certainly, but it invites unwelcome questions: Then you have ruled out, for the moment, lowering interest rates? Under what future circumstances will it make sense to lower the rates further? What are you watching as an indicator that the current rates are too high?

All of these questions must be warded off because he really does not wish to give any indication of his future course of action. Various markets would react to any hint he may give of what he is likely to do. In the circumstances, "While I've indicated to you previously that we may well have, probably do have, enough monetary stimulus in the system to create that . . ." is in every way superior to "I think we've already lowered interest rates enough." The statement is so filled with qualifications and so indefinite even with respect to its effective date or what it is talking about that it says absolutely nothing about what he may do while seeming to offer a concession. "While I said x at some point in the past," leads the audience to expect "I say y now." That is not the actual sequence, and what does follow is so much at odds with what is expected, and so entirely shapeless, that it is not immediately clear that there is actually no concession. Everything is done to leave doubt on later analysis even that he still thinks enough has been done now "to create that" (create what? the exasperated reader says), since the whole phrase is framed by "I've indicated to you previously," and does not offer the expected symmetrical statement about what the speaker is indicating now. Greenspan uses subtle verbal resources to avoid the unhedged present indicative and to erase any momentary appearance of stable assertion: modals, ambiguous reference, adverbs of doubt, locations of events in an indefinite future or an indefinite ongoing present.

This passage and a consideration of the special requirements of its exceptional scene can serve as a reminder first, that what is a vice in one style can be a virtue in another and second, that there are not merely two styles, good and bad, but many styles, some general, some highly specialized. Almost any English composition teacher would say that this passage "needs revision," and may go on to suggest what is wrong with it. In fact, there is nothing wrong with it. It is a virtuoso performance of stonewalling disguised as incoherence. There is nothing sloppy about it. It is not unplanned. It is deliberate in its contradiction of the expected symmetrical and directional image schema whose expectations it frustrates with exquisite skill. It is a performance as precise as a cat's walking though a chaos of objects on a messy desk without disturbing any of them.

This memorandum . . . deals with what might be called the least important questions confronting authors and publishers. But it is precisely because of their relative unimportance, despite their capacity for mischief-making, that we should be able to take them in our stride. The effort, in other words, is to remove them from the problem category so that we can devote our energy to matters of larger significance—authors and editors to intelligent and imaginative control of fact and expression, designers and compositors to efficient and artistic typesetting, proofreaders to rapid and precise detection of inaccuracies.

Although there are some matters of comma style (for instance, restrictive vs. nonrestrictive clauses) so well established in custom as to have become rules, nearly all are merely matters of taste. We prefer a comma before the conjunction in a series ("red, white, and blue"), and also after "i.e." and "e.g."

—"Memorandum for Authors, Editors, Compositors, Proofreaders on the Preparation of Manuscripts and the Handling of Proof," Princeton University Press, January 1990

English orthography satisfies all the requirements of the canons of reputability under the law of conspicuous waste.

It is archaic, cumbrous, and ineffective; its acquisition con-
sumes much time and effort; failure to acquire it is easy of
detection.

—Thorstein Veblen, *The Theory of the Leisure Class*

＿|

The attitude of the memorandum from Princeton University Press
might come as a surprise to readers of the guides and handbooks
used in English composition courses, where questions of capital-
ization, spelling, punctuation, and usage seem to constitute not just
the most conspicuous surface aspects of writing but practically the
whole subject. The reason for this common misordering of priori-
ties is precisely the conspicuous nature of these accidentals. That is
why Thorstein Veblen suggested in a classic work of sociology that
spelling is meant to indicate a form of social distinction based on
the leisure to learn an arbitrary and inefficient system. Such things
as the pronunciation and spelling of place names often serve as a
marker distinguishing the local population from outsiders. A distinguished American theologian who pulled off a highway to ask
directions to Beloit, which he pronounced in the French manner
(bell-wah), was quickly informed, once the laughter died down,
"Beh-LOIT, buddy. You're in Wisconsin now."

Accidentals hardly enter into the elements of style at all, but
they can cause any amount of mischief unless they are well managed because they indicate the writer's knowledge of etiquette and
protocol. The idea that dictionaries and handbooks control these
questions is a common misunderstanding. Dictionaries and handbooks try as hard as they can to keep up with the practice of a
vaguely defined set of speakers who together determine prevailing
limits of taste in such matters. Dictionary editors are in the same
position as individuals who do not wish to be conspicuous in the
wrong way. But unlike many of these individuals, the editors understand that they are observing a contest in social influence, not
recording—much less defining—a correct position.

In *Lulu in Hollywood*, Louise Brooks, who must be the best writer among all the sex symbols of the silent screen, explains that she became painfully aware of her Kansas accent because it made her sound provincial in New York. She encountered a Columbia University student at the soda fountain of a drugstore she frequented and flattered him into becoming her speech teacher. In her own words,

> "Mulk" became "milk," and "kee-yow" became "cow." Then: "Not 'watter' as in 'hotter' but 'water' as in 'daughter.' And it's not 'hep,' you hayseed—it's 'help,' 'help,' 'help'!" Within a month of fudge sundaes, this boy had picked his way through my vocabulary, eliminating the last trace of my hated Kansas accent. From the start, it had been my intention not to exchange one label for another. I didn't want to speak the affected London stage-English of the high-comedy stars, like Ina Claire and Ruth Chatterton; I wanted to speak clean, unlabeled English. My soda jerk spoke clean, unlabeled English.

Louise Brooks was no doubt right to think that in New York in the 1920s a *femme fatale* could not go around saying "kee-yow" instead of "cow," but consider how wrong she is to think that she had acquired "unlabeled" English. She had merely dropped an unfashionable label for one that was more suitable to the image she sought to project. Even if we leave her native Kansas out of the question, how would her New York soda jerk's "clean, unlabeled English" sound in Baton Rouge, Louisiana? Fort Worth, Texas? Chicago, Illinois? Or even across the bridge in Brooklyn?

The same social principle applies to many conspicuous aspects of language, none of which determines style. Consider the disappearance of the word "Negro" from contemporary American usage and the currently tenuous position of its successor, "black." At what point was "Negro" archaic usage and who decided the question? Certainly not American dictionaries. They merely surveyed current usage until they determined that the change had become general. The same phenomenon is going on today with the term "black," which itself may soon become archaic in general usage to be replaced by either "Afro-American" or "African American." The competition between these two terms will be decided by how quickly one of them is generally adopted.

All such competitions induce anxiety in many writers and speakers because the "wrong" choice can make a speaker or writer look ridiculous. For this reason there is always a market for self-proclaimed language gurus, and every bookstore has a shelf of etiquette books that pretend all these questions are settled, although inevitably these books often disagree with one another. Publishers and their technical staffs are under no illusions; they know there is no authority outside of the social hierarchy of native speakers and writers. They also know that while accidentals can cause mischief, no degree of mere correctness can possibly constitute a style and too much anxiety about accidentals can compromise one. There were plenty of actresses in the 1920s who never had to substitute "cow" for "kee-yow," but none of them projected the image that Louise Brooks did. She would have ruined that image, moreover, had she betrayed anxiety about getting it right.

Misunderstandings on this subject sometimes extend to people who have exceptional power to influence usage. *The New York Times* and *The Washington Post* gave coverage to Thurgood Marshall's decision to use the term "Afro-American" in a written opinion he filed in 1989 as an associate justice of the United States Supreme Court.

First the eminent jurist explained his motives: "I spent most of my life fighting to get Negro spelled with a capital N. . . . Then people started saying black and I never liked it."

Then he revealed how greatly he underrated his own authority: "Justice Marshall said he chose Afro-American rather than African American, now gaining currency, because 'Afro-American is in the dictionary and the other one isn't.'"

Montaigne déjà avait trouvé en sa Gascogne et dans sa tour de Montaigne, un style de génie, mais tout individuel et qui ne tirait pas à conséquence. Pascal a trouvé un style à la fois individuel, de génie, qui a sa marque et que nul ne peut lui prendre, et un style aussi de forme générale, logique et régulière, qui fait loi, et auquel tous peuvent et doivent plus ou moins se rapporter: il a établi la prose française.

[Montaigne already had found in his Gascony and in his tower at Montaigne a style of genius, but a completely individual one that drew no followers. Pascal discovered a style at once individual, marked by genius, completely his own, that no one could take from him, and yet a general style, logical and regular, with the force of law, one that everyone can and should more or less adopt as a standard: he established French prose.]

—Sainte-Beuve, *Port-Royal*

Classic style, in the hands of its master practitioners, can be distinctive without appearing to be personal. Its implicit claim is that it does not depend upon the writer's personality for its effects. Sainte-Beuve points to this feature of classic style in comparing two great French writers, Montaigne and Pascal.

It was, of course, the French educational bureaucracy in the nineteenth century that made Pascal's style something like "law" and decided that he had not merely demonstrated the powers of a style but "established French prose." Still, the apparent paradox— the claim that Pascal's style is individual yet available to everyone and even more or less obligatory—is a consequence of the classic stand on truth, presentation, scene, cast, thought and language. Pascal is a reasonable model for pedagogical purposes precisely because his style is a general one. While no student is likely to achieve Pascal's level of mastery, the great usefulness of his style as a model is precisely that it is possible for almost anyone to achieve a working competence without needing either Pascal's exceptional abilities or his exceptional passion and sense of purpose. What is personal to him lies outside the style, for his principal achievement, on this view, is more in the nature of a discovery about writing than a written expression of his own thought. Classic style disavows superior powers of introspection or exceptional personal insight or exceptional personal commitment; it never abandons the implicit claim to be merely presenting what the reader, once properly situated, can verify. Its seventeenth-century French practitioners employed the style in a variety of literary forms: in personal correspondence, in books of maxims and moral portraits, in at least one notable work of fiction, and in the memoir literature that is a feature of seventeenth-century French prose. The memoirs of both La Rochefoucauld and his rival, the Cardinal de Retz, share all the essential marks of the style. While their observations are unmistakably their own, they never ask the reader to accept what they say on the strength of something that can belong only to them. Like all classic writers, they do all the work, they do it invisibly, and they suggest that, accidents of opportunity aside, the reader could do precisely what they are doing. As one nineteenth-century editor of Retz put it,

> [L]a langue n'était évidemment pour lui [Retz] qu'un moyen de rendre sa pensée, ou plutôt de présenter habilement, sous un certain jour, les hommes, les événements, et en particulier ses propres actions.

> [Language is evidently for him {Retz} only a way of presenting his thought, or better of ably presenting, on any given day, people, events, and especially his own actions.]

Dem schreibenden Herzog bietet sich die Erinnerung an Menschen und Auftritte mit so drängender Gewalt und so viel Fülle des Einzelnen, daß seine Feder kaum mit zukommen scheint, und er ist offenbar vollkommen uberzeugt, daß alles, was ihm einfällt, für das Ganze unentberhrlich ist und sich auch ins Ganze einordnen wird, ohne daß er im voraus dafür Sorge tragen muß.

[As Saint-Simon writes, memories of people and scenes come to him so urgently and with such an abundance of details that his pen seems hardly able to keep up with it all; and he is apparently quite convinced that everything that occurs to him is indispensable for the whole and that it will find its proper place there without his having to prepare for it in advance.]
—Erich Auerbach, *Mimesis*

Je le voyais bec à bec entre deux bougies, n'y ayant du tout que la largeur de la table entre deux. J'ai décrit ailleurs son horrible physionomie. Eperdu tout à coup par l'ouïe et par la vue, je fus saisi, tandis qu'il parlait, de ce que c'était qu'un jésuite, qui, par son néant personnel et avoué, ne pouvait rien espérer pour sa famille, ni, par son état et par ses vœux, pour soi-même, pas même une pomme ni un coup de vin plus que les autres; qui par son âge touchait au moment de rendre compte à Dieu, et qui, de propos délibéré et amené avec grand artifice, allait mettre l'Etat et la religion dans la plus terrible combustion, et ouvrir la persécution la plus affreuse pour des questions qui ne lui faisaient rien, et qui ne touchaient que l'honneur de leur école de Molina. Ses profondeurs, les violences qu'il me montra, tout cela me jeta en un tel (sic) extase, que tout à coup je me pris à lui dire en l'interrompant: "Mon Père, quel âge avez-vous?" Son extrême surprise, car je le regardais de tous mes yeux, qui la virent se peindre sur son visage, rappela mes sens. . . .

[I saw him face to face between two candles, having nothing but the width of the table between the two of us. I have elsewhere described his horrible physiognomy. Bewildered suddenly by hearing and sight, I was seized, while he talked, with what a Jesuit was, who, through his personal and avowed nothingness, could hope nothing for his family, nor, through his condition and his vows, for himself, not even an apple or a drink of wine more than the others; who, through his age, was close to the moment of rendering his account to God, and who, of deliberate purpose, and brought about with great artifice, was going to put the State and religion into the most terrible combustion, and inaugurate the most frightful persecution for questions which meant nothing to him and which affected only the honor of their school of Molina. His depths, the violences which he showed me, all this threw me into such an ecstasy that I suddenly found myself saying, interrupting him: "Father, how old are you?" His extreme surprise, for I was looking at him with all my eyes, which saw it painted on his face, called back my senses. . . .]

—Saint-Simon, as quoted in Erich Auerbach, *Mimesis*

In *Mimesis*, the Romance philologist Erich Auerbach offers a series of virtuoso stylistic analyses of the type known as *explication de texte*. The passages he has selected are arranged in a chronological sequence beginning with Homer and the sacred scripture of ancient Israel and ending with selections from Virginia Woolf and Marcel Proust. In keeping with the subject of his book, whose subtitle in its English translation is "The Representation of Reality in Western Literature," the sequence of passages he discusses is conceived as an evolutionary progress of representational styles that depend increasingly for their effects on an evident asymmetry between writer and reader in their model cast. Here the classic style of Retz and Pascal is seen as formulaic and superficial compared with the next element of the sequence—the inimitably idiosyncratic performance of Saint-Simon, whose representations of individuals at the court of Louis XIV are incomparable not merely for their individuality and complexity but also for the drama of the writer's performance. Saint-Simon's prose is not a window but something like an acrobat's high wire, a platform for fantastic feats obviously beyond the reader's competence and just barely within the writer's. The writer is not so much competent as he is pushing the limits of his art, his language repeatedly tottering on the edge of syntactic incoherence but frequently achieving striking results that have the air of being part inspired genius, part happy accident.

Auerbach's claims for Saint-Simon are grounded in a conviction that the truth of human existence is very far from clear and simple; it is rather unknown and unknowable to any one individual, but reveals itself in historical processes, the dialectic counterpart of the individual projects that, seen as a sequence, unwittingly and progressively reveal what we know of human truth.

When historical particulars are seen not in the classic perspective as occasions for the revelation of eternal truth but rather in this romantic perspective as moments in the unfolding of a truth progressively revealed in history, classic style of presentation can be compared unfavorably to romantic styles of representation. This is exactly what Auerbach does.

His comparison of classic and romantic styles predictably reverses classic values. Its opening note is the preference for inspiration over rational order: the unpredictable insight that occurs in the very act of composition is preferred to the classic pattern of thought preceding speech. For a romantic like Auerbach, deliberate thought as a principle of expression guarantees a superficial and false vision; inspiration in the course of writing is a badge of authenticity and truth: "Everything that occurs to [Saint-Simon] in connection with his subject, he throws into his sentences just as it happens to come to mind, in full confidence that it will somehow fit together in unity and clearness." For Auerbach, it is not a demerit that Saint-Simon may not see this unity and clearness, that he may merely serve as an inspired conduit to make it available to a future reader.

Classic style values the order of rational analysis as being reliable and not idiosyncratic; it distrusts the order of sensation and emotion as being unreliable, idiosyncratic, and often demonstrably wrong. Auerbach inverts this scale of values:

> Saint-Simon obtains his most profound insights not by rationally analyzing ideas and problems but by an empiricism applied to whatever sensory phenomenon happens to confront him and pursued to the point of penetrating to the existential. In contrast (to mention an obvious example) the Jesuit priest of the first [of Pascal's] *Lettres provinciales* was quite clearly stylized on the basis of a preceding rational study.

This preference for following sensation as it brings unpredictable glimpses of truth is sensible on the romantic view that truth is elusive and never to be seen whole. If truth will not sit still for rational analysis, but comes only in suggestive fragmentary vision, then the writer must always write in fear that at any second whatever fragments of it have come to him will slip away. This intermittent and unpredictable pulse of revelation produces a romantic urgency to capture both the sensation and what it may suggest. This model is unthinkable in classic style, since truth is fully visible to any competent person and cannot slip away. Classic truth can never evaporate. As a result, classic presentation is characterized by calm and ease—a calm and ease that for Auerbach is a hallmark of complacency and self-deception.

> [T]he urgency of an inner impulse gives [Saint-Simon's] language something unusual, at times something violent and immoderately expressive, which runs counter to the ease and pleasantness which appealed to the taste of the time.

Auerbach conceives of the truth of human nature as consisting of "*profondeurs opaques*": perception of truth will necessarily come in exceptional fragments at exceptional moments to exceptional people. It will come when the observer does not expect it. Saint-Simon, for example, in the middle of a conversation with the

Jesuit, Père Tellier, is seized, according to Auerbach, by a revelation of "the essential nature of any strictly organized solidaritarian community." This conception of truth is of course entirely foreign to classic style. On Auerbach's view, it is a sign of integrity for a writer to present fragments of opaque profundities incompletely perceived as they offer themselves to the individual genius. On the classic view, such a presentation can only be definitive proof of failure. In classic style, the expression is a presentation of the *result* of thought. Writing that does not meet this description is incompetent by classic standards, but superior for Auerbach:

> The non-fictitious, non-precogitated quality of his material, its being drawn from immediate appearances, gives Saint-Simon a depth of life which even the great decades' most important portrayers of character, Molière for example or La Bruyère, could not achieve.

In the classic view, this judgment is simply unintelligible because the evidence offered to support the claim seems to be evidence against it. This judgment has, in the classic view, the same logic as "Guesses are better than accurate knowledge because they are more personal."

Individual genius as Auerbach describes it consists of fragmentary and unpredictable visions. The writer cannot control them. Anything that can be controlled in a rational fashion is superficial artifice, not profound truth. Genius is charismatic—blessed with prophetic, inspirational moments of vision, much as E. B. White was momentarily blessed with a glimpse into the nature of time as he recorded his impressions of the girl riding her horse around the circus ring. Neither Saint-Simon nor E. B. White can count on such revelations. They may never come to these writers again; they may never come to the reader at all. What is virtue for Auerbach is egoistical delusion for classic style.

Jane Austen's unforgettable presentation of Mr. Collins in *Pride and Prejudice*—regular and deliberate as it is—will inevitably appear to be on Auerbach's scale of values facile and superficial.

Mr. Collins was not a sensible man, and the deficiency of nature had been but little assisted by education or society; the greatest part of his life having been spent under the guidance of an illiterate and miserly father; and though he belonged to one of the universities, he had merely kept the necessary terms, without forming at it any useful acquaintance. The subjection in which his father had brought him up, had given him originally great humility of manner, but it was now a good deal counteracted by the self-conceit of a weak head, living in retirement, and the consequential feelings of early and unexpected prosperity. A fortunate chance had recommended him to Lady Catherine de Bourgh when the living of Hunsford was vacant; and the respect which he felt for her high rank, and his veneration for her as his patroness, mingling with a very good opinion of himself, of his authority as a clergyman, and his rights as a rector, made him altogether a mixture of pride and obsequiousness, self-importance and humility.

From the classic perspective, the virtue of Jane Austen's presentation is that once she has shown you where to look, her appraisal of Mr. Collins can be independently "verified" by any reader (just as it is by her characters). Saint-Simon gives a virtuoso presentation of Père Tellier and recounts his insight into the nature of the Jesuits, but while someone else might be able to verify Saint-Simon's presentation of the Jesuit of horrible physiognomy, no one else could follow the route from the physical description of one Jesuit to the revelation of the essential nature of the order. This route from the impression of one individual to a presumed knowledge of a whole community is precisely what Jane Austen means by "prejudice." *Pride and Prejudice* turns on the representation of Elizabeth Bennet's repentance for having followed this route to self-deception. What is revelation in Saint-Simon is prejudice in Jane Austen.

Mimesis is a fable about the evolutionary history of style in which later steps in the process are necessarily superior to earlier steps. It is possible for Auerbach to see a particular writer such as Saint-Simon as an almost miraculous mutation exhibiting the shape of the future: "In his level of style, Saint-Simon is a precursor of modern and ultra-modern forms of conceiving and representing life." Truth, for Auerbach, is not the property of an individual, indeed not essentially available to individuals: it resides in dialectical process—the historicist actions of epochs rather than the historical actions of individuals. The value of the individual writer consists in his degree of participation in that dialectical process. The individual genius of a great writer, then, consists in his seeing through immediate persons and events to the truth of the evolutionary historicist progression. Saint-Simon's excellence consists exactly in his being the first to glimpse a higher stage of epochal truth, as Auerbach remarks in his analysis of Saint-Simon's presentation of the duchesse de Lorge:

> We must wait until the late nineteenth century and indeed actually until the twentieth, before we again find in European literature a similar level of tone, a synthesis of a human being which is so entirely free from traditional harmonizing, which presses so unswervingly on from the random data of the phenomenon itself to the ultimate depths of existence.

On such a view, it is possible for Auerbach to place agency in epochs and their sequence rather than in individuals; to write, for example, of the "ease and pleasantness that appealed to the taste of the time," as if times have tastes, rather than individuals. In Auerbach's formulation, an earlier taste is necessarily a less adequate taste. Although earlier tastes may survive into the future to be contemporary with later tastes, they will occupy lower levels on the historicist Great Chain of Adequacy. Auerbach implies that, luckily, the taste for ease and pleasantness lies now in our evolutionary past; it is nearly unimaginable for us now—who live higher on the evolutionary scale of style—to understand the tastes that previous styles created.

Since Auerbach's measure of stylistic maturity values writing to the extent that it penetrates through local and individual human purpose to historicist truth, he naturally discounts the individual purposes of writers as impediments to the representation of truth. The more a writer includes and the less he selects according to his own purpose, the more likely it is that his writing will touch upon those truths that are essentially beyond him. The less he allows his writing to be controlled by "precogitated" individual purpose, the more likely it is that truth will work though him as its conduit. The result, in Auerbach, is a principled blindness to the individual purposes of writers he regards as superficial in comparison with Saint-Simon. Pascal's presentation of a Jesuit in the first of the *Lettres provinciales*, for example, is in the service of classic polemic; Pascal has no need or reason to present a rich and randomly detailed description of an individual Jesuit. But for Auerbach, Pascal's principle of presentation, efficiently governed as it is by his immediate purpose, makes it unlikely that truth, which always lies beyond local purpose, will work through him.

Pascal, like all classic writers, speaks for himself; writers that Auerbach admires hardly speak at all; it is the historical age that speaks through them. The voice of Auerbach's individual genius is not his own; it is the voice of Hegelian historical progress.

Since Auerbach's history presumes to know and to reveal the one ultimate purpose of writing, it can value one style absolutely above all others. Learned and inclusive as Auerbach is, his history is an ideological justification of the universal superiority of that single style, one that has not yet nor ever will be fully manifest in any text by any writer.

Classic style, a general style suitable for presenting the truth of anything, conceived as discrete and self-contained, has no continuing evolutionary history. It can be found in its perfect form in Thucydides, in Madame de Sévigné, in Jane Austen, in A. J. Liebling. It is not the style to which all previous writing aspires. Classic style is one style among many mature and consistent styles. Its virtues follow from its particular stand on the elements of style. They include the clarity and simplicity that come from matching language to thought on the motive of truth. Other styles have other virtues.

THREE

The Studio

■ Introduction

The first part of this book—which we will call "the Essay"—presents principles of style. The second—the Museum—presents exhibits and analyses of style. Once we had written the Essay and the Museum, we thought we had finished our book. Anyone who wanted to acquire the style, we assumed, had everything necessary at hand. All we had left out was the work involved in acquiring the style. Classic style pretends there is no work in writing, and we had happily skipped right over all the stages we had gone through ourselves in acquiring this most versatile and useful style. It is no secret that writing in any style is work, so we have added the Studio to our book—a place where apprentices can progress from inevitably awkward beginnings to confident mastery in semiprivacy under the benevolent eye of a friendly master who looks forward to regarding them as equals, perhaps superiors.

■ Fundamentals: Talk First

In a studio, apprentices learn fundamentals and become masters. The fundamentals, in this Studio, are taught through a set of common exercises—common in the sense that they are intended to be performed both in speech and in writing. We begin with speech because classic style grounds writing in speech.

EXERCISE 1: *Classic Joint Attention*

The radical of presentation is a scene that cognitive scientists call "joint attention." Joint attention is a familiar and common scene, one we experience routinely. In joint attention, people in one place are attending to one thing; they know they are all attending to it, and they know that by attending to it they are engaged with one another. They are jointly interacting. They may gesture and talk about what is engaging their attention, but it may be that no word is actually spoken. They are engaged in influencing one another's minds; words can help but are not essential. Joint attention does not necessarily have a practical goal. What is essential is common and interactive attention.

"Classic joint attention" is the simplest and most basic kind of joint attention. We have specified the features of classic joint attention in the Essay and in the Museum: there are just two people, paying attention to something that is directly perceptible, such as a blackbird in a tree. All of the features of classic style pertain: the motive is truth, the purpose is presentation, the scene is informal, language is adequate, truth can be known, speaker and hearer are competent, and so on. Not only do these two people see the same blackbird, but they also see it in the same mental context, a context that includes their influence on one another.

Classic joint attention is so familiar and common that we typically do not think about it or even notice it. But classic joint attention is the classic scene, the anchor of classic style. To become a classic stylist, one must be able to think about the classic scene consciously, to notice which actual scenes fit the classic scene, which are close, which are distant, and the ways in which an actual scene can differ from the classic scene. Failure to keep this classic scene in mind will result in a style that loses its anchor. Naturally, the first exercise in the Studio is to practice inhabiting an actual classic scene.

Here, then, is the first exercise: notice something directly perceptible and present it in speech to a companion who is next to you. You and your companion can be anywhere: in a park, a garden, a restaurant, walking down the street, in a grocery store, in a station waiting for a train. Recall from the Essay that to present something to someone is not merely to call attention to it, as in, "Look, there is a blackbird." Rather, to present something is to present what you want your companion to perceive. You expect your companion to be able to perceive what you are presenting once it is pointed out, as in, "That blackbird on the tree limb by the hedge has a small red stripe on each wing." What you present might be, for example, an architectural detail—something that is easy to see once your attention is directed to it, but something that just as easily could be missed. It does not have to be something visual. It could be the melody of a bird's song or the salt in the sea breeze.

Like all the exercises in this Studio, this first exercise suits the classroom. Get a partner. Observe the room, the people, what lies beyond the windows, sounds and images from a mobile device, anything in your perceptual fields. Someone might run a slideshow depicting scenes from nature, buildings, works of art, airports, city spots, a movie. Begin a conversation with your partner and make brief classic presentations as the conversation progresses. This activity may seem artificial and uncomfortable at first, because you are trying to do something consciously that you prefer to do automatically. During this exercise, listen not just to your partner, but to your own voice. As you speak, monitor what you are saying. Initially, this conscious attention to your own speech will cause hesitation and even embarrassment. Keep at it. Eventually, you will relax more and more until it feels natural to inhabit the scene of classic joint attention and speak in classic style. The instructor may wish to take the class out of the classroom, for a walk, to a café, down a city street, to an art museum, to a garden. Continue your conversation with your partner as you go, taking every opportunity for classic presentation.

TUTORIAL: *Beyond Classic Joint Attention*

Learning to focus consciously on the classic scene and to perform within it is the first step to becoming a classic stylist. But most of human communication goes beyond the classic scene in one way or another. In any act of communication, you will have in mind a network of thoughts and ideas that can be quite complicated, and this network might be too large, too detailed, and too complex to be held in mind all at once. The network might include your own identity, the identity of others, past experiences, aspirations, inferences, judgments, predictions, and many varieties of cultural knowledge. The network will also include an array of participants: perhaps you think that many people are listening to you or will listen to you. Perhaps in this network of your thoughts, there are important differences between individual members of your audience. Perhaps this network involves unknown or even fictional or imaginary participants. This mental network might involve large intervals of time—perhaps you are reacting to a criticism that someone made a week ago of a speech given by Abraham Lincoln, and you know that tomorrow someone else will comment on your response. The mental network might involve a long and complex chain of cause and effect. It might involve different and even conflicting motives or purposes. In this mental network, there might be complex ideas about how your expression will be distributed, received, and remembered. And of course, your subject in the mental network—what you want to talk about—might be very different from a directly perceptible object. We will call everything you are trying to juggle mentally "the network." A network can be close to or distant from the idea of the classic scene. Some networks will be close in some ways and distant in others. The second step to becoming a classic stylist is to learn to anchor any network in the classic scene.

When you are actually with a companion, looking at a blackbird perched in a tree, and present something about the blackbird, you are inhabiting the classic scene. But now suppose you are talking to the same person on the telephone and, let us say, telling her something you saw when she was not with you. For this telephone conversation, you are using a particular mental network. It contains what you want to present, the mode of communication, the other person in a different place, the fact that you can't see one another, the delay between perception and conversation—the list is long. A telephone call is not an instance of the classic scene. Although the difference is obvious when you focus on it, it may be invisible at first. The reason the two scenes may not seem at first to lie in two different categories is that we ordinarily structure the telephone call by the classic scene. We anchor the first in the second. We can perform in an actual scene that goes beyond classic joint attention by anchoring our performance in that classic scene. We blend a network of thought—in which, for example, we view ourselves as alone with a telephone or a computer—with our idea of classic joint attention. Writing a letter to someone is not the same as talking to that person. Writing is never an instance of the classic scene. But in writing to someone we know well, it is easy and conventional to treat this writing as if it were conversation. This is an example of what we mean by structuring one scene, writing, by another, conversation. In a way, we treat the scene in which one person is alone with a piece of paper as if it were the scene in which two people share simultaneous access to something. In writing to her sister, Jane Austen says, "I have now attained the true art of letter-writing . . . I have been talking to you almost as fast as I could the whole of this letter." Writing is not talking at all, much less engaging in conversation, but writing can be anchored in our understanding of talking and even, as here, in our understanding of a one-sided turn in a two-person conversation.

This sort of "blending" of the classic scene with a mental network that does not strictly fit that scene is fundamental to classic style. Treating something we cannot perceive—"an obvious blunder," for example—as if it were something anybody could "see" is an example of how a judgment can be treated as a perceptible object. The judgment is in the network; the perceptible object is in the classic scene. We blend them, and in the blend, treat the judgment, stylistically, as if it were a perceptible object. Often, in ordinary communication, we do quite classic things, but unless we focus consciously on the classic scene and the way in which we use it to anchor unclassic networks, our performance will be inconsistent and unreliable. Operating in the dark, we might float into and out of classic style without recognizing what we are doing. The result will be a style that is not under our control, and confusing for the reader. The classic stylist keeps clearly in mind what belongs to the anchor and what belongs to the network, and anchors the network in the classic scene. The mental networks we actually use in scenes of communication can vary greatly, but the anchor scene—classic joint attention—never varies, and this anchor sets the style.

Imagine that you are on a train, going through a landscape you have never seen before. The train stops in a rural station during the afternoon. Pointing to a tree outside the train window, you say to your companion, "That apple tree is bearing two different kinds of fruit." This is a scene of classic joint attention. Now imagine that you are writing a letter to your companion, who is back home. You write, "The train is stopped in a rural station. The apple tree outside the window bears two different kinds of fruit, one green and mottled, the other red fading to yellow." This is classic style, anchored in the scene of classic joint attention.

The goal of every one of the following exercises is to develop your ability to take things that lie beyond classic joint attention and anchor them stylistically in that scene.

Insisting on the distinction between the scene of classic joint attention and scenes that are merely structured by it may seem to be unnecessary, but recognizing that distinction is indispensable to learning classic style. In the Studio, you learn how to structure networks by the scene of classic joint attention, and to do that, you must first recognize what is being done. Once you recognize it, you can focus on it and learn to anchor networks in the classic scene. If you don't recognize what is happening, the performance remains a mystery. Recognizing what it means for a network to be structured by classic joint attention is the single most significant step to mastering classic style.

EXERCISE 2: *Hiding the Labor*

In the second exercise, introduce a single small change to the scene of classic joint attention that you practiced in the first exercise. You are still in a garden or walking down a street or in a restaurant or listening to a piece of music with someone. You direct your companion's attention to something that can be perceived, but what you ask your companion to notice is not something you have just noticed yourself. It is something you already know. In calling your companion's attention to it, however, you treat it in the same way you would treat something you observed just then. You offer no explanation of how you came to notice it yourself or how long you have known it. It is actually there to be seen, and you are not pretending that you have just noticed it; you simply point it out. There is nothing in the style of your presentation that marks it as something you already knew. Suppose that you are on your surfboard beyond the break zone of the waves, and your companion is on her surfboard five yards away. You have known for years how the pattern of the waves changes with the change in tide. And you know, too, from having studied the surf report for the day that the tide is going out just now. You say, "The tide is going out. The waves are breaking farther south, and bigger." The effect of the tide on the waves, although absolutely evident the minute you point it out, is just the kind of thing that people can look at without noticing. Your own recognition is not spontaneous; it rests upon a lengthy process of observation and study. The mental network you are dealing with goes beyond classic joint attention, but what you say is anchored stylistically in that scene. Here is the second exercise: present in speech to someone actually with you something directly perceptible that you have in fact noticed before, without marking stylistically that you knew it before.

EXERCISE 3: *Fresh Inferences*

The third exercise asks you to move on to inferences. You are making an inference, for example, when you think that someone "looks disappointed." The fact that the "disappointment" is an inference rather than something perceptible often goes unnoticed. We have to remind ourselves that a common phrase such as "You could see disappointment all over his face" is not literally true. The paradox is that throughout your life you have unconsciously treated some of these invisible inferences as things that can be perceived—but now, we are asking you to be aware that you are doing it, so that you can improve your command of style.

Here is the third exercise: present in speech to someone actually with you something directly perceptible and, in addition this time, present a related inference, but not one marked by any stylistic change in the presentation. Treat the inference the way you treat the perception. Here is an example: "That egret standing so still in the estuary is fishing." You can see the egret, the estuary, the standing, the stillness, but you cannot see the fishing. The style blends perception with inference.

EXERCISE 4: *Previous Inferences*

Here is the fourth exercise: combine exercises 2 and 3. Study a scene and think it through until you have made an inference connected to what is directly perceptible. Then, when you are joined by your companion, make your presentation without marking stylistically the difference between perception and inference, the sequence connecting perception to inference, or the archival nature of your inference. Here is an example: suppose you have deduced at some point that a restaurant dining room with an ocean view down the street from where you live must once have been an outdoor patio, now enclosed. You say to your dining companion, "We are lucky to be here with an ocean storm setting in. Those electrical outlets in the wall have covers because this room used to be outside."

EXERCISE 5: *Focusing on a Person*

The fifth exercise is the same as the fourth but focuses on a person. Among things that cannot be directly perceived—interest, disappointment, hope—many of them cannot even be inferred at a glance. They are discoveries that take time. They depend upon a series of refinements that eventually leads to an inference. But, as we said in laying out the principles of classic style, the style "does not acknowledge process or stages of discovery, does not acknowledge revision or successive refinements." Since the style does not acknowledge process, what might, in fact, be the result of observation stretching over a long period, with many stages and many revisions, is presented in the same style as something that can be observed at once, like a blackbird.

How long did La Rochefoucauld know Madame de Chevreuse before he could say she "had sparkling intelligence, ambition, and beauty in plenty; she was flirtatious, lively, bold, enterprising; she used all her charms to push her projects to success, and she almost always brought disaster to those she encountered on her way"? He could not have known this the first time he met her, but the style does nothing to draw attention to the steps by which he came to know her.

Everyone notices, after a while, features of temperament, personality, and character that are not directly perceptible. They often remain unspoken observations. Here is the fifth exercise: you and a companion are both looking at someone. Present the person. Include something you have come to notice only gradually. Your subject might be the bartender, the postal clerk, your Chinese teacher, the manager of the bicycle repair shop, or, if you are doing this in the classroom, someone you see in or from the room. Include inferences. Do not let your observation be displaced by whatever experience led to it, and do not mark the inferences stylistically as different from the perceptions.

TUTORIAL: *Two Steps to Classic Style*

You have now worked on the indispensable first exercise and four other exercises that go beyond the fundamental scene of classic joint attention. In exercises 2 to 5, you used the classic scene to structure scenes that did not fit it for one reason or another—the subject of presentation was not directly perceptible, or the recognition was not spontaneous.

This pattern—inhabit the classic scene, and then use it to manage networks that go beyond it—is the essential lesson of the Studio because these two steps are the whole art of classic style:

Step 1: Learn to inhabit the scene of classic joint attention consciously. In this first step we learn to do something consciously and consistently that we already do unconsciously and inconsistently.

Step 2: Learn how to blend the classic scene with any mental network supporting expression, so that the blend provides a familiar, consistent, manageable anchor for that network. You probably are not used to thinking of classic joint attention as a general "scene"; you probably do not consistently distinguish between what is directly perceptible, such as a blackbird, and what is not, such as a sense of the absurd. So when you are asking a companion to "notice" somebody's sense of the absurd, especially when that somebody is not actually present, you should be aware that you are not in a scene of classic joint attention at all. In the previous exercises, you already moved from step 1 to step 2. For example, when you presented an inference, you were inviting your companion to recognize your conclusion as if it were directly perceptible. This is an exemplary case of borrowing classic joint attention to structure the presentation of what cannot be directly perceived.

Often in writing, you will feel that things are getting away from you. You are not mistaken. Things are in fact getting away from you. Notice that you never feel that things are getting away from you when you are pointing out something directly perceptible to somebody next to you. You are at home in this case because the classic scene is intelligible by itself. In classic style, all other scenes become intelligible and manageable because they are structured by the classic scene. Step 2 consists of practicing how to structure everything beyond the classic scene using it as a stylistic template. When you feel that things are getting away from you, do the first exercise, and then go back to blending networks of ideas to the classic scene. These two steps will get you through any problem in classic style.

Classic style depends absolutely on domesticating realities whose borders are necessarily vague: jealousy, resentment, regret. They are never directly perceptible and can be managed in thought and language only if we treat them as what we know they are not. When we talk about "putting aside our resentment," no one is fooled into thinking that we can move our resentment out of the way as if it were a bicycle in the driveway, but if we try to handle the metaphysical character of resentment without anchoring it in something perceptible, we will be unable either to grasp the thought or to match it to language. Turning resentment into a physical object is a cognitive compression. Cognitive compression happens routinely in blending and can turn unwieldy conceptual ranges into manageable scenes. An entire mental network supporting expression can be blended mentally with the classic scene, to create a stylistic anchor for the expression. The network might involve any amount of complexity. Here is an example: In *Life on the Mississippi*, Mark Twain is writing for an unseen and indefinite audience about his boyhood experience growing up on the Mississippi before the Civil War. Classic style treats the invisible, indefinite audience as a person, treats the writing as speech, and treats "boyhood experience" in this time and place that no longer exist as if it were something directly perceptible, a thing with a definite shape, a definite texture, definite borders. This is a virtuoso, and classic, cognitive compression.

You are already a master at using simple scenes to domesticate conceptual ranges that cannot—in their undomesticated state—be held in mind. When you do that, you produce simpler, structured versions of those conceptual ranges. Language is the instrument par excellence for guiding us to that kind of structuring. In our experience, blackbirds are quite different from aspirations, but grammatically, "blackbirds" and "aspirations" belong to the same category. Nouns like *confidence, religion, nation, aspiration*, and *money* already prompt us to structure complicated concepts as things. In the structured version, they are all things that you can recognize. Single words prompt for simple structuring. So do larger grammatical constructions. Consider "Acid destroys metal," "Acid eats metal," or "Acid etches metal." These sentences prompt us to conceive of the acid as an agent and the metal as a patient. In fact, as we all know, there is a chemical reaction between the acid and the metal, and the metal is as much a cause of this chemical reaction as the acid. The grammar prompts us to seize upon a simpler version of a complex thought; the structured version depends upon a universally accessible scene, a causal scene in which an agent acts on something passive, like a sculptor working on marble.

Blending, compression, and anchoring are the heart and soul of vocabulary and grammar. In the Studio, you are extending your abilities for blending, compression, and anchoring beyond simple vocabulary and grammar to communication, especially writing. You are learning to blend a complex mental network supporting expression with a simple scene of classic joint attention. That classic scene offers a clear and direct way of communicating about a clear and direct subject of presentation. These exercises are all moves toward learning how to blend any such network involving anything and anyone with that classic scene.

EXERCISE 6: *Surfing*

This exercise has five parts. In all of them, keep these features from the classic scene:

- You are with a companion. You speak and gesture.
- You point out something to your companion that is directly perceptible.

In addition, keep a feature you practiced in exercise 2:

- Whether or not your recognition is spontaneous, present it in the same way in which classic style presents a spontaneous recognition.

But now, you are dealing with scenes that go beyond the scene of exercise 1.

In the five parts of this exercise, we use colloquial terms to mark different sources of knowledge: notably, *direct perception, inference, judgment, prediction, cultural knowledge,* and *belief.* Scientifically and philosophically, it is impossible to draw a line between perceptual knowledge and knowledge that comes from other sources, but for what follows, assume the commonplace distinction between every pair of such sources of knowledge. The goal of exercise 6 is not to create a consistent classification of sources of knowledge, but to acquire a smooth facility in moving back and forth across all such sources with no variation in the style and without marking the move from one to another.

In all five parts of this exercise, try using a single list of subjects. We provide one that has been road-tested:

1. a natural nonliving object
2. a manufactured nonliving object

3. a plant
4. an animal
5. a landscape
6. food
7. a work of art
8. a person
9. an interaction between two people
10. a public space

In the five parts of this exercise,

1. surf across perceptions and inferences
2. surf across perceptions and judgments
3. surf across perceptions and predictions
4. surf across perceptions and cultural knowledge
5. surf across perceptions, inferences, judgments, predictions, and cultural knowledge

The style never varies.

PART 1: *Inferences*

For each item on your list, present something that is directly perceptible joined with some associated inferential knowledge. In our own examples, because the style elides the distinction, we have used italics to indicate the features that cannot literally be perceived. We have provided analyses for the first three examples, because a smooth elision can go unnoticed although it becomes quite obvious with practice.

1. A natural nonliving object: The banded rocks are *formed by sedimentation.*

   You can see the rocks; you can see that they are banded; but you cannot see the millions of years of geological sedimentation that produced the rocks and their bands. The sedimentation is no longer happening. Although the distinction here is neither nuanced nor subtle, the style elides the distinction. It is as if the sedimentation were as perceptible as the rocks.

2. A manufactured nonliving object: *Any owner who recognized* that sound *would have the slipping fan belt* in that roadster *fixed.*

   You can hear the sound and see the roadster. It is an inference that the sound comes from a slipping fan belt. It is an inference that the owner does not recognize the sound because otherwise he would have had it fixed.

3. A plant: Our *struggling* lemon tree *needs less water and a little fertilizer.*

   It might take an expert to infer from the lemon tree's appearance that it is struggling, and certainly that what it needs is less water and a little fertilizer. But these inferences are presented in the same way the directly perceptible lemon tree is presented.

4. An animal: The cliff squirrels, *starved by the drought,* have extended their range *looking for food.*

5. A landscape: The sand berms *have been bulldozed up to stop* the winter waves *from eroding* the sandstone cliffs.

6. Food: The harder *goat* cheese *has been aged longer. Moisture leaves the cheese over time.*

7. A work of art: The helmeted woman leaning on her spear in this stele *is Athena, the warrior goddess, protector of Athens.*

8. A person: She has the strong wrists and forearms *of a pole vaulter or a gymnast.*

9. An interaction between two people: The host and the chef are *joking* with each other *with the familiarity that comes of being married for thirty years.*

10. A public space: There is only one person running the flower shop. Business has *returned to winter levels.*

PART 2: *Judgments*

For each item on your list, present something that is directly perceptible joined with an associated judgment.

1. A natural nonliving object: A big wave gets thinner as it
   walls up. Just before it breaks, the sunlight comes through
   for a moment, turning it an *exhilarating* green.
2. A manufactured non-living object: The reflective green of
   the surfboard *clashes* with the translucent green of the wave.
3. A plant: Monterey Pines *do not look so beautiful* toppled
   over by the storm.
4. An animal: The *adorably playful* sea otters in the bay are
   actually banging abalone open to eat them.
5. A landscape: A small port town on an island in the
   Cyclades, with its deep blue water, white-walled buildings,
   and *pure* sunlight, *is the place* to send someone if you want
   to learn whether he is *crazy or merely disturbed. Anyone
   who can stay disturbed there really does have a problem.*
6. Food: The *marvelous* beef tacos here at the seaside burrito
   shack are taken for granted by the locals.
7. A work of art: To spend an hour walking through Victor
   Horta's house in Saint-Gilles is to understand *the attraction* of art nouveau architecture.
8. A person: He keeps missing the waves. *His combination of
   athleticism, ambition, and indecision is lethal.*
9. An interaction between two people: It's not his *good* looks
   that make her nervous. It's that she knows he would like
   her to find him *good-looking.*
10. A public space: The visitors to the row of antique shops do
    not see *the fraud* because they have made a commitment
    to a certain kind of experience. *They are on holiday and
    want a good time.*

PART 3: *Predictions*

For each item on your list, present something that is directly perceptible joined with an associated prediction.

1. A natural nonliving object: The west-northwest swell *following this storm by a few days will have traveled thousands*

of miles. A swell like that loses much less of its energy than might be imagined as it travels long distances through weather.

2. A manufactured nonliving object: These houses are *future beach sculpture, once the sandstone cliffs give way.*

3. A plant: These pears *will be ready* to harvest *in a month.*

4. An animal: The mark of great racehorses is desire. Even in losing performances, they *never just give up.*

5. A landscape: When you are looking at the Swiss country-side through a train window, *the occasional buildings look offensive.*

6. Food: The price of the dinner includes *the sense of well-being that lingers through the evening.*

7. A work of art: The curator for Early Netherlandish paintings is depressed in anticipation of the *inevitable damage* to the fragile panels scheduled to be lent to an exhibit in New York.

8. A person: Her otherwise serene and beautiful mother is helpless trying to postpone her daughter's *imminent* descent into the long, dark tunnel of adolescence, in which bitterness, resentment, and sullen ingratitude are the power chords of emotional life.

9. An interaction between two people: His effervescence will evaporate *after the initial impression wears off.*

10. A public space: Improving the neighborhood *will destroy* its historic charm.

PART 4: *Cultural Knowledge*

For each item on your list, present something that is directly per-ceptible joined with an associated aspect depending on cultural knowledge.

1. A natural nonliving object: No political or financial scheme has blurred *the sharp division of rich and poor Chicago at the river.*

2. A manufactured nonliving object: Despite *indicating episcopal dignity*, a mitre makes all but the most regal bishops look ridiculous.

3. A plant: Tea is the wine of China. It even has some of wine's *sacramental character*.

4. An animal: Horses are no longer an instrument of war, but they have not been displaced as *a symbol of power*.

5. A landscape: *The English addiction to the hills of Tuscany as the earthly paradise* has always been a puzzle to the Italians.

6. Food: Both traditional French cooking before it and current techno-cuisine after it reject *the principle of nouvelle cuisine that great cooking should never mask natural savors*.

7. A work of art: James Ensor, *the only artist of the late nineteenth century who did great original religious painting*, and whose *Entrance of Christ into Brussels in 1889* was acquired by the Getty Museum in Brentwood to serve as the culmination of its collection, is famous instead for his grotesques.

8. A person: Tony went to *Flanders to study medieval architecture*, but ended up spending most of his time *surfing in Ostende*.

9. An interaction between two people: She was promoted because, as a server, she was the best presence the dining room had ever deployed, despite her tenuous grasp on the otherwise *adamantine principle that servers must not flirt with diners* because it distracts from the food.

10. A public space: Despite *the great reputation* of the experience, seeing the Piazzetta di San Marco as you arrive by boat is never a disappointment.

PART 5: *Safari*

For each item on your list, present something that is directly perceptible joined with any combination of associated inferences, judgments, predictions, cultural knowledge, beliefs, or any other such commonplace category.

EXERCISE 7: *Classic Style without Borders*

PART 1: *A New List*

We offer another road-tested list, below. Here is the exercise: For each of the items on the list, present something that is directly perceptible, along with associated inferences, judgments, predictions, cultural knowledge, beliefs, and anything else that is not directly perceptible.

1. an article of casual clothing
2. an architectural feature
3. a piece of furniture
4. a uniform
5. a passage of music
6. a physical sensation
7. a taste
8. an electronic device
9. a piece of luggage
10. an actor engaged in a performance

PART 2: *Another New List—Your Choice*

When you have finished your exercises with this second list, move on to invent your own list of ten categories. You will find possibilities everywhere. Consider a photograph of someone's face. When you see one, it is almost impossible to resist forming a quick sense of the character of the subject. Of course, all you can see is the photograph. But a classic presentation of the photograph can include inferences, judgments, predictions, cultural knowledge, in fact recognition of any sort. Raymond Chandler's Marlowe, the detective in *The Big Sleep*, is shown a photograph of a man he is looking for: "He pushed a shiny print across the desk and I looked at an Irish face that was more sad than merry and more reserved than brash. Not the face of a tough guy and not the face of a man who could be pushed around much by anybody. . . . A face that looked a little taut, the face of a man who would move fast and play for keeps." Here is the exercise: Invent your own list of ten categories, and then, for each item, do what you did in exercise 6. Enjoy the waves.

EXERCISE 8: *Describing Is Not Presenting*

Exercises 6 and 7 focused on blending any subject with a directly perceptible object. Now we turn to blending any purpose with presentation. The nature of presentation is fully discussed in the Essay and exemplified in the Museum. Recall that in presentation, writers take responsibility for everything. The reason writers speak in classic style is to present something they judge to be worthy of presentation. In particular, in classic style, writers are not following orders or a template.

In this exercise, we refine our concept of presentation by contrasting it with a different purpose, one with which it is often confused—description. Although the term "description" is elastic, it is quite different from what we mean by "presentation." Description, as we use the term, is a performance in which the speaker is a delivery device. In some cases, the speaker performs a monitoring service, giving a running account of the salient features of a subject, the way an announcer might for a sporting event. In others, the speaker fills in a pre-existing template. In all cases, the speaker follows a protocol that comes from someone else. A description is inadequate if it leaves out part of this protocol. Presentation, by contrast, is something for which an individual is entirely responsible—responsible for what is included and for what goes unmentioned. A presentation may have uses, but its goal, stylistically, is not utilitarian. If you describe a painting, for example, the painting's dimensions are essential, as is its support (panel or canvas). This is the sort of information you expect to find in a descriptive catalogue. In a presentation, these features could conceivably be included, but they needn't be.

When Julien Green offers a presentation of the Ghent Altarpiece, he deals with just one of that polytych's panels. If your knowledge of the altarpiece were limited to the details that Green chooses to present, you would have no idea that it consists of a dozen sections when open and nine others when closed. You would have no idea that it is an oak panel with wings and that the wings are painted on both sides. If Green's presentation were meant to be a description, it would be completely inadequate, but he is not working for the editor of a catalogue; he is offering what he finds worth presenting. What Green says in his presentation is informed by his distinctive imagination and intelligence. What he presents can be seen once he has presented it, but it is not necessarily what someone else in his place would find worth presenting. If a professional art historian or curator were offering a description of the painting, it would be identical to what any other competent professional would offer as a description. You would be able to recognize the painting from the description just the way you would be able to recognize a book from a description in a rare book dealer's catalogue.

It is not yet time to start writing, but in this exercise, while as always retaining the scene of classic joint attention as the anchor of the network, give up actually being next to your listener. Here is the exercise: Call someone on the telephone, or through some kind of voice chat, and in the course of the conversation describe something you can see. Then call someone and in the course of the conversation present the same thing. The two activities should feel very different.

This exercise is intended to draw a distinction between presentation and description. You can repeat the exercise—first description, then presentation, until you command the difference—by choosing different items on the lists used in previous exercises. You might first choose a concrete, definite, visible object, like a chair. Then advance along a scale: a tree, a bird, a dress, the way a particular animal moves, the way a particular person talks, a local environment—such as Mount Vernon Square in Baltimore—, a city, someone's character, a legal concept such as perjury.

EXERCISE 9: *Conversations*

Here is the exercise: When you are with a companion, recall a conversation you had with her in the past. Present it in classic style. Notice that it is normal to treat this previous conversation as something present, something that you and your companion can jointly see, even though each of you is dealing with a separate memory, a separate mental representation, which can be and probably is quite different for each of you. The basis of classic style is that any scene of communication can be blended with the classic scene to bring it to intelligible and congenial human scale. You are familiar with this sort of blending, and often do it without thinking about it, as in the case of recalling and presenting the conversation. What this exercise asks you to do is something you have been doing practically all of your life. It is a simple step from presenting a perception ("The blackbird on the tree limb has red markings on its wings") to the presentation of a memory ("Your response to my suggestion two days ago that we go away for the weekend was unexpected"). You can see both the blackbird and the red markings, but both the response and its unexpected nature, although they can be presented in the same style as the blackbird and its markings, are unavailable to perception. Consistent classic style requires recognizing that these features lie beyond the classic scene, yet domesticating them by anchoring them in that scene.

EXERCISE 10: *Stealth Argument*

Classic style characteristically avoids explicit argument and never seems to press for agreement since it is structured by a scene where neither argument nor urgency has a place. Your project is to accomplish the goals of argument by what is ostensibly simply presentation. If you ask a companion to notice an owl whose coloring makes it difficult to distinguish the owl from the tree and the foliage where it is perched, you don't have to persuade your companion that the owl is actually there; she can see it for herself as soon as she knows where to look. When classic stylists are interested in persuasion, they engage in a kind of stealth argument that is conducted as if it is simply presentation. In the Museum, we analyzed argument-as-presentation in Descartes, in Mark Twain's discussion of the experience of war, in Liebling's dismissal of the BBC's account of the Normandy Invasion, and in the Smithsonian presentation of the dragoon tie, where commercial motives are disguised as art historical presentation. Andrew Hodges on Alan Turing, Junichirō Tanizaki on Terukatsu, Jane Austen on Mr. Collins, and La Rochefoucauld on Madame de Chevreuse all engage in argument as presentation. Here is the exercise: Review these passages and then offer a similar stealth argument of your own.

EXERCISE 11: *Arrivals and Departures*

Many situations impose a style—contractually or by convention. An official conducting a marriage must do so according to a protocol, and fulfill that protocol. These situations arise in life as soon as one represents a group. A child selling cookies may say, "Hello, we belong to Girl Scout Troop 27, and we are selling cookies to raise money for a field trip to the Getty Museum where we will earn our visual arts badges." This is extremely unclassic, and all the participants in the conversation probably know that the Girl Scout has been taught to say exactly this. But when the Girl Scout is asked about the differences in the kinds of cookies, she may switch into classic style. After her classic presentation, she may switch back into the scripted sales conversation in order to complete the transaction, thank the customer, and otherwise create goodwill. Switching into and out of the classic scene serves a great range of situations, from selling Girl Scout cookies to presenting a case before the Supreme Court. Such situations often come with a scripted protocol. The moments that serve the protocol are highly unclassic because they are formal and because they are imposed. Yet the speaker or writer can switch into and out of classic style and keep the protocol to a minimum. The result can be a piece that has all the required parts but still feels classic most of the time.

In official style, the speaker is the agent of a system. A passport controller at the Brussels airport, for example, after asking the required questions about your travel plans, may drop straight into classic style. "What is the purpose of your trip?" "Cultural. I want to see the James Ensor paintings in Antwerp." "You won't be disappointed. Ensor lived in Ostende, but his best paintings are in Antwerp."

Suppose two people are interviewing you for a job. This is an encounter so complex, unfamiliar, and difficult to navigate that many people find it paralyzing. The actual cast and purpose are far from classic. The scene can induce terrible anxiety; efforts to control it are often immediately apparent to the interviewers. But the job interview can be done in classic style. It just happens that what you are presenting is yourself, but in the way you would present the blackbird. You are pointing out what you expect the interviewers to recognize once you show them where to look. When asked, "So, what did you do in college?" you answer, "I divided my time between molecular genetics and surfing." The exercise is to carry out a job interview in classic style. The reader of the Studio might not have the opportunity to do this assignment in the field. But it can be done in imagination, or with a friend, as a mock interview. Similarly, a letter of application for a job falls into a protocol. If it does nothing more than follow that protocol, it will be impossible to distinguish it from a hundred others. There is a real advantage in being able to include a passage in classic style even in this most unclassic situation. The situation need not—and usually should not—dictate the style.

Here is the exercise: Begin in a nonclassic style—official style or practical style, for example—and then switch out of it into classic style.

EXERCISE 12: *Talking to Strangers*

We began with the scene of classic joint attention, which has a cast of two. This scene and its cast anchor classic style, although in most forms of writing and in many forms of broadcast speech the audience could consist of any number of people, known or not, visible or not. Any audience is treated as if it were a single individual. Consider Alec Guinness's speech accepting an honorary Academy Award, in which he wittily presents the defining moment of his formation as a film actor. (You can find it on YouTube.) Although his speech sounds informal, there are many reasons to think it has been carefully prepared: there are no false starts or awkward sentences, grammatical mistakes, syntactic bobbles, or hesitations. Contrast this to Dustin Hoffman's introduction. Sir Alec's intonation, cadence, and pace are perceptible; their preparation and his forethought are neither perceptible nor, at first, even evident. He sounds natural and spontaneous. Although he probably wrote his speech and memorized it, it sounds like conversation. He is talking to a group, but it sounds as if he is talking to one person—you. Of course, he doesn't call you by name, but the model for the interaction is one person addressing a companion.

Now, do the same thing. Here is the exercise: Make a presentation to a group of people, but anchor it in the classic scene, treating the group, stylistically, as an individual.

■ Fundamentals: Write Second

If you have completed the common exercises in speech, you are probably ready to do them in writing. If you are wondering why there has been such a lengthy oral preliminary to the acquisition of a style of writing, our answer can be found in the opening paragraphs of this book. Writing is an intellectual activity. To achieve good prose styles, writers must work through intellectual issues, not merely acquire mechanical techniques. The heart of classic style is the root scene of classic joint attention. The actual scene of writing is blended with the classic scene so that writing is treated as speech. No matter how many people are addressed, no matter how indeterminate this "audience" is, no matter where they are, the style treats them as if they were a single person to whom the writer is speaking. Inferences, judgments, predictions, and cultural knowledge are treated as "things" that can be directly perceived. Neither the concept of classic joint attention nor an ability to blend an actual scene with the classic scene can be acquired simply by writing and then doing some local revision. Blending complex networks to the classic scene defines classic style, and while it is possible to acquire this ability through imitation of classic models, it is a chancy and inefficient path. In the Studio, we are offering a tested and secure path. If you work out the intellectual issues first, the activity of writing will be defined by a concept of style. You can then proceed with confidence.

You have already practiced the common exercises in speech. Now is the moment to observe that what works in speech cannot be directly transfered to writing. Go through the common exercises anew, this time in writing. We are not asking you to transcribe what you have already said, offering it in written form. Approach the exercises now with the resources of writing; do not cling to the resources of speech. Anchoring writing in speech is not pretending that writing is speech. Anchoring a mental network supporting expression in the classic scene is not pretending that you are in an actual classic scene; it is more subtle. It may sound paradoxical to say both that having done the speech exercises will help you to master a style of writing and that writing is a very different activity from speech because it lacks the resources of speech. But both are true and for a crucial reason: classic prose style blends speech with writing. A classic prose stylist must be able to supply by imaginative blending the structure of classic joint attention that the actual environment of writing lacks.

In what follows, we will add some comments on doing these common exercises in writing.

TUTORIAL: *Blending Scenes*

Writing is not a scene of classic joint attention, but in classic style the writer will use the classic scene as an anchor so that, in the blend, writing becomes speaking, the indefinite audience that is not present becomes a single person who is right there, and the subject becomes something that can be perceived. If writing is not a scene of classic joint attention, neither is reading—and writing, especially in classic style, assumes a reader, so it is part of the writer's task to induce the reader to anchor her activity in the classic scene as well.

Neither writer nor reader is deluded. They both know they do not share an environment they can refer to directly, but the writer anchors the actual scene to the classic scene in order to provide a consistent style.

TUTORIAL: *Lost in Words*

In writing, you lose the effects of the charm you may have in person. You lose the effects of gesture, proximity, warmth, intonation. In person, you can command and hold attention by being attractive, but all of that is gone in writing. All you have is the appeal of the presentation—the attraction of thought and of language. A speaker of some personal charm can give a pastiche of clichés the illusion of meaning, but in writing, a pastiche of clichés will always look like a pastiche of clichés. Presence is crucial to the classic scene. But in classic writing, there is no speaker, no shared environment, no interaction between speaker and listener. Presence must be supplied by the writing itself. Bernard Shaw, a dramatist who wrote his plays to be read, was especially sensitive to this distinction. He once remarked that there are fifty ways of saying the word "yes," and five hundred ways of saying the word "no," but just one way of writing them down.

TUTORIAL: *Onset and Dismount*

A written text has a beginning and an end—a first sentence and a last. Sections of writing have beginnings and ends too. Typically, speaking is not so discrete. When you drop into classic style in speaking, there may have been quite a bit of speech before it—greetings, small talk, and obligatory ceremonial questions and answers—and always after it the dribbling little bits of farewell, which the Viennese used to call "Goodbye without leaving." Your first words are unlikely to be taken as the start of a coherent presentation. In classic prose, it is automatic. The first sentence is the onset. The last sentence, at least of the section, is the dismount. Crisp onset and dismount carry a premium in classic writing beyond their value in classic speech.

■ Advanced Writing

Every classic stylist encounters novel situations. We explained in the Essay how some occasions call for a sequence of styles, or a blend of styles, or the development of a special style based on a general style. A style, after all, is defined by a coherent and consistent stand on the elements of style, expressed as a short series of questions about truth, presentation, writer, reader, thought, language, and their relationships. These questions are addressed to fundamental issues that must be answered deliberately or by default before we can write at all. Style is an intellectual matter of thinking through these questions in any situation. Someone who has worked through the curriculum of the Studio is equipped to recognize and work on new projects without further coaching by thinking through the elements of style and drawing on techniques learned in the Studio. In what follows, we suggest a few encounters with novelty.

EXERCISE 13: *Sketchbook*

Most of the writing instruction in the United States focuses on revision. This approach is fatal for the student attempting to master classic style. The essential ability of the classic stylist is to inhabit the style and to work within it. It is almost always a mistake to try to drag a piece of writing that was unclassic at its inception over rocks and through vegetation in a misconceived attempt to move it somehow to classic heights. Inhabiting the style means imaginatively blending the classic scene with the mental network supporting expression. The blend anchors the network and provides the stylistic structure. It is the platform from which the classic stylist works from beginning to end. The classic stylist learns to speak directly from inside that blend, even if the initial performances are weak. A piece conceived and written from within classic style can be improved, but no draft written without a settled style can be revised into classic style. The conventional advice to think of "style" as a final touch leads to disaster because style is not a surface decoration that can be added during revision. Style must be considered at the outset. Forget entirely the idea that "working on your writing" begins after you have something down on paper.

Consider that students in an art studio are often asked to take their sketchbook out into the field to do speed sketching. They see something and sketch it rapidly, never erasing but instead flipping quickly to a blank page to sketch something else. Later, they review their sketches, but they do not revise. In this Studio, the sketchbook exercise asks you to do in writing what the art student does in speed sketching. Here is the exercise: Recognize something in the field; step into classic style; present your recognition. Do not revise. Continue until you have ten prose sketches. As you begin to advance in your sketchbook exercises, you might move up, as you did in the common exercises, to subjects that are less and less directly perceptible, always blending them stylistically with what is directly perceptible. Once you have finished your ten speed sketches in classic style, put the work of your session aside. Review it later, but do not revise it. Tomorrow, do the sketchbook exercise again. A daily dose of the sketchbook exercise for a couple of weeks seems to have the power to move students rapidly. At first, they find this extremely difficult and seem to make no progress, but after a few days the style starts to come naturally. Some students get past their previous conditioning only after a couple of weeks of the sketchbook exercise has purged them of bad habits.

EXERCISE 14: *Coherent Mixed Styles*

It may seem paradoxical in a Studio devoted to classic style to include the study of styles that are only partially classic. But classic virtues can come from even a few classic ingredients, and the opportunity to deploy such mixed styles arises frequently. Instruction manuals have a practical motive, but they do not have to be impersonal; the cast can be collusive; the thought and language can be distinctive. The voice does not have to be one job description speaking to another. We can instead match a practical motive with a classic presentation, to produce a mixed style that might be called classic practical style, a style whose attraction and power do not depend exclusively on accomplishing a practical goal. Imagine reading a cookbook even if you have no intention of cooking. A cookbook in classic practical style might be attractive purely for the virtues of its classic presentation. There are many styles that can be mixed with classic ingredients to create an unmistakably classic flavor.

Here is the exercise: Pick a subject you understand well and write a "how-to" piece. The subject can be anything: how to identify a tree from its leaves, how to avoid probate, how to give a dinner party. The piece will be practical, of course, but experiment with the inclusion of classic ingredients. These classic ingredients might include a classic voice, a collusive cast, a full command of language, a crisp onset and dismount, truth as a complementary motive, presentation as a complementary purpose.

EXERCISE 15: *Lists*

Can a list be written in classic style? Of course. The material does not determine the style. The writer of a list could accept the stand of slavish adherence to a template, like a notary providing an inventory. But the writer can take the classic stand—someone recognizes something worth presenting to someone else. The writer can assume full responsibility for the selection.

A menu is a list, but if it is written in classic style, it can present the character and tradition of a restaurant and the nature of a cuisine. There is an owner, chef, or dining room manager standing behind the presentation. In classic style, neither the menu nor the wine list is a helter-skelter list of what happens to be available to eat and drink. A wine list can present the knowledge, culture, and taste of the sommelier. In the previous exercise, you practiced writing something in classic style that had an additional practical purpose. Menus and wine lists can similarly be written in classic style even though their ostensible purpose is practical. For someone interested in food and wine, a classic menu or wine list can be read for pleasure, even if the restaurant is a continent away or has been closed for years.

Menus and wine lists are only one example of lists that can take the classic stand and can accordingly be read and enjoyed independent of any practical goal. Georges Perec, in *La vie mode d'emploi* (*Life A User's Manual*), presents lists of the contents of basement storage lockers of an imaginary apartment building. Each is a masterful presentation in an individual voice not just of the items but also of the owner's habits, history, and character, and their cultural resonance. Here are two:

Bartlebooth's cellar:
In Bartlebooth's cellar there is some left-over coal on top of which still lies a black enamelled metal scuttle with a wooden grip fitted on its wire handle, a bicycle hanging on a butcher's hook, now unoccupied bottle racks, and his four travelling chests, four curved chests covered in tarred canvas, braced with wooden slats, with brass corners and hasps, and lined throughout with a sheet of zinc to ensure waterproofing.

The Rorschachs' cellar:
A bottle rack, wire, plastic-coated, is placed to the left of the slatted door. The lower level of the rack holds five bottles of fruit brandies: kirsch, apricot, quetsch, plum, raspberry. On one of the middle rows there is the score—in Russian—of Rimsky-Korsakov's version of Pushkin's *Golden Cockerel*, and a probably popular novel entitled *Spice, or the Revenge of the Louvain Locksmith*, with a cover depicting a girl handing a bag of gold to a judge. On the top row, a lidless octagonal tin containing a few novelty chessmen made of plastic, crudely imitating Chinese ivory pieces: the knight is a kind of Dragon, the king a seated Buddha.

Ernest Hemingway is said to have written a six-word short story—"For sale. Baby shoes. Never worn."—that provides the inspiration for this exercise. Here is the exercise: Locate some suitable publication that carries classified advertisements, and write for that publication a list offering items for sale. Take the classic stand.

EXERCISE 16: *Résumé*

A résumé is a list presenting a person. Its writer can take the classic stand. Often, résumés are completely unclassic, signaling—through their formatting and phrasing—anxiety and desire. Résumés often appear simultaneously pushy and defensive, with ungenerous margins, scarce white space, compressed fonts, hyperbolic and aggressive vocabulary ("High-powered self-starter seeks management position with superpotential for advancement"), and the listing of every conceivable fact that might sway a reader ("Second-place, all-class essay competition, 7th grade, East Nowhere Middle School"). Academic résumés often expose self-inflicted wounds under "Publications" ("Genetics of the ALDH2 locus. *Science*, submitted"). Anyone established in the academy knows that anybody can submit anything anywhere; a submission is not a publication. A classic résumé, by contrast, is one whose writer, stylistically, is self-possessed, unconcerned, merely presenting. Stylistically, the writer has no anxiety. The writer does not want anything from the reader. The motive is truth—not desire for a job—and there is symmetry between writer and reader. A classic résumé typically has pleasing margins, ample white space, and a classic font. Its phrasing is calm. It is often distinctive for the range of lower-level detritus it leaves out. The style is not affected at all by insecurity, fear of unemployment, or sense of urgency, regardless of what is in the writer's mental network.

Here is the exercise: Write a résumé strongly influenced by classic style for a historical person: Anne Boleyn before her marriage, Einstein when he worked in the Swiss patent office, Hannibal before he invaded Europe, Grace Kelly before she made her first movie, Vermeer applying to the painters' guild.

EXERCISE 17: *Admissions Essay*

The essay, or statement, that an applicant submits for admission to a program belongs to a real scene that, like the résumé and the job interview, is unclassic in cast and purpose. But the applicant can write the essay entirely in classic style and may by doing so distinguish the application from a mountain of predictable rival submissions. Here is the exercise: Imagine such a case and write an admissions essay in which you, someone you know, or a historical or fictional person is the candidate.

EXERCISE 18: *Science*

Classic style is often the ideal style for scientific writing. Here is the exercise: Write a scientific piece in classic style. Point out where your reader should look and present the recognition. Stylistically, your reader is with you in a scene of classic joint attention, and pleased to be there.

Accomplished scientists often eschew stridency of any sort, since after all it is presumably the science that is the subject rather than the scientist or the scientist's chapel. Treating scientific writing as adversarial argument disguises the fact that almost all of a mature scientific piece is presentational: it presents the relevant tradition of research, and it presents the facts, events, and evidence that the reader needs.

Your own writing for this exercise will not resemble Sir Isaac Newton's prose, because he wrote in the early eighteenth century, but it may come as a surprise to see how often Newton used a style close to classic. Here is a passage from the *Opticks* (1704):

> In a very dark Chamber, at a round Hole, about one third Part of an Inch broad made in the Shut of a Window, I placed a Glass Prism, whereby the Beam of the Sun's Light, which came in at that Hole, might be refracted upwards toward the opposite Wall of the Chamber, and there form a colour'd Image of the Sun. The Axis of the Prism (that is the Line pass-

ing through the middle of the Prism from one end of it to the other end parallel to the edge of the Refracting Angle was in this and the following Experiments perpendicular to the incident Rys. About this Axis I turned the Prism slowly, and saw the refracted Light on the Wall, or coloured Image of the Sun, first to descend, and then to ascend. Between the Descent and Ascent, when the Image seemed Stationary, I stopp'd the Prism, and fix'd it in that Posture, that it should be moved no more. For in that posture the Refractions of the Light at the two Sides of the Refracting Angle, that is at the Entrance of the Rays into the Prism, and at their going out of it, were equal to one another.

EXERCISE 19: *Obituaries*

Obituaries often follow a template closely and exclude classic presentation. Such obituaries are conventional descriptions of mainly surface information—date and place of birth, education, professional accomplishment, cause of death. In these routine performances, there is often no indication that the writer is responsible for selecting details or exercising independent judgment. There are, however, exceptions. Jeremy Pearce's obituary for John L. Bull, one of the authors of *The Audubon Society Field Guide to North American Birds, Eastern Region,* from which we quote in the first entry of the Museum, appeared in *The New York Times* for 15 August 2006. He includes the obligatory descriptive information but takes the classic stance in presenting what he has judged to be worth presenting. Here is how he ends the obituary:

> Mr. Bull was often accompanied by his wife, an educator at the [American Museum of Natural History], on birding journeys. In 1989, the couple collaborated on a book, "Birds of North America: Western Region: A Quick Identification Guide for All Bird-Watchers."
>
> Remarking on the mourning doves that he spotted in Central Park, Mr. Bull observed: "They are the most mo-

nogamous birds I've ever watched. They always travel in pairs."

This is classic presentation; it follows no template. The writer, in offering an analogy between the travels of Mr. Bull and his wife, and the travels of the mourning doves that Mr. Bull observed, decides what is significant and appropriate. His perfect dismount is a classic achievement, one that belongs to a writer, not to a template. Now try writing a classic obituary of your own.

EXERCISE 20: *Real Estate Pitch*

Like obituaries, real estate prose of the sort one finds in multiple listings of properties for sale is typically entirely impersonal. It is marked by obligatory hyperbole and artificial effervescence. Here is the exercise: Study some real estate prose and then present a house as if it were for sale, offering in classic style what the reader would want to know if that reader were shopping for a house. You might want to present a property not actually for sale: the Ca' d'Oro in Venice, Jacques Cœur's *hôtel particulier* in Bourges, the Rockoxhuis in Antwerp, the Getty Villa in Malibu, the White House during the federal government's bankruptcy sale.

EXERCISE 21: *Restaurant Review*

In classic style, direct perceptions, inferences, and judgments can all be treated as recognitions and can all be presented to a companion who will share these recognitions once they are pointed out. Restaurant reviews are not merely replete with inferences and judgments; they are an outstanding example in contemporary writing of discussions of taste, subject to endless debate and qualification. In classic style, taste can be treated as if it were as perceptible as a table setting. A restaurant review in the hands of a classic stylist treats its standards of judgment as obviously appropriate and writes as if the reader would agree not merely with the evaluation of the flavors in the *ris de veau en salade* but with the standards that produce that evaluation. The style is indifferent to what those standards might be. They might devalue mere novelty or they might value novelty above all. A classic restaurant review could either criticize a formal restaurant for using exotic instead of common ingredients in a traditional dish or praise it for innovating the traditional dish by using exotic ingredients. The classic restaurant review consists, in large measure, of placing the reader in a position to perceive both the validity of the judgments and the appropriateness of the standards—as if such matters are impossible to miss once obstacles are cleared out of the way and the reader has an unobstructed view of things.

Consider:

> On a November evening in Dijon, Jean-Pierre Billoux serves wild duck, in its own juice, roasted with apples. This is the refinement of a classic by a master cook. There is no stridency or forced originality. The eight-year-old Corton Grancey seems to have been made for this perfectly roasted duck. This dish is the culmination of a tradition that has its historical roots in Guilaume Tirel's "Chapitre de Fricassure"; it reflects the accumulated wisdom of a six-hundred-year-old craft that translates nature and seasons, and their immemorial recurrence, into textures, fragrances, and flavors that allow you to feel yourself a part of them. It is rooted in a place too; it is not a cuisine suitable for "international hotels." The seasons, the fragrances, the flavors of Burgundy are not the seasons, the fragrances, the flavors of Kyoto, or London, or Las Vegas.

The superiority of a cuisine rooted in a place and in a season over a cuisine suitable for "international hotels" is not asserted but treated as if it were as obvious as the duck and its apples.

Here is the exercise: Write a classic review of a restaurant and post it to one of the many online sites carrying restaurant reviews. Focus especially on including judgments in passing, almost incidentally, as if they are not personal judgments at all but rather elements of the restaurant that any competent diner could recognize, once pointed in the right direction.

EXERCISE 22: *Travel Writing*

Travel pieces—like cookbooks, restaurant reviews, and real estate descriptions—can be utilitarian. The reader is going somewhere and looks for facts and information in order to organize a trip. But in all of these genres, the practical purpose can be subordinated or even ignored. Travel writing can be completely presentational, and when it is, it can incorporate indefinite ranges of history, judgments, and cultural commentary, treated as if they can be seen.

The Michelin Green Guides are the gold standard of commercial travel writing. Here is a passage from the entry on the Abbey of Fontenay from the Michelin Green Guide to Burgundy:

> Cistercian architecture first appeared in Burgundy in the first half of the 12C (Cistercium was the Latin name for the town of Cîteaux). It is characterized by a spirit of simplicity in keeping with the teaching of St Bernard. He objected bitterly to the luxury displayed in some monastery churches, opposing the theories of some of the great builders of the 11C and 12C with extraordinary passion. His argument against the belief of abbots such as St Hugh, Peter the Venerable, and Suger, who believed that nothing could be too rich for the glory of God was expressed for example in the letter he wrote to William, Abbot of St-Thierry, in which he asks, "Why this excessive height in the churches, this enormous length, this unnecessary width, these sumptuous ornaments and curious paintings that draw the eyes and distract attention and meditation? . . . We the monks, who have forsaken ordinary life and renounce worldly wealth and ostentation for the love of Christ, . . . in whom do we hope to awaken devotion with these ornaments?"

Fontenay, which is now a historic site and has not been a functioning church since the French Revolution of 1789, is one of the finest surviving examples of the austere beauty characteristic of Cistercian architecture, but no current visitor to Fontenay encounters Saint Bernard, his mentality, the opposition between styles of spirituality, or the architectural expression of that opposition in the uncluttered severity of Fontenay contrasted to the rich iconography of its Burgundian rival to the south, Cluny.

On reflection, it is not a surprise that the recognitions presented by the classic travel writer might lie beyond perception. As Mark Twain, launched on his career by his travel writing, observed, "[L]ife does not consist mainly—or even largely—of facts and happenings. It consists mainly of the storm of thoughts that is forever blowing through one's head." Classic style domesticates these vast conceptual networks by blending them with the classic scene. Travel writing is an exemplary genre for such capacious classic presentation.

Here is the exercise: Write a classic travel piece, a presentation of a place or places, ranging wherever thought takes you, and without foregrounding any practical purpose.

EXERCISE 23: *Prejudices: What about Peanut Butter?*

A prejudice is something that has been accepted without the benefit of considered judgment: a preference for Swiss chocolate or Chinese tea, let us say, when they have not actually been compared to any alternative: Belgian chocolate or Indian tea. Everyone has such prejudices, but they are rarely presented as such. If you loathe baroque architecture and find art nouveau architecture pleasing because you have paid close attention to the style you like and haven't paid any attention to any other style, your taste has been affected by prejudice, but that is not necessarily a bad thing—especially in classic style, because the style has a fundamental prejudice of its own for human scale, and life is too short to give an impartial and considered judgment to every variety of chocolate or every style of architecture.

Someone with a narrow taste guided by prejudice can in fact offer a thoroughly excellent presentation of what falls within this restricted taste. Someone whose taste for art nouveau architecture has become a prejudice might be just the person whose essay on Victor Horta you will find most informative and even well-judged. Paul Erdös, the subject of a biography called *The Man Who Loved Only Numbers*, referred to anyone who had stopped doing mathematics as "dead." For him, nonmathematicians were not alive. This legendary and, for Erdös, personally debilitating prejudice against anything but numbers did not mean that he was not worth listening to when he was talking about mathematics.

A presentation that covers many alternatives is not necessarily as good as a presentation—even if driven by prejudice—that focuses on just one. Here is the exercise: Present something you know and love without being defensive about it at all, without worrying about being fair or balanced. Belgian beer, baroque music, surfing in Southern California. Ignore that voice that says, "What about German beer? Gregorian chant? Alaia surfing in Australia? What about peanut butter?"

EXERCISE 24: *Tethered Excursions*

For this advanced exercise, select and present in classic style a subject as far away from the blackbird in the tree as possible, something that requires thought branching over almost every kind of conceptual geography. Our example—just one—is the concept of privacy. Privacy is something that cannot be directly perceived at all. It is a concept that stretches over all of human history, with remarkable differences across cultures in the placement of the dividing line between the private and the public. It is a highly nuanced concept that has never settled down. On the contrary, every aspect of it, from legal to moral to psychological, seems to be contested in our own time and place. It involves indefinitely many people, including unknown people. Presenting the concept of privacy is maximally uncongenial to the scene of classic joint attention. If you can blend the conceptual network for thinking and talking about privacy with the classic scene, we think you can blend anything with the classic scene, and you can consider yourself a competent classic stylist.

■ Conclusion

Every great artist was once an apprentice who learned fundamentals from someone much less talented. Velásquez was a much greater painter than his teacher. Newton was a much greater mathematician than his teacher. Neither could have progressed without a formation in fundamentals. Now that you have obtained a formation in fundamentals and experimented with a few advanced exercises, you have completed the apprenticeship offered in this Studio. But artists never really leave their studios. They continue to refine their grasp of fundamentals and extend their reach. There is no end to this refinement or extension. If there were a final exercise in the Studio, it would be to keep your eyes open for new opportunities to advance your command of style while keeping your presentations clear and simple as the truth.

FOUR

Further Readings in Classic Prose

Classic guidebooks are a natural place to begin. They form a large and universal genre in which actual scenes and casts are almost identical to the model scene and cast of classic style. They accordingly require little covert substitution by the writer, and in that respect are simple to analyze. *The Audubon Society Field Guide Series*: Subjects include Birds; Butterflies; Fishes, Whales, and Dolphins; Fossils; Insects and Spiders; Mammals; Mushrooms; The Night Sky; Reptiles and Amphibians; Rocks and Minerals; Seashells; Seashore Creatures; Trees; Weather; Wildflowers. *The Michelin Green Guide Series*: Places include all the regions of France; many European countries, including Greece and Italy; and several metropolitan regions, including Paris, Rome, London, and Washington, D.C.

Classic guidebooks include guides and descriptions of historical sites and monuments, for example, Branislav Brankovic's *Les vitraux de la cathédrale de Saint-Denis*, a pamphlet by the curator of the former abbey church, meant to be used by visitors. Works of art history from a period before documentary photography became routine have a close affinity to guidebooks and are sometimes presented as guides to past mentalities. Émile Mâle's foundation work on medieval Christian iconography, *L'art religieux au XIIIᵉ siècle en France* (1898), is a prominent example. For inaccessible art works such as illuminated manuscripts, the style is still used, as it is in Virginia Wylie Egbert's work on the reflection of everyday life in an illuminated manuscript: *On the Bridges of Mediaeval Paris: A Record of Early Fourteenth-Century Life*.

Sophisticated classic guidebooks often take the form of travel writing and the literature of places, including the political geography of the historic past and descriptions of imaginary places. Colin McEvedy, *The Penguin Atlas of Medieval History*. Jacques Hillairet, *Dictionnaire historique des rues de Paris*. Georges Perec's presentation of the street where he grew up, "Allées et venues rue de l'assomption," *L'Arc*, volume 76, and his virtuoso presentation of an imaginary Paris apartment building, *La vie mode d'emploi*. Jonathan Raban, *Arabia: In the Labyrinth*. Mark Twain, *Innocents Abroad*.

The following examples, arranged by period and topic, provide an overview of classic style.

Classic style in classical antiquity: Thucydides, *The Peloponnesian War*. Plato, *Apology*. Euclid, *The Elements of Geometry*. Euclid is often overlooked as a master of classic style, although the Euclidean proof in *The Elements* is classic in almost every sense and received a detailed analysis from Proclus in late antiquity that specifies its classic features. The typical Euclidean proof makes something evident. Its motive is truth, its purpose presentation. There is symmetry between writer and reader. Reading *The Elements* is like reading La Rochefoucauld's *Maximes:* both works imply that seeing truth requires consistent discipline, but that the discipline is possible and its results valuable. Like one of La Rochefoucauld's maxims, a Euclidean proof is complete and self-contained. Although it prepares from the beginning for its end, and builds momentum as it proceeds, its end is not predictable, however evident once seen. The labor is hidden, and there is a delightful vigor and freshness in its shape.

Classic style in the French seventeenth century: Descartes, *Discours de la méthode*. Madame de Lafayette, *La princesse de Clèves*. Pascal, *Lettres provinciales*. The Cardinal de Retz, *Mémoires*. La Rochefoucauld, *Maximes* and *Mémoires*. Madame de Sévigné, *Lettres*. La Bruyère, *Les Caractères*. See also Sainte-Beuve's classic nineteenth-century history, *Port-Royal*.

Classic style in Britain: The eighteenth century saw the development of a class of professional journalists and reviewers whose routine job was to produce something for print. These journalists sought to show the reader what they saw. Samuel Johnson is the most enduring of the first generation of such journalists. A line can be traced from his *Rambler* papers to Addison and Steele's *Spectator* to the journalism of Bernard Shaw. Neither Johnson nor Addison and Steele consistently used classic style, which is not fully formed in British journalism until Shaw.

Classic style in America: Although Thomas Jefferson did not write consistently in classic style, it is fully formed in his writings when he chooses to use it, as it is in Mark Twain, another great writer who uses classic style, among others.

Biography and autobiography: Edith Wharton, *A Backward Glance*. Mark Twain, *Life on the Mississippi*. Ralph Kirkpatrick, *Domenico Scarlatti*. Louise Brooks, *Lulu in Hollywood*.

Cultural anthropology: Clifford Geertz, *Works and Lives: The Anthropologist as Author*.

Food: Jean-François Revel, *Culture and Cuisine*. Waverley Root, *Food* and *The Food of France*. Prosper Montagné, *Larousse Gastronomique* is the classic encyclopedia on gastronomy. Its entries are small masterpieces of the genre. Under "chèvre" we find: "On consomme surtout la chèvre en Espagne, en Italie et dans le midi de la France, mais pour des raisons qui n'ont rien de gastronomique." Under "lait" we find: "Malgré son état liquide, le lait doit toujours être considéré comme un aliment et non comme une boisson, et doit être *mangé*, plutôt que *bu*, c'est-à-dire *mâché* et insalivé, ingurgité lentement; de cette façon, il se coagule dans l'estomac en petits fragments facilement attaquables par les sucs digestifs; avalé au contraire tout d'un trait, il forme dans l'estomac un caillot volumineux, indigeste, parce que les sucs digestifs le pénètrent difficilement; pour la même raison, il est plus digestible sous forme de potages ou de bouillies, parce que son mélange avec des farines favorise cette fragmentation du caillot, aussi est-il mieux toléré sous cette forme, même par les entéritiques."

Scholarship and academic writing: Frederick Crews: *The Critics Bear It Away*. This book, mainly a collection of review articles from *The New York Review of Books*, aims at making academic disputes accessible to any intelligent reader and connects those disputes to larger political ideas and temperaments. It is not polemical in the sense that Pascal's *Lettres provinciales* are, but it shares Pascal's conviction that academic questions can be made accessible to a general audience and can have broad cultural relevance. There is a basic appeal to common sense as opposed to sophistic theory: "I believe that critics, without abandoning their sense of history, should . . . [put] preconceptions in abeyance and [follow] the writer's individual path wherever it may lead." Crews rejects the replacement of writers by "what Michel Foucault belittled as 'the author function.' Once writers have been discounted as the primary shapers of their works, critics are free to 'liberate signifiers from the signified'—that is, to make a text mean anything or nothing according to whim."

For a similar analysis of academic historiography, see J. H. Hexter, *Reappraisals in History* and *Doing History*.

Science: James Watson, *The Double Helix*. Antoine Laurent Lavoisier, *Traité élémentaire de chimie*. Richard P. Feynman, *The Character of Physical Law* and *QED: The Strange Theory of Light and Matter*. Oliver Sacks, "A Neurologist's Notebook: To See and Not See," *The New Yorker*, 10 May 1993.

Sports: Queene Hooper Foster, *Boating Etiquette*; see especially "Care of the Seasick." Bill Surface, *The Track: A Day in the Life of Belmont Park*.

Technical writing: It is a universal and accurate complaint that manuals that come with machines—from computers to automobiles—and books of instruction that come with everything from tax forms to garden furniture are unintelligible. Frustration at this unintelligibility is intensified by the certain knowledge that the writer of the manual or instruction booklet actually knows what the reader wants to find out. The reasons for this infelicity are many, but one of the most prominent is that no individual passage, not even the first one, seems to be independently intelligible. In a manual or instruction booklet that succeeds, the writer is trying to fulfill the classic scene: he is trying to put the reader where the writer is standing. He already knows how the thing works, and he is trying to position the reader to know the same thing. Because the official manuals and instruction booklets are worthless, there is

an enormous market for unofficial manuals and books of instruction, the best of which adhere closely to the classic scene. A legendary example is Alan Simpson's unofficial *Mastering WordPerfect 5.1
for DOS*, which found a very large and eager audience. To understand why, check Simpson's treatment of any individual function
or procedure. Both the whole treatment and the individual sentences are almost always independently intelligible—a feature they
share with Euclid's proofs, La Rochefoucauld's maxims, and the
Audubon Field Guide's descriptions of birds.

History: John Keegan, *The Second World War* and *Six Armies in
Normandy*. Tony Judt, *Postwar: A History of Europe since 1945*.
Large historical topics have no perceptible shape and no perceptible borders, but the nature of a topic does not control the style in
which it is presented. An event such as the Second World War, the
Normandy Invasion, or the recovery of Europe from the devasta-
tion of the Second World War can be treated as a "thing" and so
presented in classic style. The writers of such classic presentations
in effect invent their subject, giving it an objective shape and definition it never had for participants. The books by Keegan and Judt
are prominent recent examples of how a very large and complex
network of events can be presented as something the reader can
perceive as if it were a cedar tree in an arboretum.

The reader may find it helpful to consider a few works on the intellectual foundations of styles. Although the view of styles as deriv-
ing from conceptual stands is now uncommon in writing manuals,
it has been the foundation of seminal analyses from Aristotle to
Claude Rawson. The indispensable sources from classical antiquity
are Longinus, *On the Sublime*, and Aristotle, *Poetics* and *Rhetoric*.
Morris Croll's essays on Renaissance topics, collected in *Style,
Rhetoric, and Rhythm*, offer an extended analysis of prose style as a
branch of intellectual history. The identical conception of style can
be found in a surprising range of analyses from the scholarly to
the mordant. Claude Rawson, in "The Character of Swift's Satire"
(in *Order from Confusion Sprung*), contrasts the styles of Swift's

and Samuel Johnson's satire as manifestations of their underlying conceptual dispositions. Rawson deals with specific differences at the level of verbal choice by uncovering the conceptual reasons for these differences: Johnson's "rectitude so open and so doggedly committed to plain palpable fact . . . cannot lightly allow itself the distorting obliquities of verbal wit. . . ." In *Life on the Mississippi*, Mark Twain identifies a particular style as the central catastrophe in American intellectual history. Beginning from the fixed verbal phrase, "the beauty and the chivalry of New Orleans," Twain traces the surface marks of what he calls "the southern style" back to their source in a complex of ideas he calls "the Sir Walter disease"—a conceptual monstrosity combining contemporary observation with an atavistic chivalric ideal derived from *Ivanhoe*. Twain demonstrates that the faults of the "the southern style" have nothing to do with verbal skills. When a Southern writer is not enchanted by Walter Scott's "sham chivalries," he is capable of "good description, compactly put." Verbal blemishes at the surface derive from systemic intellectual disease at the core. "The beauty and the chivalry" is a surface eruption of an intellectual disease whose effects are only incidentally verbal—in Twain's account, this underlying conceptual stand was also "in great measure responsible for the war."

While this list could be extended indefinitely, we would like to close with the largely overlooked career of a master in a largely undervalued form: modern American literary journalism. A. J. Liebling (1904–1963) is a major American writer, all of whose work falls into the category of reporting and journalism. His subjects include the Second World War (*Mollie and Other War Pieces, The Road Back to Paris*); American politics (*The Earl of Louisiana*); urban scenes (*The Jollity Building, The Telephone Booth Indian, Chicago: The Second City, Back Where I Came From, The Honest Rainmaker*); boxing (*The Sweet Science, A Neutral Corner*); gastronomy (*Between Meals: An Appetite for Paris*); memoir and historical retrospective (*Normandy Revisited*); and social institutions (*The Press*).

Almost all of this material originally appeared in *The New Yorker*. Liebling's reputation suffers because of a deeply entrenched prejudice against journalism as literature. His eccentric range of interests and his ability to treat the observational temperament as a "thing"—itself the subject of reporting—would not have been readily welcomed in any other American magazine published in his working lifetime. *The New Yorker* published writers in many styles—such as John Updike, Roger Angell, and E. B. White, the finest contemplative stylist of his era. But it was especially receptive to classic style, and its own self-presentation was essentially classic almost from its inception. Many of its writers—whether their form was reporting, cultural criticism, fiction, memoir, casual essay, political commentary, or any of the other conventional forms available to contemporary writers—were classic stylists: James Thurber, Ann Beattie, Joseph Mitchell, Richard Rovere, Harold Rosenberg, Susan Sheehan, Donald Barthelme, Philip Hamburger, Audex Minor, Xavier Rynne, Jorge Luis Borges—the list could be extended at will.

Three successive editors—Harold Ross, William Shawn, and Robert Gottlieb—opened its pages to a remarkable variety of writers on an equally remarkable variety of subjects. Its stance was always that it found a contribution interesting because its writer made it so, and the editors decided to pass such a piece on to readers because of its intrinsic interest, not for any practical reason. The famous covers, many of them by major artists, were not keyed to current events except in the most oblique ways and ordinarily had no tie-in with any specific piece in the magazine. There was no overprinting on the covers, except for the magazine's name, date, and price, and under these editors, there were no photographs in the magazine except for those in advertisements. At one time, *The New Yorker* refused advertisements it thought were too strident or otherwise not suited to the ethos of the magazine—which was never commercial, and was always, in its own idiom, casual. "Nature is coming to an end," the magazine might announce in unsensational language—Bill McKibben's small book *The End of Nature* first appeared as an article in *The New Yorker*; John Hersey's *Hiroshima* was almost the entire editorial content of one issue of the magazine—but in classic fashion, the magazine wanted nothing from the reader but her attention. It never asked its readers to *do* anything, above all never asked its readers to *buy* anything. This attitude gave the magazine unparalleled respect among readers, especially if those readers were themselves writers, but it proved to be ultimately impractical in a commercial enterprise.

In 1985, the magazine was purchased by a company that publishes many other magazines, all of them vehicles for commerce, all of them engaged in conventional ploys to get the reader's attention and divert it to the interests of its advertisers. *The New Yorker* that writers and readers respected above all other contemporary magazines and whose back issues are an anthology of distinguished writing and graphics no longer exists. While many of the classic writers associated with *The New Yorker* would have flourished without it, Liebling was perhaps the magazine's preeminent gift to American literature. *The New Yorker* allowed this reporter the time, space, and scope he needed to become the outstanding classic stylist in modern American literary journalism. Liebling is the great successor in American classic style to the Mark Twain of *Life on the Mississippi*.

Notes

Page 1   "J'ai sur-tout à cœur": Jean-Baptise Le Brun, "Discours préliminaire" to *Galerie des peintres flamands, hollandais et allemands.* 3 volumes (Paris: Le Brun, 1792–1796), 1:i and iv.

Page 7   "the most formidable man": William Butler Yeats, *The Autobiography of William Butler Yeats* (New York: Macmillan, 1953), page 169.

Page 13   Rivarol on the French language: *De l'universalité de la langue française* (1783) (Paris: Pougens, 1800).

Page 13   "The English language": T. S. Eliot, *What Is a Classic?: An Address Delivered before the Virgil Society on the 16th of October 1944* (London: Faber and Faber, 1945), pages 26–27; reprinted in *On Poets and Poetry* (London: Faber and Faber, 1957), pages 53–71, quotation from page 66.

Page 14   "Mme de Chevreuse": La Rochefoucauld, *Mémoires* (1662), in *Œuvres complètes*, edited by L. Martin-Chauffier and Jean Marchand (Paris: Gallimard [Bibliothèque de la Pléiade], 1964), page 40.

Page 15   "That praises are without reason": Samuel Johnson, "Preface to Shakespeare" (1765), in *Johnson on Shakespeare*, edited by Arthur Sherbo, 2 volumes (New Haven, Connecticut: Yale University Press, 1968), 1:59–113, quotation from page 59.

Page 16   "The truth is rarely pure, and never simple": Oscar Wilde, *The Importance of Being Earnest* (1895), in *Oscar Wilde*, edited by Isobel Murray (New York: Oxford University Press [The Oxford Authors], 1985), page 485.

Page 20   "Dramatic sentiment": Charles Rosen, *The Classical Style: Haydn, Mozart, Beethoven* (New York: Norton, 1972), all quotations from page 43.

Page 20   "A profound symbolism": Émile Mâle, *Religious Art in France: The Late Middle Ages* (1908), translated by Marthiel Mathews (Princeton, New Jersey: Princeton University Press [Bollingen], 1986), page 211.

Page 21   Books on style: *The Chicago Manual of Style*, fifteenth edition (Chicago: University of Chicago Press, 2003). *MLA Style Manual and Guide to Scholarly Publishing*, third edition (New York: Modern Language Association of America, 2008). Willams A. Heffernan and Mark Johnston, *The Harvest Reader*, second edition (San Diego: Harcourt, Brace, Jovanovich, 1991), chapter 7, "Style." Kate L. Turabian et al., *A Manual for Writers of Research Papers, Theses, and Dissertations*, seventh edition (Chicago: University of Chicago Press, 2007). William Strunk, Jr. and E. B. White, *The Elements of Style*, third edition (New York: Macmillan, 1979). Joseph M. Williams [and Gregory G. Colomb], *Style: Toward Clarity and Grace* (Chicago: University of Chicago Press, 1990).

Page 28   "The prize fighter": A. J. Liebling, *The Sweet Science* (1956) (New York: Penguin, 1982), page 249. An earlier version appeared as "A Reporter at Large: Next-to-Last Stand, Maybe," *The New Yorker*, 16 April 1955, pages 90–106.

Page 29   "an exact knowledge of the past": Thucydides, *The Peloponnesian War*, section 1.22, translated by Rex Warner (Harmondsworth: Penguin, 1954), page 48.

Page 33   "Having, without the form": Jeremy Bentham, *The Book of Fallacies*, as quoted in Kenneth Burke, *A Rhetoric of Motives* (1950) (Berkeley and Los Angeles: University of California Press, 1969), page 94.

Pages 35–36   "In spite of its liquid state": Waverley Root, *Food* (New York: Simon and Schuster, 1980), page 257; taken from the entry "lait" in Prosper Montagné, *Nouveau Larousse Gastronomique* (Paris: Larousse, 1967), which reproduces the sentence from Prosper Montagné, *Larousse Gastronomique* (Paris: Larousse, 1938), page 629: "Malgré son état liquide, le lait doit toujours être considéré comme un aliment et non comme une boisson . . ."

Page 36   "Unusual among songbirds": John Bull and John Farrand, Jr., *The Audubon Society Field Guide to North American Birds, Eastern Region* (New York: Knopf, 1977), page 514.

Page 37   "As far back as the records go": Waverley Root, *The Food of France* (1958) (New York: Vintage, 1992), page 3.

Page 47   "[W]ere I persuaded that Charlotte": Jane Austen, *Pride and Prejudice* (1813), edited by R. W. Chapman, third edition (London: Oxford University Press, 1932), page 135.

Pages 48–49   "Many attempts have been made": C. H. Dodd, *The Interpretation of the Fourth Gospel* (1953) (Cambridge: Cambridge University Press, 1968), pages 289–290.

Page 51   Foucault on "What Is an Author?" in *Language, Counter-Memory, Practice*, edited by Donald F. Bouchard, translated by Donald F. Bouchard and Sherry Simon (Ithaca, New York: Cornell University Press, 1977), pages 113–138.

Page 61   "To shun English": "French May Be Language of Love, but for Science . . . ," *The Wall Street Journal*, 21 October 1983, page 1.

Page 63   "[I]f you want to understand what a science is": Clifford Geertz, "Thick Description: Toward an Interpretive Theory of Culture," in *The Interpretation of Cultures* (New York: Basic Books, 1973), page 5.

Page 63   "The fact is that the subtlety": Janel Mueller, *The Native Tongue and the Word: Developments in English Prose Style 1380–1580* (Chicago: University of Chicago Press, 1984), page 13.

Page 66   "By his manner, his looks, his voice": Longinus, *On the Sublime*, section 20, translated by W. Hamilton Fyfe, in *Aristotle* (Cambridge, Massachusetts: Harvard University Press [Loeb], 1932), 23:190.

Page 66   Demetrius on linguistic construction: *On Style*, section 1.1–2, translated by W. Rhys Roberts, in *Aristotle* (Cambridge, Massachusetts: Harvard University Press [Loeb], 1932), 23:295–297.

Page 66   "Long journeys are shortened": Demetrius, *On Style*, section 2.46, in *Aristotle*, 23:331.

Page 66   The role of image schemas: "Image schema" is Mark Johnson's term. See *The Body in the Mind* (Chicago: University of Chicago Press, 1987), page xiv. The term and concept are treated in Mark Turner, *Reading Minds: The Study of English in the Age of Cognitive Science* (Princeton, New Jersey: Princeton University Press, 1991), pages 57, 101, and 151–271. The conceptual instruments according to which we align image schemas of thought and language in poetry are analyzed in George Lakoff and Mark Turner, *More Than Cool Reason: A Field Guide to Poetic Metaphor* (Chicago: University of Chicago Press, 1989), pages 155–157.

Page 68   Aristotle, in the *Rhetoric*, on styles: *Rhetoric* (1413b), edited and translated by John Henry Freese (Cambridge, Massachusetts: Harvard University Press [Loeb], 1926), page 419.

Page 68   "stand in irreconcilable opposition": Demetrius, *On Style*, section 2, in *Aristotle*, 23:322–323.

Page 68   "comes from trying to outdo the sublime": Longinus, *On the Sublime*, section 3, in *Aristotle*, 23:130. (Translation by Mark Turner.)

Page 68   "from the same cause": Longinus, *On the Sublime*, section 5, in *Aristotle*, 23:136. (Translation by Mark Turner.)

Pages 68–69   Aristotle on surface techniques: *Poetics*, section 22, translated by W. Hamilton Fyfe in *Aristotle* (Cambridge, Massachusetts: Harvard University Press [Loeb], 1932), 23:84–91.

Page 70   "For the effect of genius": Longinus, *On the Sublime*, section 1, in *Aristotle*, 23:125.

Page 70   "inventive skill and the due disposal": Longinus, *On the Sublime*, section 1, in *Aristotle*, 23:125.

Page 70   "the command of full-blooded ideas": Longinus, *On the Sublime*, section 8, in *Aristotle*, 23:141.

Page 70   "Now, since the first, I mean natural genius": Longinus, *On the Sublime*, section 9, in *Aristotle*, 23:143.

Pages 70–71   "The machinery of grace": Michael Donaghy, "Machines," in *Shibboleth* (Oxford: Oxford University Press, 1988), page 1.

Page 73   "It is necessary to express what is true": La Bruyère, *Les Caractères* (1688), edited by Robert Garapon (Paris: Garnier, 1962), page 70.

Page 73   "And ten low Words": Alexander Pope, *An Essay on Criticism* (1711), in *Poems of Alexander Pope*, edited by John Butt (New Haven, Connecticut: Yale University Press, 1963), page 154, line 347.

Page 75   "The brooding note": Clifford Geertz, *Works and Lives: The Anthropologist as Author* (Stanford, California: Stanford University Press, 1988), pages 14–16, 23.

Page 82   "Although a dirty campaign": Julian Barnes, "Letter from London," *The New Yorker*, 4 May 1992, pages 78–92, quotation from page 80.

Page 82   "With peer pressure and whippings": Ruth Baer Lambach, "Colony Girl," in *Women's Experiences in United States Communal Societies*, edited by Wendy Chmielewski, Marlyn Dalsimer, and Louis Kern (Syracuse, New York: Syracuse University Press, 1993), pages 241–255, quotation from page 243.

Page 82   "In the same year": *Greece*, Michelin Green Guide (Paris: Michelin, 1987), page 24.

Page 82   "It is from this weighing of delights": A. J. Liebling, "Memoirs of a Feeder in France: II. Just Enough Money," *The New Yorker*, 18 April 1959, pages 49–76, quotation from page 49; reprinted in *Between Meals: An Appetite for Paris* (1962) (San Francisco: North Point Press, 1986), quotation from page 57.

Page 83   "As she emerged in front of us": E. B. White, "Letter from the South," *The New Yorker*, 7 April 1956, pages 39–49; reprinted with a postscript as "The Ring of Time" in *The Points of My Compass: Letters from the East, the West, the North, the South* (New York: Harper

& Row, 1962), pages 51–60; and in *Essays of E. B. White* (New York: Harper & Row, 1977), pages 142–149.

Page 86   "My disappointment was immense": Marcel Proust, *Remembrance of Things Past* (French original, 1913–1927), translated by C. K. Scott-Moncrieff and Terence Kilmartin, 3 volumes (New York: Random House, 1981), 1:190–193. (This edition is a revision by Terrence Kilmartin of Scott-Moncrieff's translation as completed by Andreas Mayor after Scott-Moncrieff's death.)

Page 90   "Here, before the Lord" and "Take no account of it": 1 Samuel 16. Translation from *The New English Bible*.

Page 90   "The Word of the Lord came to me": Jeremiah 1. Translation from *The New English Bible*.

Page 91   "Woe is me!": Isaiah 6. Translation from *The New English Bible*.

Page 92   "Let us recover the joy of battle": Homer, *Iliad*, 19.149–161, translated by Robert Fitzgerald (Garden City, New York: Anchor, 1974), page 462.

Pages 93–94   "[W]e know that many purely formal patterns": Kenneth Burke, *A Rhetoric of Motives* (1950) (Berkeley and Los Angeles: University of California Press, 1969), page 58.

Page 94   "Our love of what is beautiful," "No doubt all this will be disparaged," and "In this way Pericles attempted" (Pericles' Funeral Oration, subsequent oration, and Thucydides' analysis): Thucydides, *The Peloponnesian War*, sections 2.35–46 and 2.60–65, pages 144–151 and 158–163.

Page 100   "because its favorite point of view": Hilary Putnam, "Two Philosophical Perspectives," in *Reason, Truth and History* (Cambridge: Cambridge University Press, 1981), pages 49–74, quotations from page 49 and page 50.

Page 109   Bull and Farrand: *Audubon Field Guide* (New York: Knopf, 1977). Tufted Titmouse, pages 658–659; Northern Shrike, page 514; Hairy Woodpecker, page 644; Western Meadowlark, page 512.

Page 116   *Los Angeles Times*: Douglas Frantz and Glenn F. Bunting, "Weathering the Storm, Cajun-Style," 28 August 1992, page 1.

Page 117   Murrin: *The Allegorical Epic* (Chicago: University of Chicago Press, 1980), page 3.

Page 117   Feynman: *QED: The Strange Theory of Light and Matter* (Princeton, New Jersey: Princeton University Press, 1985), page 4.

Page 117   McKeon: "Philosophy and Method," *Journal of Philosophy* 48 (25 October 1951): 653–682, quotation from page 667.

Page 120   Twain: *Life on the Mississippi* (1883) (New York: Penguin, 1984), pages 45 and 64.

Page 122   "In the North one hears the war mentioned": Twain, *Life on the Mississippi*, page 319.

Page 123   Tanizaki: *The Secret History of the Lord of Musashi and Arrowroot* (1983), translated by Anthony H. Chambers (San Francisco: North Point Press, 1991), page 9. (Original Japanese book publication of *The Secret History*, 1935.)

Page 124   Descartes: *Discours de la méthode*, in *Œuvres et lettres*, edited by André Bridoux (Paris: Gallimard [Bibliothèque de la Pléiade], 1953), pages 126–179, quotation from pages 129–130.

Page 125   Pascal: *Pensées*, in *Œuvres complètes*, edited by Louis Lafuma (Paris: Seuil, 1963), page 611, number 847. The corresponding number in Léon Brunschvicg's edition is 893.

Page 125   Blake: *The Marriage of Heaven and Hell* (?1790–1793) in *William Blake's Writings*, 2 volumes, edited by G. E. Bentley, Jr. (Oxford: Clarendon, 1978), 1:84.

Page 128   La Bruyère: *Les Caractères* (1688), edited by Robert Garapon (Paris: Garnier, 1962), page 70.

Page 128   Madame de Sévigné: *Correspondance*, 3 volumes, edited by Roger Duchêne (Paris: Gallimard [Bibliothèque de la Pléiade], 1972–1978), 2:601, number 638. For Duchêne's gloss on *poésie*, see page 1384.

Pages 130–131   Liebling: "A Reporter at Large: Cross-Channel Trip 1," *The New Yorker*, 1 July 1944, pages 34–41, quotation from page 34. Reprinted as "Cross-Channel Trip" from "And So to Victory" in *Mollie and Other War Pieces* (New York: Schocken Books, 1964), page 117.

Pages 131–132   Mueller: *The Native Tongue and the Word* (Chicago: University of Chicago Press, 1984), pages 278–279.

Pages 136–137   Chastel: *Le Mythe de la Renaissance 1420–1520* (Geneva: Skira, 1969), page 29; translated by Stuart Gilbert as *The Myth of the Renaissance 1420–1520* (Geneva: Skira, 1969), page 29.

Page 138   Borges: "Los traductores de las 1001 noches" (1935), in *Historia de la eternidad* (Buenos Aires: Emecé, 1953), pages 99–134, quotation from page 101.

Page 140   Root: *The Food of France* (1958) (New York: Vintage, 1992), page 21.

Pages 140–141   Friedländer: *Die Altniederländische Malerei*, 14 volumes (Berlin: Cassirer [volumes 1–11] and Leiden: Sijthoff [volumes 12–14], 1924–1937): volume 4, *Hugo van der Goes* (1926), page 8. Translation taken from *Early Netherlandish Painting*, 16 volumes, translated by Heinz Norden (Leyden: Sijthoff; Brussels: Éditions de la Connaissance, 1967–1976): volume 4, *Hugo van der Goes* (1969), page 9.

Page 141   Steiner: *The Colors of Rhetoric: Problems in the Relation between Modern Literature and Painting* (Chicago: University of Chicago Press, 1982), pages 68–69.

Page 144   Madame de Lafayette: *La princesse de Clèves*, in *Roman et Nouvelles*, edited by Émile Magne (Paris: Garnier, 1970), page 376.

Page 146   Hodges: *Alan Turing: The Enigma* (New York: Simon and Schuster, 1983), pages 117–118.

Pages 146–147 Jouvenel: "Introduction" to Hobbes's translation of *The Peloponnesian War*, 2 volumes, edited by David Greene (Ann Arbor: University of Michigan Press, 1959), 1:xiii–xiv.

Page 148   Wilde: *The Importance of Being Earnest* (1895), in *Oscar Wilde*, edited by Isobel Murray (New York: Oxford University Press [The Oxford Authors], 1985), page 485.

Page 148   Geertz: "Thick Description," in *The Interpretation of Cultures* (New York: Basic Books, 1973), page 14.

Page 149   La Rochefoucauld: *Maximes* (1678), number 56, in *Œuvres complètes*, edited by L. Martin-Chauffier and Jean Marchand (Paris: Gallimard [Bibliothèque de la Pléiade], 1964), page 410.

Page 149   Pope: From *An Essay on Man* (1733–1734), in *Poems of Alexander Pope*, edited by John Butt (New Haven, Connecticut: Yale University Press, 1963), page 502.

Page 149   Oakeshott: *Experience and Its Modes* (1933) (Cambridge: Cambridge University Press, 1966), page 20.

Page 150   Shaw: *Back to Methuselah: A Metabiological Pentateuch* (1921), in *Complete Plays with Prefaces*, 6 volumes (New York: Dodd, Mead, 1963), 2:10.

Page 152   "The concept of spatial form": The first two sentences of W.J.T. Mitchell, "Spatial Form in Literature: Toward a General Theory," *Critical Inquiry* 6, number 3 (1980): 539–567. W.J.T. Mitchell is the editor of *Critical Inquiry* and Gaylord Donnelley Distinguished Service Professor of English Language and Literature at the University of Chicago.

Page 152   "Rembrandt was a very young man": Suzanne C. Pipes, "Rembrandt: *Old Man with a Gold Chain*" (unpublished manuscript).

Page 153   Lavoisier: *Traité élémentaire de chimie présenté dans un ordre nouveau et d'après les découvertes modernes* (Paris: Cuchet, 1789), pages ix–x.

Page 153   La Rochefoucauld: *Maximes* (1678), number 49, in *Œuvres complètes*, page 409.

Pages 153–154 Descartes: *Discours de la méthode*, page 131.

Page 154   Descartes: *Discours de la méthode*, page 126.

Page 155   Barthelme: "Daumier," *The New Yorker*, 1 April 1972, pages 31–36, quotation from page 36. Reprinted in *Sadness* (New York: Farrar, Straus and Giroux, 1972), pages 161–183, quotation from page 183.

Page 157   Larkin: *High Windows* (London: Faber and Faber; New York: Farrar, Straus and Giroux, 1974), page 30.

Page 159   Robert Martin Adams: *Bad Mouth* (Berkeley and Los Angeles: University of California Press, 1977), page 104.

Page 159   La Rochefoucauld: *Mémoires* (1662), in *Œuvres complètes*, page 40.

Pages 161–162 Liebling: "The Great State: 1—Waiting for the Imam," *The New Yorker*, 28 May 1960, pages 41–91, quotation from page 41. Reprinted in *The Earl of Louisiana*

(New York: Simon and Schuster, 1961), quotation from pages 8–9.

Page 162   Morrison: *Playing in the Dark* (Cambridge, Massachusetts: Harvard University Press, 1992), pages 63–64.

Page 162   "the style she employs to make her points": Lehmann-Haupt, "2 Voices as Far Apart as the Novel and the Essay," *The New York Times*, 2 April 1992, page C21; review of Toni Morrison, *Jazz* (New York: Knopf, 1992) and *Playing in the Dark: Whiteness and the Literary Imagination* (Cambridge, Massachusetts: Harvard University Press, 1992).

Pages 166–167 Milton: *Areopagitica*, in *Complete Prose Works of John Milton*, 8 volumes, general editor, Don M. Wolfe (New Haven, Connecticut: Yale University Press, 1953–1982), volume 2: *1643–1648*, edited by Ernest Sirluck (1959), pages 486–570, quotation from page 539.

Page 168   "If you hear me defending myself": Socrates, *Apology*, in *The Last Days of Socrates*, translated by Hugh Tredennick (1954) (Harmondsworth: Penguin, 1969), page 45. Reprinted in *Collected Dialogues of Plato*, edited by Edith Hamilton and Huntington Cairns (New York: Pantheon [Bollingen], 1963), pages 3–26, quotation from page 4.

Page 169   Greenspan: Quoted in Steven Greenhouse, "The Fed's Master of Obfuscation," *The New York Times*, 20 April 1992, national edition, page C1.

Page 173   Veblen: *The Theory of the Leisure Class* (1899) (Harmondsworth: Penguin, 1979), page 399.

Page 174   "'Mulk' became 'milk'": Louise Brooks, *Lulu in Hollywood* (New York: Knopf, 1983), pages 10–11.

Page 175   "I spent most of my life fighting": Thurgood Marshall, "Justice Marshall, on 'Afro-American': Yes," *The New*

York Times, 17 October 1989, page A21; also reported in "Talking Points," *The Washington Post*, 18 October 1989, page A29.

Page 176   Sainte-Beuve: *Port-Royal* (1840–1859), 3 volumes, edited by Maxime Leroy (Paris: Gallimard [Bibliothèque de la Pléiade], 1953–1955), 1:135.

Page 177   "[L]a langue n'était évidemment": Louis-Adolphe Régnier, *Lexique de la langue du Cardinal de Retz* (Paris: Hachette, 1896), page [i].

Page 178   Auerbach: *Mimesis: Dargestellte Wirklichkeit in der Abendländischen Literatur* (Bern: Francke, 1946), pages 370–371. Translation from *Mimesis: The Representation of Reality in Western Literature*, translated by Willard R. Trask (Princeton, New Jersey: Princeton University Press, 1953), page 420.

Page 179   Saint-Simon: Quoted in Auerbach, *Mimesis*, pages 427–428.

Page 180   "Everything that occurs": Auerbach, *Mimesis*, page 421.

Page 181   "Saint-Simon obtains his most profound insights": Auerbach, *Mimesis*, pages 428–429.

Page 181   "[T]he urgency of an inner impulse": Auerbach, *Mimesis*, page 433.

Page 182   "the essential nature": Auerbach, *Mimesis*, page 428.

Page 182   "The non-fictitious, non-precogitated quality": Auerbach, *Mimesis*, page 423.

Page 183   "Mr. Collins was not a sensible man": Jane Austen, *Pride and Prejudice* (1813), edited by R. W. Chapman, third edition (London: Oxford University Press, 1932), page 70.

Page 184   "In his level of style, Saint-Simon": Auerbach, *Mimesis*, page 431.

Page 184   "We must wait until the late nineteenth century": Auerbach, *Mimesis*, pages 425–426.

Page 193   "I have now attained the true art of letter-writing": *Jane Austen's Letters,* 3rd edition, ed. Deirdre Le Faye (New York: Oxford University Press, 1995), page 68. Letter #29, to Cassandra Austen, Saturday 3–Monday 5 January 1801; complete letter, pages 66–69.

Page 206   "He pushed a shiny print": Raymond Chandler, *The Big Sleep* (1939) (New York: Vintage [Vintage Crime/Black Lizard], 1992, pages 123–124.

Page 218   "Bartlebooth's cellar": Georges Perec, *Life A User's Manual,* translated by David Bellos (Boston: Godine, 1987), chapter 72, "Basement 3," page 344.

Page 218   "The Rorschachs' cellar": Georges Perec, *Life A User's Manual,* translated by David Bellos (Boston: Godine, 1987), chapter 67, "Basement 2," page 325.

Page 220   "In a very dark Chamber, at a round Hole": Isaac Newton, *Opticks or A Treatise of the Reflections, Refractions, Inflections &Colours of Light* [Book One, Part I: Prop II, Theor. II], 1704 (New York: Dover, 1952 [reprint 1979]), pages 26 and 28.

Page 224   "Cistercian architecture first appeared in Burgundy": *Burgundy Jura* (London: Michelin Apa, 2007), pages 76–77.

Page 225   "[L]ife does not consist mainly—or even largely—of facts and happenings": *Autobiography of Mark Twain,* volume 1, edited by Harriet Elinor Smith et al.; Mark Twain Papers (Berkeley and Los Angeles: University of California Press, 2010), page 256.

Index